Schools for America

Schools for America

Report of the AASA
Commission on School Buildings

American Association of School
Administrators
1201 Sixteenth Street, N.W.,
Washington, D.C. 20036

Foreword

On two former occasions, the American Association of School Administrators has produced and widely distributed major publications on school building planning. The first, *American School Buildings,* published in 1949, was virtually a handbook on school building planning. For a full decade it was used extensively by administrators, school board members, and school plant specialists.

In 1960 the Association, through a special commission, produced and published *Planning America's School Buildings.* This was a completely new book that reflected basic changes wrought in approaches to school plant planning and the character of facilities during the decade of the fifties, when as many as 70,000 classrooms were being constructed in a single year and annual capital outlay expenditures, mostly for school buildings, approached the $3 billion mark.

The need for more and better school building space has increased rather than diminished during the first half of the sixties. Each year public elementary and secondary school plants have been expanded to accommodate a million additional pupils. This growth in enrollment has continued uninterruptedly over a 15-year period, and there is no indication that the trend will turn downward in the near future. Furthermore, additional demands for school plant facilities have been made as the educational program has been extended downward to enroll a greater number of children at the early childhood level and extended upward through vocational and technical schools and community colleges to meet diversified educational needs at the post high school level.

But the challenge to people re-sponsible for school plant planning is far more than to provide space. They are challenged to provide the best possible learning environment for a growing pupil population with an increasing range of interests and capabilities. The school plant that does not facilitate instruction has fallen short of its purpose. It must accommodate such new media of instruction as mechanical aids, paperbacks, consumable pamphlets and brochures, recordings, tapes, slides, teaching machines, programed instruction facilities, and a wide range of electronic equipment. Provisions must be made for large-group instruction that will use a variety of electronic aids and the skills of exceptional teachers to full advantage, and at the same time facilities must provide opportunities for small, intimate teaching-learning relationships between the pupil and his instructors.

The whole process of urbanization has cast school building problems into a new perspective. As people in increasing numbers have moved from sparsely settled areas toward large centers of population, schools have inevitably become larger, and school planners are challenged to create an environment in which the pupil can maintain his individuality and circumstances in which the unique qualities of his personality and his special interests can be recognized and nurtured. Pressed to meet this important educational need, administrators and architects are focusing attention on the total environment of the school plant facility and striving to build into its design, orientation, and ap-pointments the warmth and friendliness needed to give young people a sense of belonging, a sense of security, and a feeling of identity with the school, even when the enrollment is large. Study carrels, courts, seminar rooms, student commons, special play courts, little theaters, snack bars, and reading alcoves represent but a few of the approaches that have been made to dealing with the problems of bigness.

With increasing urbanization, the cost of sites has risen almost astronomically in many localities; at the same time, the processes of site acquisition have become more complicated. Congestion, the flow of traffic, parking space, and health and safety features are problems that have been recognized by school planners throughout the years. But with urbanization and the increasing size of schools, they become more complicated and more pressing.

The assist people responsible for school plant planning in neighborhoods and communities throughout the country in meeting these persistent problems and new ones just emerging, the Commission on School Buildings was appointed in 1964 and charged with responsibility for exploring the whole spectrum of school plant planning in this country and reporting to the membership and to the general public. To the extent that this Commission has provided herein new information, new insights, and guidelines that will lead to better school plants wherever they are constructed, it will have served its purpose.

Forrest E. Conner
Executive Secretary
American Association of
School Administrators

Dedicated to Shirley Cooper

Of all the activities in which the American people engage as they live and work together in their local communities, counties, and states, perhaps none expresses in material form so many aspects of our culture as school-building construction. With its roots deeply embedded in the past, the school building is a symbol of the ideals of a free, self-governing people. This was true of the rough log cabin that housed a meager educational program in the frontier community. It is equally true of the well-planned school plant which houses a comprehensive educational program in a present-day suburban school district. Its classrooms, its libraries, its laboratories, and its shops, filled with eager, inquiring children and hopeful, questioning youth, are as alive to the present as a busy street or a buzzing industrial plant.

With a look toward the future, the school building reflects the ambitions, the hopes, the aspirations, and the dreams of a people that is striving to move forward and upward to a way of life that is better, fuller, richer, and more rewarding than that which it now knows. At its best in form and appearance—as it stands majestically on the highest hilltop in the village, or nestles quietly and unobtrusively on the bank of the small stream in the valley, or affords a pleasing contrast to the dull, monotonous tones of a tenement district in a congested metropolitan area—it is an expression of the aesthetic values of the people and their sense of what is pleasing and beautiful.

—Shirley Cooper
*Deputy Executive Secretary and
Director of Inservice Education
American Association of School Administrators
September 1949-July 1966*

Acknowledgments

Schools for America is the result of two years' work by an outstanding commission assembled by Dr. Shirley Cooper, the prime mover and architect of this document, to whom the publication is dedicated. Chapters herein were prepared by individual members of the AASA Commission on School Buildings and revised through successive meetings so that the final draft—this document—represents the best judgment of the Commission as a whole. The American Association of School Administrators expresses most grateful thanks to each member of the Commission who gave so generously of his time and talents.

Throughout the period of preparation of this book, the Commission drew heavily on the knowledge, wisdom, and experience of a great many people, as many as possible of whom are identified on page 167. The Commission acknowledges their specific assistance, and the Association expresses its appreciation for their invaluable help.

Special acknowledgment from the Commission and the Association is due Beatrix Sebastian of the AASA staff for indispensable aid and painstaking care in preparing this report.

AASA COMMISSION ON SCHOOL BUILDINGS

C. William Brubaker, AIA
The Perkins and Will Partnership
Chicago, Illinois

B. Melvin Cole
Assistant Superintendent in
   Instruction and Personnel Services
Baltimore County Schools
Towson, Maryland

Carroll F. Johnson
Superintendent of Schools
White Plains, New York

F. Lamar Kelsey, FAIA
Lamar Kelsey and Associates
Colorado Springs, Colorado

Robert Billsbrough Price, FAIA
Tacoma, Washington

G. E. Rast
Director of Research and Curriculum
College of Education
University of Bridgeport
Bridgeport, Connecticut

K. G. Skaggs
Specialist in Occupational Curricula
American Association of
   Junior Colleges
Washington, D.C.

Richard F. Tonigan
Associate Director for Administration
Dormitory Authority of
   the State of New York
Elsmere, New York

Table of Contents

Chapter 1 / *Tomorrow's School*

As man casts off the bonds of earthbound knowledge and soars to new intellectual heights, he must unlearn as well as learn. Only yesterday, the atom was thought to be the immutable unit of matter; now it has been split, with consequences both fearful and wonderful. And learned scholars, considering strange rays of light, again dispute a question once believed settled—the very origin of the universe. In the laboratory, life can be created in a test tube. Breathtaking advances in new knowledge and understanding are being made not only in nuclear physics and mathematics, but also in biology, in chemistry, and in the social sciences. One revelation leads swiftly to a dozen others in irreversible geometric progression.

The changes in perspectives this new knowledge requires, the mental revisions it demands, and its implications for social and cultural change place a heavy responsibility upon this generation of students and upon their teachers. Learning cannot be limited to acquisition of facts. As knowledge burgeons, selection, analysis, and objective interpretation become more imperative in the educational process.

Relations between people will gain a new depth and subtlety. At a time when communications are instant and global, when misunderstanding can bring catastrophe, our current modes of relating to one another just won't do. That is the negative side. On the positive, what goes on between human beings is the ultimate turn-on. The landscape of love and friendship has endless vistas, and the future will find us new and better ways of journeying into those vistas.[1]

These are not new dimensions of educational needs. Thoughtful educators and forward-looking school systems in the United States are well aware of the pressing need to help young people grasp the outlines of a new epoch filled with seemingly contradictory concepts and are seeking ways to accomplish this end. The results of their efforts have led to more accurate methods of teaching students and better ways of grouping them. Computerized data processing enables administrators and teachers to handle records more efficiently. Architectural plans are geared to individual-study needs. Curriculums in biological and physical sciences, in the humanities, and in English have been revised and reorganized. In-creasing emphasis is given to community colleges and to post high school vocational training. Television has become a medium for continuous training from early childhood through old age. National responsibility for education is acknowledged and in evidence in the National Defense Education Act, the Economic Opportunity Act, and the Elementary and Secondary Education Act.

No Time for Complacency

But let us not be complacent; we have only begun. We cast about for answers but do not find them. Often, we seem to stumble from one crisis to the next and to exhaust our energies in putting out fires instead of preventing them. Hard pressed, we are too willing to settle for expedience and too content to let the future take care of itself.

Since the beginning of public education in this country, schoolmen in every age have been deeply concerned about the salient characteristics of the times and how cultural circumstances affect the educational needs of people. But

---

[1] Leonard, George B. "Where the California Game Is Taking Us." *Look* 30:114; June 28, 1966.

comprehending circumstances, even with clarity, and recognizing the educational needs of children and youth are but preliminary steps. Administrators must go beyond this point and bring about changes in the educational programs necessary to meet new needs and to cope with new circumstances.

Consider this paradox: As change accelerates, life becomes more leisurely. At the turn of the century only about 25 percent of total U.S. national time (inhabitants x 24 hours x 365 days) was devoted to leisure pursuits; at midcentury the proportion of national time devoted to leisure had increased to 34 percent; and it is estimated that by the year 2000 more than a third—38 percent—of our time will be leisure time.[2] But this will be a frantic leisure, frayed at the edges, unless meaning can be found in a world where change is the only constant. Where shall man begin his quest? The human nervous system is already taxed by the rate of change it is obliged to endure. Will man be able to respond rationally when the

twenty-first century subjects him to a relentless barrage of new stimuli?

Ways predicts that acceleration will become so rapid that trying to "make sense of change" will actually become our basic industry. Aesthetic and ethical values will be affected; no widely held system of ethics can contain in ready-to-use form the norms by which to judge many next-century eventualities. Because education is the primary social instrument of human adjustment, a cautionary note should be sounded. Change—even radical change—should not be confused with absolute randomness. There will be some continuity, some persistent patterns, difficult though they may be to discern.

In looking for patterns, we do not start from scratch. Neither men nor society determine objective truth, and a change in society will not change truth. But the perception of truth by men—what they perceive and how they perceive it—is surely affected by changes in society. Many truths of history, science, philosophy, and religion have been perceived as transcending change. In a time of great social flux the truths perceived as transcendent may be fewer—and therefore more precious. They may be perceived as more abstract—and therefore harder to apply to actual life. A tremendous effort will be required to build the intermediate links be-

tween the novel patterns of a changing society and abstract, enduring truth.[3]

New Yardsticks

In designing tomorrow's curriculum, which in turn will determine school design, we must neither take for granted the old methods of imparting values nor despair of finding new ways to inculcate ethics and elevate aspirations. Yet if man's mooring is not to be a stable code of values, by what else shall he secure himself? In an age when radical change is a condition of life, how shall pupils be taught to judge right and wrong, good and evil, art and sham if the old yardsticks of fixed length cannot be applied to what man says and does and creates? How shall we find for ourselves and reveal to students those links between change and abiding truth?

It might be tempting to give comfort to younger children—while they are yet so small, so very vulnerable—by evading the issue. But a developmental curriculum cannot be constructed on evasion. Evasion nurtures insecurity. One who fol-

[2] American Academy of Political and Social Science. *Leisure in America: Blessing or Curse?* (Edited by James C. Charlesworth.) Philadelphia: the Academy, 1964. p. 10.

[3] Ways, Max. "The Era of Radical Change." *Fortune* 69:113 ff.; May 1964.

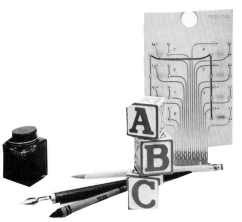

lows a course of evasion with children and youth will eventually be forced to confess his evasion. The truth is that there is no unchanging answer to any question in man's changing world.

The role of reason and understanding in dealing with the forces that surround us and the belief that the focal point of reason is lodged in the individual have been central values in public education in this country since the beginning. If they are to continue to be key values in education, these principles must be applied in new and volatile situations virtually alive with phenomena that do not readily check with existing value patterns just as rigorously as they have been applied in simpler circumstances in the past.

We cannot be fearful; we must be positive; we must continue as we always have to identify standards and inculcate ethics from the time a child is capable of rudimentary communication with his fellow beings. Ways must be found to teach him to love, to understand, and to be compassionate toward others; to find joy in truth and satisfaction in the search for knowledge; to recognize beauty and to cherish perfection; and to realize that man lives not by bread alone. If we can-

not promise pupils that virtue will always be rewarded and evil always punished in the changing world about them, we must help them to achieve personal integrity which will be its own reward.

The Challenge of Change

At a time when staggering change is the primary fact of life, we shall have to embrace the facts of life as they are and teach pupils to exult in the challenge change presents. Pupils from the earliest prekindergarten stage throughout their school careers will be encouraged to inquire, to probe, to sift, to weigh, and to appraise every object and concept they encounter—much as their kinesthetic perception is now developed with modeling clay. The excitement which stems from discovery has always been fostered by discerning teachers. Now the school will have to nurture the combined emotional and intellectual satisfaction-in-depth which comes from applying one's entire critical faculties—ethical and intellectual— to new ideas, situations, and objects in order to anticipate their farthest-reaching implications.

Change can be an exhilarating experience for pupils—not something to be feared, but something to be greeted eagerly, to be examined minutely, and to be judged wisely. Unless pedagogy at the

primary and even prekindergarten levels is reoriented, the school cannot effectively help the children and youth whom it serves to develop the intellectual and moral capacity to cope with questions of science and ethics which they will be forced to answer for themselves. One frightening example will serve to underline the point: In the spring of 1966 at a meeting of scientists in Los Angeles, Professor Elof Carlson, a UCLA zoologist, confidently predicted that within a century or two it will be possible to analyze the genetic code revealed in the dried tissue of Egyptian mummies, to copy the code, and to implant it in fertilized ova. The result, Professor Carlson said, will be new human beings who exactly duplicate mental and physical attributes of such geniuses as King Tutankhamen. He further asserted that the world could thus breed another musical genius like Mozart, if only Mozart had been mummified at death![4]

Now how can a fixed, inflexible code of ethics be applied to a scientific evolution which will shortly confront civilization with all the moral, social, economic, and politi-

---

[4] Associated Press. "Recreate Mummified Geniuses." *White Plains Reporter Dispatch,* April 12, 1966. p. 1.

cal implications of the ability, not only to create life in a test tube, but to control precisely the genetic code of the human race? Our grandchildren possibly and our great-grandchildren certainly must be ready to face the day when this Pandora's box flies open.

But there are other frontiers with relevance to education. The most challenging American frontier is in the social and the psychic world. This is a frontier of thought, of relationships among people, of joy and ecstacy, of sorrow and despair, and of powers within the human spirit that have as yet been but vaguely recognized. Grasping at the outlines of this new frontier, young people are questioning almost everything and are rejecting much tradition. There is a confused groping for something better. Their behavior and the questions they raise cry out for open confrontation with great questions and the meaning and purpose of events. They are trying to think their way through to a stable position when the very ground under their feet is shifting. The schools must help them explore with an open mind the noblest ideas and the best sources of mature values. It must help them to communicate better with their fellows,

with thoughtful adults, and with the ever-widening universe of ideas, concepts, and knowledge.

Points of Beginning

In response to these and other challenges appearing on the horizon, educators today are turning to nongraded grouping, independent study, self-starting techniques, and programs in which each pupil progresses at his own pace. They are slowly but surely becoming aware that lock-step, grade-by-grade education simply will no longer do the job which must be done.

Finding new ways to educate children for a new world applies to those who deal in bricks and blueprints as well as those who conduct classes, administer school systems, handle finances, and plan new curriculums. For the school building is education's environment, and as such, it shapes the product. Those who design school buildings symbolize values and transmit to the students in tangible form a sense of priorities in the educational program. If the building, with its appointments and its arrangement of space and equipment, facilitates independent study; encourages quiet contemplation of the true, the beautiful, and the good; and engenders respect for craftsmanship, skill, and perfection, then the building will enhance and reinforce the teacher's efforts.

In designing buildings that will facilitate teaching and learning, we shall have to examine blueprints carefully and look for more than economy and efficiency in planning the arrangements of rooms and the equipment of interiors. To illustrate, in preparation for compensatory programs, we might consider putting carpets and fireplaces in the schools to give deprived youngsters a facsimile of the mid-twentieth-century middle class suburban home. Do we judge carpets for their symbolic value or for their intrinsic beauty, utility, and acoustical properties? Is a school fireplace needed for warmth? Does it have value in terms of education, or is it just a pleasant monument to a vanishing way of life? It may be that both carpets and fireplaces are desirable; it may be that one is and the other is not desirable. But in any case, let us make the decision advisedly.

Technology and Leisure

Increase in leisure time and the technology of automation are major forces in the rate of change. It is difficult to comprehend their full implications. "The rapid development of new knowledge, unaccompanied by the technology of automation,"

Brown observes, "might well be a drastic happening; but, coming together—new knowledge plus automation—the two forces complement each other." These two forces may be a classic example of Edward Teller's observation that two problems can sometimes be united into a solution.

Since society does not have to be largely occupied by work it can focus attention upon the other big theme which is pulsating through the culture—the rapid explosion of knowledge.

Since the economy of the future will provide substantial blocks of uncommitted leisure time for all persons, then Americans must begin the search for another fulfillment. This can be found only in education. In essence, if an individual is to experience self-fulfillment to any considerable degree, then he must be equipped with highly developed skills for learning.[5]

Emphasis must be on skills which enable an individual not only to learn, but to *reason*—to compare, to deduce, and to project consequences. Recognizing this necessity, many serious thinkers have become more and more concerned with the negative implications of an automated technology. But automa-

tion need not make automatons of mankind. We can and must harness technology for the good of mankind as we have harnessed the gigantic forces of nature to relieve people from unnecessary toil and to make life better. We need not and will not, if we choose otherwise, become an Orwellian society of assembly-line beings.

The Computer in Instruction

Consider, for instance, what the computer can do in education if its versatility is applied imaginatively to curriculum, pupil scheduling, records, and testing. In getting away from rote learning and overreliance on the textbook-question-and-answer type of program, we can look to the computer to project realistic hypotheses in chemistry, social studies, and even in music. In this manner students will be able to explore alternatives and view—or hear and view—the results.

One of several well-advanced experiments in simulated-environment instruction is being conducted by the Board of Cooperative Educational Services in the First Supervisory (School) District of Westchester County, New York, with the advice and technical assistance of IBM

specialists. Teachers from some ten school systems in this upper Westchester County area have spent several summers working in task forces to prepare programed syllabi in chemistry, in music, and in social studies.

The chemistry program is designed so that each step in a laboratory experiment is flashed on a screen. A pupil responds by indicating the next step, and the computer responds, in turn, by showing him the result of his decision—even including an explosive result produced by the "wrong" combination of chemicals. Extended to an entire series of laboratory experiments, such a computerized, simulated chemistry program would greatly enhance flexibility of scheduling lab work for an entire class. Moreover, it would enable pupils to make up work at times of their own choosing or to do additional work in study or free periods and forge ahead into new territory at will.

The simulated environment for social studies developed by this Board of Cooperative Educational Services is similar to the computerized economic model used by some graduate schools and by economic planners in various governments. The first environment programed by BOCES was based on the socioeco-

5 Brown, B. Frank. *New Concepts in School Plant Design: An Accent on Accessibility.* Melbourne, Fla.: Melbourne High School, 1966. pp. 6-7.

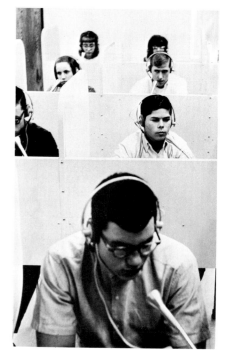

nomics of ancient Sumer. It gives social studies students a chance to "help" the Sumerian priest-king make some important guns-or-butter decisions and to project the social and economic consequences of those decisions.

In this teaching-learning situation a whole series of alternatives in response to a given situation or a particular course of action can be explored and their consequences evaluated. The wheel has been invented. If the order is given to put wheels on carts so grain can be moved more quickly, will an economy of abundance result? What happens to leisure? To employment? To the rate of invention? To the growth of villages? Will there be inflation in Sumer? If less Sumerian energy is required for food distribution, where will the surplus energy be diverted—to military activity or to artistic achievement?

The possibilities for realistic study of the effects of technological development on the production of economic goods, on employment, on the use of natural resources, on long-established value patterns, on income, on standards of living, and on the places where people live and the hours they work are readily recognized. When relevant data and the consequences of different courses of action are dramatically and forcefully brought within the realm of student comprehension, learning will undoubtedly take place at a much more rapid pace than is possible through the reading of printed materials and the discussion of questions and issues.

Learning Resources

No longer will the library be a collection of printed matter with, perhaps, some tapes and records in a soundproof carrel to one side of the room. The library in tomorrow's school will contain instant information in three dimensions: printed, animated, and with sound. A student will be able to sit in a library booth equipped with television screen, earphones, and a device resembling today's stock ticker or teletype receiver. If the desired printed material is not on file locally, relevant excerpts will be supplied by the interlibrary teletype receiver which will be plugged into a statewide, perhaps nationwide, network of libraries encompassing schools, colleges, medical schools, museums, the Library of Congress, and gradu-

ate centers. Programed instruction sequences, films, television documentaries, and other visual library references will be instantly available on an individual viewing screen in the library booth at the student's own school. Great works of music, rare recordings, and tapes of outstanding musical performances will come to him through his library booth earphones at pushbutton command. The advanced student will be able to obtain instantaneous computer translations in his own language of any scholarly work or scientific paper he may wish to read. Education will truly be a matter of probing, analyzing, and interpreting all the information in man's collective storehouse of knowledge.

Measurement and Evaluation

As education moves to independent pursuit of knowledge from today's group-textbook technique of instruction, testing and test records will be revised drastically. The IQ test, standard achievement scores, percentiles, and other "norms" upon which we have relied in this century will be anachronisms. Pupil progress will be analyzed in terms of profiles of individual growth rather

than in terms of collections of "right or wrong" answers to categorical questions. Multivariate analysis of longitudinal studies made possible by the computer will provide a continuous profile of each student's mental, emotional, and physical growth.

The computer—or, at least, data-processing equipment—is already being used in many school systems. But in most instances its use is limited to clerical tasks without its contributing to any notable advance in evaluating a pupil's individual progress. If we do not take advantage of the computer's ability to answer questions and interpret data, the need for its use in analyzing and evaluating instructional programs and the progress of individual pupils will be inconsequential. What is needed is "a summary of test score evidence with respect to particular questions, questions with educational and career relevance for each student." [6]

With effective use there will be an input consisting of scores, grades, biographical (including family) information, and the student's school and career plans. Output will then be in the nature of appraisal of the

direction in which the student is moving and prediction of probable success and satisfaction to be expected. Presumably, stumbling blocks could be anticipated and current obstacles to achievement eliminated. A computer programed with sufficient information could help in selecting an appropriate sequence of books, films, courses, lectures, and other material for each student. With appropriate use of computers, it will be possible for teachers and administrators to identify students whose achievement-growth curves have headed downward, analyze school practices in terms of student behavior and achievement, do better jobs of college and vocational placement, identify latent abilities of adults whose jobs have become obsolete as a result of technological advance, and develop retraining programs and placement procedures on an objective basis.

Form and Substance

The form and substance of the educational program for tomorrow's school is just emerging. Like the

glow of the sun on the eastern horizon, it gives promise of a new day that is not yet born. The program in this school will have greater breadth and depth than the program in today's school. Prekindergarten classes will be universally accepted as an integral part of the educational program. Essential compensatory educational experiences will help the child from the culturally deficient rural area or the urban slum to get an even start with the child who comes to school from more fortunate circumstances. Vocational training and retraining programs will help young people move from the schools directly into employment where they can earn a living and make useful contributions to society. Adult education programs will help young people move in developing their potential for new employment.

Much of the content in the instructional program will be shifted to more appropriate grade levels, and irrelevant and obsolete content will be discarded and replaced by concepts and information that have relevance in a life characterized by dramatic cultural change. Public education will be extended beyond the traditional twelfth grade to provide the understanding needed by everybody for effective citizenship

[6] Cooley, William W. "A Computer-Measurement System for Guidance." *Guidance in American Education II: Current Issues and Suggested Action.* (Edited by Edward Landy and Arthur M. Kroll.) Cambridge: Harvard University Press, 1965. pp. 265 ff.

and to serve older people as well as youth who want to continue their education on a part-time basis.

Those who are responsible for shaping this new educational program, mustering the support it must have, and designing the school facilities that will house it and make it functional will be guided by full understanding that the school is called upon to meet the needs of a generation of youth who must make a place for themselves in a world of change—in a culture they did not create, in a world they did not make, and amidst pressures that have baffled and perplexed their elders. These are overtones of the educational programs for the school of tomorrow.

A new type of school facility will be needed. This facility will not appear overnight; but it will not appear at all unless serious thought is given to what it should be. It must provide a functional environment for education moving into a state of unending transition. It must provide a visual environment which reassures and inspires—which says to students that change is challenge, not threat. It must encourage innovation and lend itself to modification as the educational program grows and changes. It must be a community rallying point, a focus of community learning from cradle to grave. Above all, it must not force the educational program into a restrictive architectural mold.

Those who are most successful in designing the new schoolhouse will look closely at the emerging social, economic, and cultural conformations which will determine the anatomy of the twenty-first century. The educational facility of tomorrow, whatever form and shade it takes, must be as much a part of its world as the little red schoolhouse was a part of yesterday.

Chapter 2 / *The Vista*

There are 3 billion people on the earth today. Unless present population trends change substantially, this number will double by the year 2000. The world supply of food, economists and demographers tell us, must be tripled during the next 35 years. Yet during the time that the supply of food must be increased so dramatically, the steady growth of industrialization and urbanization will continue. Scholars at the Athens Center of Ekistics look ahead to Ecumenopolis (literally, world city) when industrialization will have erased the disparity between Western industrial and Eastern rural nations and to the time when the earth may have a population of 50 billion persons.[1]

Already impatient hands are reaching out all over the world not only for food but for dignity, freedom, and, most eagerly of all, for knowledge—that "open sesame" to the better life. In Asia, in Africa, in South America, and even in our own prosperous continent, human appetites and aspirations hunger for long-denied satisfaction. If civilization as we know it is to endure and to continue to lead mankind a little closer to the destiny he seeks, it will be through education. Education is the key to employment in our own society and holds most promise for easing social tensions here and elsewhere.

Education increases the productivity of workers. It enhances their skills, it improves their health and strength, it enhances their responsibility and self-discipline, it enables them to operate advanced technologies which would otherwise be foreclosed by lack of literacy and understanding. Education also produces the scientists, engineers, businessmen, and government officials who are needed to invent, develop, and apply new technologies. . . . Instead of technology being the given to which people must adjust, the qualities and abilities of the people are the given, and it is to them that technology must adjust. Technological advancement can proceed only as fast as the educational advancement of the society will permit. . . . I see as the task of highest priority for our society the extension of education to the disadvantaged elements of our society, both rural and urban and both white and black, and the deepening of education for all groups. I see this not so much as a way to full employment as a means to achievement of ever higher technologies and thus to economic progress.[2]

The main purpose of education is, however, neither economic nor technological, but rather the development of individual talents and the building of a rich and creative civilization. Bowen further observes that he is "amazed and pleased by how little conflict there is between the best in education for human development and the best in education for economic and technological progress." With John Stuart Mill, he believes that the "drawing out of the powers of the human being is the best education for life as well as for economic productivity."[3]

It is not change per se which the schools of tomorrow must foster, but the *capacity* for change. Senator J. W. Fulbright, chairman of the Senate Committee on Foreign Relations, has pinpointed a fundamental challenge to educa-

[1] McBroom, Patricia. "Civilization in 2100 A.D." *Science Newsletter* 88: 298-99; November 6, 1965.

[2] Bowen, Howard R. "Technological Change and the Future of Higher Education." Paper read at the closing general session on "Technological Changes in the Future of Higher Education," Twenty-First National Conference on Higher Education (sponsored by the Association for Higher Education), Chicago, March 16, 1966.

[3] *Ibid.*, p. 5.

tion, "freeing our minds from the dead weight of habit and prejudice and stereotype and . . . bringing to bear on foreign policy the rich and diverse resources of liberally educated men."[4] While this comment was directed specifically to foreign policy, it applies equally well to the entire spectrum of education.

It would be folly, of course, to look to the future with the eyes of an isolationist. There are no cultural islands left on earth, and no longer can we be insular in educational planning. Education must be viewed in worldwide perspective, for it is against a world backdrop that the human drama of the late twentieth and early twenty-first centuries will be enacted, and educators must write a script which will make sense in that setting.

Perceptions of the Future

What can we now perceive of the future? Some of its dimensions are quite clear, others hazy. There is no doubt that we must continue to cope with phenomenal population growth.

[4] Fulbright, J. W. "Higher Education and the Crisis in Asia." Paper read at the second general session on "Higher Education and the Crisis in Asia," Twenty-First National Conference on Higher Education (sponsored by the Association for Higher Education), Chicago, March 14, 1966.

The technological revolution already well under way will pit the importance of the individual against the benefits of automation and cybernetics. We can foresee with considerable clarity increasing worldwide urbanization and growing intensity in the struggle between the "haves" and the "have nots." If social stability and economic equilibrium are to be achieved, it is urgent that instructional programs be recast and reorganized to re-educate unemployed adults; to give culturally handicapped youngsters compensatory education; to extend equal educational opportunities to all children, youth, and adults; and to prepare people to meet and cope with problems emerging in an age of unending change.

The cost of retooling our educational systems for the job ahead will be staggering; it will make today's school budgets look small in retrospect. Planning and initiating an educational program that will do what must be done and mustering the necessary financial support will require all our imagination and all our ingenuity. It will also require a new partnership among local school authorities, state governments, the federal government, and world agencies such as the United Nations and UNESCO.

Sarnoff has predicted that science and technology will advance further during the remainder of this century than in all the millennia since man's creation. The moon and other parts of the solar system will be brought within the human domain, he forecasted, and man will have machines which can multiply thought and logic a millionfold. Despite advancing industrialization, or perhaps because of it, Western nations will be able to produce twice as much food as they can consume and to extend production and conservation techniques to less favored parts of the world. Large-scale desalinization of ocean waters and the tapping of vast underground freshwater lakes will substantially increase man's supply of pure water, and food crops harvested from the sea will alleviate his ancient dependence on the soil.

With the construction of nuclear power plants, unlimited energy is at hand. Atomic science and electronics are revolutionizing diagnostic medicine and surgery. As noted earlier, it will soon be possible to manipulate the individual human genetic code and control the transmission of hereditary characteristics. Audio and visual commu-

nication between continents and among planets will be inexpensive and instantaneous, and travel so swift and effortless that man will rocket from one end of the earth to the other as casually as he now drives to the supermarket.

"Despite these enormous changes," Mr. Sarnoff reassuringly concludes, "the machine in the year 2000 will still be the servant of man. The real promise of technology is that it will release man from routine drudgeries of mind and body and will remove the final imprint of the cave. . . . Man's mind will then be free for the creative thinking that must be done if the impact of science is to be harmonized with man's enduring spiritual, social, and political needs."[5]

Yet let us not be lulled into complacency by such reassurances. The United States, because of its pre-eminence in the world's socio-economic power structure, can expect to assume major leadership responsibility for advances in education. If we fail to do it, who can? And who will? The outlines of an educational program necessary to meet these challenges are perhaps less discernible than projected scientific achievements. As one looks

ahead to an emerging, unfolding instructional program, nevertheless, he sees greater reliance on non-graded grouping and individually paced study, closer tailoring of educational programs to student career plans, training for occupations beginning in the elementary grades, closer cooperation between economic enterprise and the schools, and inservice programs for teachers and administrators that will keep them sensitive to the implications of cultural change and fully acquainted with new information.

Education, in a new sense will be the main purpose of life. Learning is what human life is. Humanity has traveled a long way to arrive at that essential truth. Man in the past may have been a hunting animal, a fighting animal or a working animal. Future man will be a learning animal, not just during what we now think of as the school years but during all of life. To go on learning, to go on communicating that learning to others, will be considered a purpose worthy of man's enormous and ever-expanding capacity.[6]

Good schools will become better. But unless the whole public comprehends the educational challenges emerging in this new era and exerts extraordinary efforts, the gap between good schools and poor schools is likely to widen until the ills growing out of the disparity awaken disinterested and indifferent people in great numbers from their lethargy. Many thoughtful people question the capacity of the schools to rise to this new challenge.

The growing national concern for the improvement of education is undoubtedly one of the most pronounced phenomena of the times. This concern has led to negative criticism of the schools as they are and of what they try to do as well as to constructive suggestions for improvement. In truth and fairness, it should be pointed out that much of the criticism of public education that comes from this penetrating analysis is not criticism of the schools so much as criticism of the culture. For the schools in general have tended to reflect those parts of the culture which have deep and abiding meaning to all people. In this character, they have tended to remain a few paces behind the tempo set by the drummer. Their

[6] Leonard, George B. "Where the California Game Is Taking Us." *Look* 30: 116; June 28, 1966.

[5] Sarnoff, David. "By the End of the Twentieth Century." *Fortune* 69: 116-19; May 1964.

chief deficiency may well be their failure to affect the culture rather than merely to be a function of it.

On the one hand, the schools are pressed to take a leading role in correcting the social ills imposed by segregated housing, racial discrimination, low economic income, and poor physical and mental health. On the other hand, strong pressures are exerted on the schools to keep teaching and learning free from and unsullied by the realities of life about them. As the philosophy that undergirds the institution of public education is reviewed in light of new circumstances, new needs, and new demands, the schools will undoubtedly be affected by these divergent viewpoints.

Full utilization of manpower by the schools, as in other segments of the culture, is not among the least of the multiple dimensions of the new educational challenge. In this age when the United States is called to her most arduous world responsibility, her working force— the productive segment of society —will be proportionately smaller than at any other time in her history. According to the Bureau of the Census, the labor force—persons aged 22 to 64—in 1950 con-

stituted 55 percent of the total population; persons from birth to age 21, 36.9 percent of the population; and persons 65 and over, 8.1 percent. By July 1970, Census projections indicate, the working age group will decline to 46.9 percent of the total population, while the birth-to-21-year segment will have grown to 43.7 percent and the over-65 group to 9.4 percent of the population.

This pattern of population age distribution is expected to persist to the end of the century. The population swell of the post World War II baby boom has reached the colleges, and the crest of the wave will enter the labor force during the next five years. But if present trends of early marriage and child-bearing are sustained, there will be an almost simultaneous increase in the birth-to-five-year age group as people born in the immediate post-war period produce a new crop of infants. Meanwhile, at the other end of the scale, life expectancy increases and swells the ranks of senior citizens.

More of Everything

The implications are clear: more classrooms, more teachers, more money will be needed. Local taxpayers, with the heaviest levy on residential real property, will find it increasingly difficult to meet ris-

ing costs of education. More will be demanded of the schools than ever before, and they will be expected to meet those demands more efficiently and more economically.

Numerically, the prospect is awesome. The traditional 5-to-17-year-old school-age group increased from 31 million in 1950 to more than 43 million in 1960 and is expected to reach 54 million by 1970. Note the phrasing, "traditional school-age group." The idea of a given "school age" is rapidly becoming an anachronism. Learning is, by man's nature, a life-long process, but its depth and breadth have heretofore depended upon the individual's own initiative once he passed beyond the age of "formal schooling." No longer is this true. Society is now insisting that formal education be stretched almost from cradle to grave and that it be the acknowledged responsibility of the public schools. Consequently, we are not talking about educating 54 million youngsters in 1970; we are talking about community demands for liberal arts, science, and vocational education for a total popula-

14

tion of 213 million by 1970 and perhaps twice that number by 2000.

The rapid growth rate of the oldest and the youngest age groups in this country inevitably means increasing demands for all types of social and governmental services—especially education. People under the age of 21 and over the age of 65 generally pay less or even no property and income taxes. As the proportion of the total population in these age groups increases, the financial burden on the productive age groups becomes increasingly greater. And this happens at a time when education is stretching vertically to meet the needs of every age group and extending horizontally to provide a wider range of opportunities to meet diversified needs and interests.

Getting a job, earning a living, and making a useful contribution to society are uppermost in the minds of most people and in particular young people. Recognizing that education now more than ever before stands clearly between them and the jobs they want, they turn to the schools to provide the skills, the information, and the understandings necessary for purposeful and useful employment.

This emphasis on vocational education is not merely a concern of the individual. The manpower needs of business, industry, agriculture,

and service institutions and agencies depend upon appropriate, adequate, and continuous education. Education has been recognized by the federal government in recent legislation, by business and industrial leaders, and by local and state governmental officials as a promising way to solve the unemployment problem, to reduce delinquency, and to help people move from poverty-stricken conditions into circumstances where they can have good homes and lead useful lives.

The educational needs of newcomers to the cities whose ways of life have been disrupted by technological changes that affect employment opportunities and the children of migratory agricultural workers who follow the crops from one part of the country to another, seldom remaining in one locality long enough to profit substantially from a well organized educational program, are especially great. Teachers, administrators, health officials, welfare workers, and community leaders must approach the problem of meeting the special educational needs of these people with imagination, with boldness, and with readiness to make adaptations in

existing programs. These adaptations may well lead in some instances to taking the school to the learner if the learner cannot come to the school.

Alger Retires

After many years of resistance, the American people now seem willing to inter the Horatio Alger legend. They are conceding that in a highly specialized, technological society personal enterprise alone is no substitute for specialized training. In a simpler agrarian society, a strong back, a hard muscle, a willingness to work, and an aggressive spirit were all a youth needed to get and hold a job and to make a place for himself in the world. The implements he used were simple and easily understood. High priority was placed on physical strength, power of endurance, and ability to stand up under the rigors of hard labor.

Such circumstances no longer prevail. The implements and mechanical devices that workmen now use are no longer simple; they are complicated; and each productive operation is synchronized with a hundred others. In this new age, high priority is placed on mental alertness, on highly developed skills, and on ability to work cooperatively

15

as a member of a team or a large group and to fit into an enterprise with which the employee had no direct acquaintance until the day he was employed.

Vocational training, once considered at a simple, mechanical level, is now regarded by many laymen and educators as highly technical training. Continuing provision for retraining workers is needed as rapidly advancing technology eliminates old jobs and creates demands for new skills. Housing and equipment for vocational training which will cut unemployment rates and meet requirements of industry will be two to three times as expensive as facilities for college preparatory programs.

With society becoming more complex and with great groups of people concentrated in urban agglomerations becoming more dependent on intricate, interwoven networks of specialization, all sorts of skills and talents will be needed for a multitude of roles and functions. We have trouble enough imparting the knowledge and wisdom we wish to transmit to students in a conventional setting on a traditional 9- or 10-month schedule. To do the job ahead, more and more school systems will turn to a 12-month

school program and to 13 or 14 years of schooling. These extended programs may offer two streams of education—one for future technicians and skilled tradesmen and one for those who will later proceed to higher studies in science, engineering, medicine, and the liberal arts. California has already led the way in community college development, and other states are following suit with community colleges closely attuned to regional needs.

The college preparation function of the secondary school and the costs of meeting the demands for higher education in the years ahead will make tremendous demands on educational resources. As graphically shown in the accompanying chart, enrollments in colleges and universities during the next 25 years will increase approximately 175 percent, while increase in the population will be a little less than 50 percent. In other words, the proportion of the population enrolled in institutions of higher education 25 years from now will be about three and a half times greater than now.

Not only will there be more people in colleges and universities, but they will be better prepared for college work than they have ever been before.

Several colleges and universities with high admittance standards are finding that their

"best freshmen are getting better—getting better *fast*," as Lee DuBridge, President of Caltech, affirms in a recent issue of his institution's *Quarterly*. He notes "a rise of from 10 to as much as 40 points on the percentile scale (of CEEB test scores) for the average freshman in the past ten years" at universities such as Caltech, Harvard, Yale, Princeton, Stanford, and M.I.T.[7]

Yesterday, Today and Tomorrow [8]

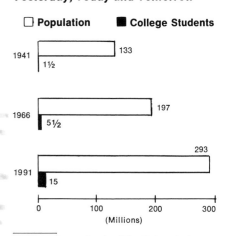

□ **Population**   ■ **College Students**

[7] Killian, James R., Jr. "The Return to Learning." *New Curricula*. (Edited by Robert W. Heath.) New York: Harper & Row, 1964. pp. 260-61.

[8] Lindow, Wesley, and Tickton, Sidney G. "Yesterday, Today, and Tomorrow." Paper presented before the State Chairmen of the Savings Bond Division of the U.S. Treasury Department, February 9, 1966. Washington, D.C.: Savings Bond Division of U.S. Treasury, 1966.

Improvements in the qualifications of young people enrolled in less renowned institutions are undoubtedly comparable—and the end is not yet. Academic standards and the quality of work in liberal arts institutions and graduate schools will continue to rise.

The Peripatetic Population

The frustrations encountered by educators as they try to cope with internal migration and the patterns of population distribution in the United States will be most vexing of all. We are a nation on the move. Each year in the past decade, 30 million people have moved from one house to another—about 20 million to a new location in the same county, 5 million across county lines, and 5 million across state lines. There is good reason to believe that mobility will accelerate as new industries springing up across the land attract craftsmen and professionals to new opportunities.

The population of urban areas increased from 64.0 percent of the total population in 1950 to 69.9 percent in 1960. And there are indications that this trend toward urbanization will persist. But there is a paradox here. While urbanization continues and metropolitan districts increase in size, the population of many cities is declining. Families are moving from the central cities to satellite suburbs. Eight of the 10 largest cities in the United States lost population between 1950 and 1960.

Sections of cities vacated by prosperous families are being occupied by less affluent people. Crowded into city quarters, these newcomers have created problems and conflicts that have all too frequently remained unsolved and unresolved by city school systems caught in the crosscurrents of social change. The need for all sorts of educational and other governmental services increases at a time when the financial base of the city is being weakened by the influx of people with low incomes. As viewed from the point of view of the school board and the superintendent, the cost of an adequate educational program has increased phenomenally while the city's financial ability to support schools has been substantially weakened. These are facts of life that must be forthrightly faced in projecting education programs to meet the needs of great cities in a period of transition.

The Negro's Urban Plight ✳

The difficulty of the educational problem in large city school systems has been accentuated by the preponderance of Negroes in inmigration. As they have come in increasing numbers from the agricultural lands of the rural South to take heavy jobs in city factories, technology is doing away with the jobs they came to fill. Lacking the skills required for ready employment in business and industry, many are left stranded and bitter in the city ghetto. The unemployment rate among Negroes in 1964 was twice the unemployment rate among white people. These circumstances are particularly trying for the teen-age Negro. To illustrate, 15 percent of all American teen-agers seeking work in 1964 were unemployed; but 23 percent of Negro teen-age boys and 31 percent of Negro teen-age girls could find no work. In such circumstances they are beginning adult life with a perspective of uselessness and hopelessness.

But one cannot fruitfully think for long in terms of a single Negro community in a large city. Each metropolis has at least two Negro communities—one characterized by fairly good income, comfortable housing, and reasonable security; the other by instability, high rates

17

of unemployment, and social values that lead to frustrations and conflict rather than self-confidence and stability.

It scarcely needs to be said that the educational needs of the second group are different from those of the first. The traditional forms of academic instruction common in existing schools are largely irrelevant to the needs of this second group. It is estimated that there are now more than 100,000 Negro youngsters, ranging in age from infancy to the late teens and early twenties, in New York City alone who are denied love, dignity, patrimony, and the tradition of any culture but television. "They rock around on the deck of an unstable society, their bread given to them by underpaid welfare workers, their hopes zero, their mothers despised, their hearth the gutter, a subculture in a general American urban culture which itself does not know where it is going."[9]

Can we who teach avert our faces from such wants, such needs, and such misery?

[9] White, Theodore H. *The Making of the President, 1964.* New York: Atheneum Publishers, 1965. p. 230.

School Is for Everybody

Tomorrow's school will be for everybody—the young and the old, the gifted and the handicapped, the academically talented and the youth with a mechanical bent. Schools will be different but, rather than having disparity in quality, they will have diversity in excellence.

Tomorrow's school will reach out to the places that enrich the human spirit—to the museums, the theaters, the art galleries, to the parks and rivers and mountains.

It will ally itself with the city, its busy streets and factories, its assembly lines and laboratories—so that the world of work does not seem an alien place for the student.

Tomorrow's school will be the center of community life, for grown-ups as well as children—"a shopping center of human services." It might have a community health clinic or a public library, a theater and recreation facilities.

It will provide formal education for all citizens—and it will not close its doors any more at three o'clock. It will employ its buildings round the clock and its teachers round the year.[10]

[10] Johnson, Lyndon Baines. Acceptance of the American Education Award at the 1966 convention of the American Association of School Administrators. *Official Report: Your AASA in 1965-66.* Washington, D.C.: the Association, 1966. p. 191.

The success of Operation Head Start dramatically illustrates what can be done through local-federal cooperation. As a result of the Head Start program, thousands of youngsters have entered kindergarten with a little more confidence and a little less disadvantage than would otherwise have been the case. Education will continue to reach down to the prekindergarten level in an effort to give the disadvantaged child, the shy child, the slow learner, and the physically handicapped youngster a true head start. Research has clearly shown that children are most susceptible to environmental influences during the first few years of their lives and that their ability to learn, rather than being fixed by genetic factors at birth, emerges as it is nurtured. And one can be sure that the people of this country will insist that these opportunities be extended to include young children in all segments of the population.

The Educational Policies Commission has unequivocally recommended that all children from the age of four be enrolled in school at public expense.[11] Such an ex-

[11] National Education Association and American Association of School Administrators, Educational Policies Commission. *Universal Opportunity for Early Childhood Education.* Washington, D.C.: the Commission, 1966.

tension of the educational program brings with it a host of problems, not the least of which are securing competent teachers, providing adequate plant facilities, and gaining better understanding of the patterns of physical growth and behavior of children at these earlier ages. Schools must be designed and scaled to the interests and behavior patterns of children. Their natural eagerness to learn must not be throttled by overpowering corridors; discouraging stairways; and big, impersonal classrooms. Some spaces in every elementary building must be special places for little folks—rooms with doors opening directly onto pleasant, grassy playgrounds; rooms furnished with colorful, light-weight furniture which can be rearranged by small hands; rooms where windows and windowsills are conveniently close to the floor.

The new schoolhouse will have separately accessible wings with special entrances for elderly students and for adult committee meetings or general community use. Multipurpose space will be common. For example, a single room may have a small stage and a general meeting area flanked by alcoves with movable partitions. There will be spaces for small-group discussion, individual study, committee projects, instructional materials, displays, and other special uses.

The requirements of space age science, technology, industry, social services, and government will be so great and so staggeringly diverse that human resources cannot be wasted. Practical as well as humanitarian considerations will re-emphasize the importance of the individual in all schools and in every part of each school, whether space is used by prekindergarten children, elementary and secondary students, vocational students, handicapped youngsters, elderly persons, geniuses, or dullards.

In acknowledging the need for diversity in school plant planning, we are only echoing what Thoreau said so long ago: "If a man does not keep pace with his companions, perhaps it is because he hears a different drummer. Let him step to the music which he hears, however measured or far away."[12] So that each student can "step to the music which he hears," new schoolhouses will provide quiet places for individual reading, scientific experiments, artwork, and independent research. Each student will have access to television, to sound tapes, and to books in small private places where he can go to pursue his own interests. Lecture halls for large groups; small- and medium-sized meeting rooms for smaller groups; and shops where students can work with many kinds of tools, materials, and equipment will be standard features. These features of the school plant will not be luxuries, and they need not be expensive. Indeed, a school tailored to individual needs should and can be more economical and more efficient than an unimaginative structure in which people are herded together like sheep.

A 1960 study by Educational Facilities Laboratories counsels educators, architects, and citizens to—

—Anticipate—schools are usually planned too fast.

—Think of what you want the school to produce before you decide what to put in it.

—Don't plan in isolation—your neighbors have the same problems.

—Don't buy permanence at the expense of performance. We're in a period of rapid cultural change; don't saddle us with unchangeable schools that will some day "sit beside the road, a ragged beggar, sunning."[13]

13 Educational Facilities Laboratories. *The Cost of a Schoolhouse.* New York: the Laboratories, 1960. p. 138.

12 Thoreau, Henry David. *Walden.* New York: Random House (Modern Library edition), 1950. p. 290.

New materials just appearing on the market and new uses of old materials make the building of new schools exciting. New possibilities are opened by versatile structural steel, precast concrete, aluminum alloys with unusual strength, laminated wood, new adhesives, and plastics which can be molded to order in any shape from rectangle to hyperbolic paraboloid. These and other materials will be imaginatively used in constructing buildings to facilitate the operation of the new educational program—a program that will cast off nineteenth-century shackles of tradition and teach people to think for themselves. The ability to think independently must be further developed. It is impossible to teach a generation of children all the facts relevant to a satisfying and productive life and to impart all the information accumulated through the ages. Old and young alike must be taught how to learn, how to gather information, how to organize and evaluate it, how to reason, and how to think. The new educational program must inspire them to want to learn and to keep on learning every day of their lives.

If teachers, administrators, and parents want to foster in young people the desire to be daring, to be bold, to try new ways, and to discover the truth, then they must set an example by daring to design buildings which exemplify and embody these aspirations. If children are to learn to love beauty, to respect wisdom, and to seek peace, then the school building must be a visible testament of the commitment of communities of mature people to these values.

In projecting this goal for school plant planning, two recognized leaders in school plant planning—one an educator, the other an architect—in 1949 challenged architects, administrators, school board members, and all others with responsibility for planning to "create school plants which will be living realities of the best American life. Plants which will embody the best of American idealism. Plants in which people can grow and be happy. In which communities can be born. School plants which demonstrate what can happen when free men work together toward common, worthy ends."[14]

This challenge to translate the philosophy and the broad outlines of an educational program into functional and aesthetically pleasing school buildings for tomorrow's children is as apropos to this generation of school builders as it was 20 years ago and perhaps even more vital to the ongoing course of educational improvement.

[14] Cocking, Walter D., and Perkins, Lawrence B. Schools. New York: Reinhold Publishing Co., 1949. p. 1.

Chapter 3 / *New Instructional Procedures*

Every dimension of education —purposes and content, methods and materials, financial support and status—has been dramatically influenced during the past decade by forces inherent in rapid cultural change. Its recognition as a force in shaping the destiny of a free nation and a free world is unmatched in the history of the nation. Buildings, teachers, books, programs, policies, and the achievement of pupils have all been subjected to the close scrutiny of a concerned people. Educators in every corner of the nation have examined the educational process with the full realization that the future of this nation and the free world depends in large measure on the excellence of education in the United States.

In recent years there has been a flood of so-called innovations in education. Attention has been sharply focused on broadening the program, lengthening the school day, increasing the length of the school year, extending the program to pre-first-grade levels, expanding the college, and improving adult education. None of these approaches to strengthening the

schools is new, but each has been given new impetus. At the same time there has been a mighty tug-of-war between long-established and traditional methods of teaching and newer techniques and procedures. Team teaching, along with all that it implies, has had a powerful impact on education. The need for grouping children in groups of varying size has been more clearly recognized. The trend toward individualized teaching, independent study, and student research has emphasized the need for smaller instructional areas. These shifting emphases and the increase of evening high schools, growing interest in the middle school, concern for the deprived child, and a virtual explosion of production of teaching media have triggered experimental and pilot programs of education across the country.

Tempo of Change

Materials of instruction, undreamed of a few short years ago, are now in the wings of the educational stage. Some school communities, recognizing the potential of these new and varied teaching tools, are finding ways to use them to teach more and to teach better. Teaching machines, audiovisual devices, listening devices, microfilming equipment, and many other new tools are claiming places on the educational scene.

One cannot help feeling change in the tempo of our educational programing. Teachers are pressed to help children learn more. Pressure to learn more and to learn better is felt by children. Some subject matter is being moved downward to lower grade levels. Some skills formerly taught only in secondary schools are now taught at elementary grade levels. These changes in programing and increases in educational tempo are having profound effects on educational planning.

The ferment of ideas in education affects every feature of the school plant, from temperature control to the electronics laboratory. Since buildings call for major investment of educational funds, since they are of such permanent nature, and since they have such a direct and definite influence on the educational process, educators and community leaders have rightfully been concerned about their design and their potential for meeting educational needs.

Space

How can we plan the school building for tomorrow from what we know today and under the influence exerted upon us by our yesterdays? Upon what factual information and background of experience can we draw to gain this vision? We know not the answer to either of these questions, but there is one concept which has great implications for school building design. This concept is *space.* This does not merely suggest that more space is needed or that pupils and teachers can get along with less space. Rather, it focuses attention on a kind of space that can be adjusted to changing needs with minimum delay and cost. We need fluid space, flexible space, variable space, multiple-use space, and space which is not restrained by tradition. Spaces need not be more costly, but they must be more functional and productive in the education of boys and girls.

Individualized Learning

Perhaps the one major trend which has exerted the greatest impact on planning new schools is the growing recognition of the individual in instruction. For decades educational leaders have given lip service to the need for each individual student to progress at his own rate. The decade of the sixties is seeing this concept translated into bricks and mortar. The good school building today has many kinds of spaces and maximum ability to convert and reconvert spaces as the need arises. Study carrels are provided for individual and small-group use. Many of them are specially equipped for visual and audio presentations as well as for quiet study and research. Classrooms, too, are designed to facilitate individual study as well as participation in groups of various sizes. Interesting little corners with a variety of educational toys and games, places where a child can manipulate objects or put together a model, and spaces for quiet reading or viewing filmstrips can bring great rewards in the achievement of young people.

Emphasis on individual learning should not be interpreted to mean that normal-sized classrooms or instructional areas are being abandoned. The more traditional-sized classrooms and spaces for individuals and small groups are needed as well as areas to facilitate large-group instruction. The modern school building properly designed for all sizes of instructional groups, therefore, loses the neat pattern of rows of identical classrooms separated or joined by corridors. By design, the spaces differ in size, function, and equipment.

The Changing Classroom

The classroom, long regarded as the very core of educational facilities, is feeling the impact of change from many sides. As the kind and amount of information increases and teachers and administrators devise new ways to help children learn more and learn it faster and better, the traditional classroom is feeling the tugs of change. Mass communication media, already proven to be educationally valuable, are claiming their share of space. The increasing amounts and kinds of education materials and tools used are changing the face of the classroom. The need and the demand for an extended school year is necessitating air conditioning, and heavier reliance on artificial lighting is decreasing the need for wide, expansive

window areas. Feeling the push from many directions, permanent walls are giving way to provide more flexible space for teaching and learning.

If there is a key to designing the classroom of today, that key might well be *flexibility of space.* Efficient deployment of staff is high among the priorities being set at every level of education in America. Classrooms are no longer regarded as the private property of the individual teacher established in the self-contained room. Teams of teachers want classroom facilities shaped to fit the needs of the present as they attempt to meet the educational goals set for them by society. A classroom should probably be anything but permanent and should certainly reflect to the highest degree possible its potential as a laboratory of learning. New ways will continue to be sought to provide large and small classroom spaces readily adaptable to change.

The Changing Curriculum

Many people believe that we may be on the threshold of a renaissance of the humanities. The last decade brought a tremendous surge of interest in the sciences; now the humanities are demanding their rightful places. Thoughtful planners of good school facilities are including in their plants well designed theaters or auditorium-theaters where children come together to debate and to sing, to hear concerts and see pageants, and to participate in dramatic productions. Provisions are being made for art instruction and well designed areas for art displays throughout the building. Band, choral, and music practice rooms are being provided to give students varied opportunities to become better acquainted with the world of music. These facilities are not considered to be frills in construction but functional areas specifically designed to meet the educational, psychological, and emotional needs of children. Why should not the school planner be just as concerned for the potentially talented artist as for his counterpart in the academic field? Why should he not provide for this student, too, the laboratory of learning which may kindle and develop his skills in his own particular field of interest? And, since concern is increasing for the emotional and psychological well-being of pupils, why should not the school planner give adequate consideration to providing facilities to meet these needs?

In developing building plans, administrators sensitive to children's needs give prime attention to providing areas other than conventional classroom spaces. For even young children, there are spaces for library books, growing plants, science collections, and art displays, appropriately designed and equipped for the age level. There are spaces for creative play, for sitting, visiting, and relaxing. There are gardened areas rich in beauty where children learn through experience not only to enjoy beauty, but to respect and protect it. The auditorium and assembly rooms give live, first-hand experiences in the performing arts—orchestral, dramatic, and choral performances —all appropriate to the child's age level. Other parts of the building contain museum and laboratory facilities to further acquaint the child with the world in which he lives.[1]

Many recent school buildings contain facilities that lend themselves well to role playing in education. Here one might expect to see a "mock court in action" or a "legislature in session." These areas

[1] American Association of School Administrators. *Imperatives in Education.* Washington, D.C.: the Association, 1966. pp. 81-82.

need not be expensive in design or construction and certainly should not be so overdesigned as to restrict their broad usage in many programs. Such areas serve well as theaters-in-the-round for dramatic productions.

Many recently constructed secondary schools have included animal and micro laboratories in their science departments. Students derive great benefits from programs in animal care. Opportunities to work with animals, to handle them, to feed them, to test their reactions to diet and environmental conditions, and to learn their habits enrich the science program far beyond the cost of physical facilities needed for such programs. School planners should contemplate the need for such facilities in a new secondary school.

An art museum in the community elementary or secondary school brings interest, curriculum enrichment, and still another tool to the teacher as she reaches out to help each child. Such a museum serves the whole community in the evenings and on weekends as well as pupils and teachers during the school day. Here children and even some adults get their first real learning about and enjoyment of the world of art. A well-designed art museum, with simple but attractive furnishings, proper lighting, and ap-

propriate acoustics may well become one of the busiest and most popular spots in the community.

Because of the current great interest in science, especially in space conquest, some schools are incorporating modest planetariums into their buildings. Such a facility, with a competent instructor, adds great impetus to the school program. In large school districts a planetarium may well serve students from several schools as well as adults during nonschool hours. It affords opportunities for young and old alike to grasp the greatness of the universe and the immensity of the task faced in probing into outer space. The magic of the projector, the simulation of the evening skies, the mystery of the constellations, and the glory of the sunrise and the sunset come close to reality in this working tool of education.

A greenhouse can add new dimensions to a science program at modest cost. A work area where students can experiment with plants, try out conditions for growth, and study the effects of soil and fertilizers can bring school alive for some students whose interests lie in plants more than in books. The abilities of these students lie more

in their hands and their feeling for living plants than in academic pursuits. Even a small and inexpensive greenhouse can bring new interest and vitality into the science program and broaden its scope.

Foreign language departments, primarily in secondary schools, have moved steadily toward the use of language laboratories. This technique requires a radical departure from the classroom in which Latin was taught in years past. The use of electronic equipment and the atmosphere of the room itself require change in size and a change in decor. Large schools or schools with an emphasis on foreign language instruction may find that the language laboratory is fully scheduled and in almost constant use by classes in foreign languages. Other schools, wanting to make better use of facilities, have found that language laboratories serve other educational programs—English, social studies, and the sciences—to advantage. Multichannel communication units can serve more than one group at any given time.

Instructional Resources Center

Libraries, too, are changing and becoming much more than reading rooms and repositories for books and pamphlets. To be sure, these are major functions of this educational space, but there are other needs to be met. The library area might be more appropriately designated as the instructional materials center or the learning resource center. In a center developed in this broader context, the user finds the information he needs in print, on film, in photographs, and in models. In small rooms and booths and carrels there are facilities for small groups to listen to recordings and view projections. If educational television is used in instruction, one may find in the library complex the major control room for the school. Here, also, are facilities for the storage, control, and distribution of the audiovisual equipment used in the school. This instructional center is designed to serve teachers as well as students and is in use in the evenings and on Saturday as well as throughout the school day. It is the resource center for the total educational program.

The first step in planning library facilities is a comprehensive survey of the school's educational program and the requirements for teaching and learning resources. The growing amount of knowledge in nearly all fields, the interrelation of these fields, and the global scope in which they function require that students in today's secondary school be given opportunities to learn more, in many subject matter areas, than specialists a few years ago knew. Every student must develop a greater capacity and a greater desire for learning than students in former years needed to have. The central purpose of the school library is to provide the materials, the inducements, and the environment to make this possible.

The architectural concept of a good school library has dramatically changed in recent years. Earlier, the library in many schools was little more than a study hall—a classroom lined with bookshelves and furnished with large study tables. Not infrequently the students were barred from access to the bookshelves by formidable counters and an overly protective librarian. As educational needs have changed and the amount of information essential for nurturing the maturing minds of young people has virtually exploded, the character of the library has changed. It has become larger and more functional. Students are put into a more intimate relationship with books, pamphlets, and other media used in transmitting ideas and information.

A functional school library, operating as an instructional materials center, should include rooms or space for—
—books, magazines, pamphlets
—professional materials
—individual study
—conferences
—classroom work
—listening and viewing
—audiovisual equipment and materials storage
—preparation of instructional materials
—librarian's office
—library workroom
—storage for printed materials.

The library in a secondary school should be located for maximum accessibility, convenience to academic classrooms, and protection from disturbing sounds in shops, music rooms, and cafeterias. In a growing school system, space should be allowed for future expansion also. Appropriate provisions should be made for extra-hour use (evenings,

summers, and Saturdays) and for adequate security when the library is in use and school is not in session.

Specific space requirements will be determined to a considerable extent by the size of the student body, the character of the school program, and the number and kinds of materials to be housed. But nothing much will be accomplished by an adequate, or even impressive, collection of books, materials, and equipment if limitations in space and facility arrangements prevent convenient and effective use. If there is one single space above all others in the school building that should be easily and readily accessible and that should have an inviting quality and a relaxing and contemplative atmosphere, it is the library.

In overall appearance, the library should be attractive and comfortable, as well as functional. An atmosphere that is harmonious, pleasant, and inviting will do much to encourage maximum student use. No longer is a school library an isolated corner shrouded in silence. As an integral part of the total school program, it is an active center for learning.

A library classroom is an important part of the school library suite. The trend toward independent study accentuates the need for students to learn how to use library resources efficiently. It is logical that this instruction be given by the librarian in the library. There are also many times when teachers wish to devote an entire class period to the use of library materials and to aid students in applying them to the subject at hand. Such activities in a general reading room may be annoying to other library users, but they can be carried on without disturbance in an adjoining classroom.

The library will be incomplete if provision is not made for a small professional library for teachers. This facility should have shelving, a periodical rack, a few desks, and comfortable chairs. If space is not available elsewhere, suitable equipment should be available for previewing audiovisual materials. The librarian also must have office space where she can perform her administrative duties. This office should open off the reading room and be connected to the workroom where processing is done. The workroom may include space for the preparation of instructional materials, but ideally the preparation room should be a separate facility, because different machines, materials, and equipment are used. When com-

binations are necessary, it is better to place racks for the storage of printed materials in the library workroom and audiovisual storage in the preparation room.

Despite all the attention audiovisual aids have received, particularly in recent years, very few plants have been planned to use the potential of these teaching media to best advantage. Lack of display space to invite the curious mind is one of the most obvious limitations in many newly constructed schools. Rather than enclosed spaces for untouchable objects, there is need for open lobby display areas, where larger numbers of people congregate or move through exhibits of artifacts and working models that stir the curiosity of young and old alike. Young people learn through many sensory approaches—the handling of objects, the intrigue of the working model, and the drawing power of the strange artifact. Displays that appeal to the sense of smell as well as sight, touch, and hearing can be created.

The potential of slides, filmstrips, and films for teaching and learning has scarcely been touched in many schools. Their use, as compared with the use of textbooks and other printed material, is incidental, something extra, or something special. It should be no more unusual for a student to study a set of slides or view a film in seeking to gain better understanding of an issue or some physical phenomenon than it is for him to read a textbook or to consult a standard reference. All are important; all should be readily available; and all should be used when the problem or circumstance calls for their use. Group use as well as individual use is essential. The day of the traveling projector, the blacked-out classroom, a screen in the storeroom, and a teacher in every room who doubles as a technician in audiovisual aids has just about passed. Provisions for educational television and film projection in classrooms by conduit circuits are designed into today's school. A good educational program will be made better by such facility planning.

Multiple Use of Space

Increasing emphasis on a comprehensive program of health services has caused school building planners to give serious considera-

tion to the activities a multipurpose room can be expected to accommodate. The adequacy of the traditional multipurpose room to serve so many functions—dining, assembly, and physical education—is being questioned. In increasing numbers gymnasiums are being planned as functional units in elementary schools. To be sure, they are not replicas of college or high school gymnasiums, nor should they be. Designed for a sequential program of physical development, these facilities serve a total program of education. If appropriately designed and equipped, the elementary gymnasium may serve the community effectively during evening hours when school is not in session. Such dual use increases the value of this school facility to the community and thus justifies even more the investment of funds in construction.

In many elementary schools dining rooms and assembly hall facilities are one and the same. The stage built at one end of the dining

hall and demountable dining tables make it possible to use this area as an assembly hall when it is not in use for dining. Further use can be made of this large area by dividing it into smaller instructional spaces through the use of movable partitions. With such an arrangement, groups of children can be brought together either in the large area for large-group instruction or in the smaller subdivided sections for a more intimate type of instruction. Ideally there should be a facility specially designed for each major function, but the hard facts of economics in most communities make some compromises necessary. The procedures suggested here are most commonly used in circumstances where facilities must be planned for multiple use.

The Atypical Child

The school has a commitment to serve all children and should insofar as possible provide an educational facility and an educational climate that is suitable for all children—the handicapped as well as the normal child. Severely handicapped children are best served in schools designed specifically to

meet their needs, but many handicapped children can and should attend regular schools in their own communities.

A physical handicap, no matter what its nature, in some measure sets the child apart from other children; it constitutes a barrier in his association with them. Segregating handicapped children to gain the advantages of physical arrangements and equipment tends to make this barrier higher and more nearly impenetrable. In consideration of the long-range educational needs of the handicapped child and his psychological reactions to his own difficulties and to other people, serious efforts should be made to develop a program and to construct facilities that will permit him to attend school with more fortunate children. With but little additional cost, provisions can be made to permit seriously handicapped children to live and work with other children to good advantage. If their needs and their limitations are kept in mind in the planning of school facilities, none but the most severely handicapped need be sent to special schools.

Community Use

Schools are no longer 6-hour, 5-day, 9-month institutions. No longer are children and adults repelled by No Trespassing signs on school property. The tide of isolation from community life has changed and is flowing strongly in the opposite direction. Schoolhouse doors are open, and signs everywhere read "welcome." This welcome is extended through arrangement of facilities, through policies pertaining to use of facilities, through appointments and furnishings, through avenues of access, and by the posture of the administration and instructional staff.

The school of today is of the community rather than just in it. Through its program, its organization, and its operation, it emphasizes unity with community life rather than aloofness from it. Buildings are available around the clock for education, recreation, meetings, and other use by citizens of the community.

Needless to say, school plant facilities intended for dual use by the community and by students must be carefully planned. Shops, auditoriums, libraries, seminar rooms, laboratories, swimming pools, and gymnasiums used frequently by adults during the evening hours must be readily accessible and lo-

cated so that the parts of the plant not in use during the evening hours need not be heated, cooled, lighted, or supervised.

The community service function of the school must be near the forefront in educational planning. The unique character of the community will determine to a considerable degree the nature of the services the school provides to people in the community. To illustrate, the vocational agriculture department should be ready and willing to check the butterfat content of the milk from a dairy herd, to run soil tests for the suburban dweller who is planting azaleas or rhododendron, or to recommend the kind of fertilizer needed for a new planting of strawberries; the League of Women Voters should be able to get new insights into a proposed change in the tax levy in a seminar sponsored by the economics department; and the housewife who wants to develop her interests in painting should be able to enroll in an evening course

in art to develop her talents and learn new techniques in the use of color and design.

Office Space

As school systems become larger and more complicated, responsibility for curriculum planning, instructional improvement, and professional leadership is being decentralized to a considerable degree and placed with the administrative staff in neighborhood and community schools. Such organization gets closer to the people and improves communication between the school and the community. In designing facilities to serve the administrative staff in such a school, adequate space must be provided for locally assigned personnel. This means that there must be more than an office for the principal and the secretary. School administration and instructional improvement are not separate and distinct functions, but tend to merge into one and the same thing. They resist separation. The principal assumes responsibility for the improvement of instruction and should be given adequate personnel to perform the task. He is the educational leader. His office is the nerve center for the entire school—the center

for coordination, for community educational leadership, and for setting the overtones of the school's philosophy.

The principal's office and the administrative suite designed to meet these needs should be located near the entrance to the school building. There should be a general reception area that is easy to locate, pleasant in design, and inviting in appearance. Counters, storage areas, and arrangement of office spaces are designed for free and easy access rather than as barriers between the staff and those who come to the office for assistance. The facilities themselves, by their arrangement and design, should be inviting to the teacher who is looking for guidance and to the pupil who is seeking advice, as well as to the anxious parent or interested citizen. The principal's office is an information center, and its doors are open, but the principal cannot always be out in the open. He must have office space which provides opportunities for him to have some

time alone to think, to read, to ponder, to speculate, and to counsel.

Offices are provided for other personnel also, such as vice-principals, guidance counselors, health officers, and secretaries and clerks. Adequate storage and shelving spaces are provided for all school personnel. Adequate provision is made for the communications system; it is easy to find, easy to enter, pleasant to be in, and designed to facilitate movement of people and provide privacy when necessary. Teachers, too, are provided with adequate office space for planning, for conferences with individual students, and for preparation of instructional materials. Critics who are prone to label administrative office space as a frill requiring unnecessary expenditure of public funds often fail to understand the importance of this facility in the total educational program.

Communication

The impact of the explosion of communication aids has been felt in school design. The good school is designed to make the use of these aids easy and effective. Built-in screens, means for easy transmission of films to any instructional area from a central source within the building, intercommunication systems between all areas in the build-

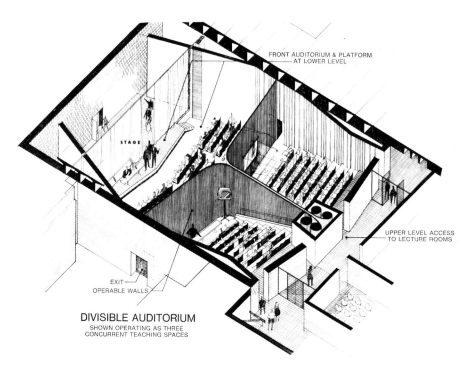

FRONT AUDITORIUM & PLATFORM
AT LOWER LEVEL

STAGE

UPPER LEVEL ACCESS
TO LECTURE ROOMS

EXIT
OPERABLE WALLS

DIVISIBLE AUDITORIUM
SHOWN OPERATING AS THREE
CONCURRENT TEACHING SPACES

ing, semiprivate corners in classrooms for viewing and listening, and tack boards and chalkboards are but some of the devices provided to make communication easy and instantaneous. Many teachers are discouraged from using screens and projectors because they are fearful of the mechanical procedures necessary or because such equipment is difficult to secure from a central storage area. Too many schools today have heavy investments in audiovisual equipment of the mobile type which is not being used as often as it might be.

Few, if any, educators are still debating the usefulness of educational television. They may well be debating how educational gains can best be accomplished, but not whether television is useful as an educational tool. Properly programed and executed, television can greatly enrich school programs. Thoughtful school planners, therefore, incorporate facilities which make these opportunities available to the instructional program. Students benefit not only from television programs brought to their classrooms but also from opportu-

nities to share in the preparation and production of programs. Television also provides new opportunities for kindling the imagination of an otherwise disinterested student and for challenging the gifted student to share his talents with his peers.

Adaptability to Change

As thoughtful teachers and administrators seek new and improved ways to help children learn more and learn better and forward-looking architects seek better ways to provide facilities adaptable to changing curriculum and methods, attention is focused on flexibility in the use of space. The need and cry for flexibility is not new. For a quarter of a century schoolmen have sought facilities that were readily adaptable to changes in instructional programs, in teaching techniques, and in educational goals. Flexibility, however, is no cure-all. It means but little unless instruction is improved by its utilization.

Flexibility in school design means many things to many people. School buildings have been designed with operable walls which form rooms at the touch of a button. This kind of flexibility may be useful in the day-to-day operation of the school. Buildings constructed with walls that are relatively easy to

move, remove, or install—although not folding or operable in nature—provide a different kind of flexibility involving a time factor. Obviously, all buildings possess a kind of flexibility; all can be changed, given the time and the funds to do so.

In its initial design, the good school building incorporates every conceivable characteristic which lends itself to easy adaptability of physical facilites. The location of services, the relationship of one unit to another, the location and number of loadbearing walls, the movability of units of furniture and equipment, the extent or lack of permanent fixtures, and the amount of multiple-use space all have implications for those who plan today's building for tomorrow's youth.

A Beckoning Challenge

The task of building a school has never been an easy one, and the task facing today's school planners and builders is perhaps more complex now than it has ever been before. It is not easy to provide effectively for the boundless enthusi-

asm of youth. There is no single, sure blueprint to the provision of channels for the curiosity of the young and growing mind. There is no simple way to provide a multi-programed curriculum to meet the needs of all children. But this is a beckoning challenge and not an insurmountable one. New materials and equipment, new insights and know-how, and new methods and techniques are available to today's planner. Physical facilities must reflect this challenge. Broad and rapid changes are occurring in our time; the potential for change in the future promises to exceed that of the present. The people of this country look to education as the key to the life of a free democratic society. The home of education is the school. To plan for it, to design it, to build it, and to make it function effectively is a challenge and an opportunity to the school administrator, the teacher, the architect, and all who plan schools for tomorrow.

Chapter 4 / *Beauty—An Indispensable Element*

The school building at its best engenders a climate that brings out the best in people. In its totality—site, building mass, form, design, and overall relationships — it is pleasurable to the senses and exalts the mind and the spirit. Whether it is a small, simply designed rural elementary school nestled among the pines on a sloping hillside; a sleek, multistoried urban high school in the center of a bustling industrial city; or a huge community college complex of buildings on an extensive park-like site, the good school building symbolizes the highest purposes of education and expresses the ideals and aspirations of the community it serves. Beauty is an indispensable element of its composition.

To serve its function well, to meet the educational expectancies of its students and the community, to be truly great, the school building must be more than a container for the educational program. Merely meeting all the criteria of areas and spaces to accommodate the educational program is not enough. The building must have certain intangible qualities, many of which may not be openly apparent but which are necessary if the school is to be more than an envelope for teachers and students. The building must become an inspiration to the student, the teacher, and the community it serves. It should be friendly, attractive, and stimulating. It should impart to all whom it serves a feeling of security and well-being and a sense of pride.

To the skilled architect, this indispensable extra quality for school design becomes a major objective. In addition to satisfying all program requirements, the school building must have the quality of design required of any fine piece of architecture—for school design is the art of architecture in the fullest sense. From the first interpretation of the program and the selection of the site on through the preliminary sketches to the completed plant, the program requirements, the function, the massing, the form, the play of light and shade, the judicious use of materials, the element of surprise, the feeling of purpose and the ability to inspire a sense of belonging, and an awareness of beauty all stand together as a responsibility of those charged with creating a school.

Impact on the User

The goals, aims, and aspirations of the ultimate user should perhaps be expressed more tangibly in the American public school of today than in any other form of architecture, for the goals, aims, and aspirations of education in the United States are as noble as any conceived by man. The high purpose of the public school should be reflected in the character of the plant. For many communities, as well as for many who will use the facilities, a truly fine school can be an adventure never before experienced—a chance to appreciate a truly fine environment. Should not the school then express the very best in today's architecture?

A good school building is an important teaching tool. It has an impact that is over, above, and beyond its functions of shelter, provision of equipment, and serving as a framework for organization. A well designed building can give pleasure, it can stimulate, it can relax, and it can minimize internal and external traffic and disciplinary problems. It should capture the spirits of young people and consciously seek to make favorable impressions on their lives. A truly fine school can become a symphony of delight.

For the very young child, the school building may be his first experience with the outside world—his first contact with the beautiful—fine architecture, integrated with art and sculpture. Here, as in all good architecture, scale is of special importance; one must always remember the user. To the more mature youngster, the school is a bigger world removed from the protection of the elementary years; it's a first experience of "boy meets girl"; it's a world of new responsibility, of ambitions, and of dignity. He is in a period of formation. The school should aid proper formation not only of educational aims, but also of the cultural aesthetics and spiritual values so necessary in today's rapidly changing culture.

The high school student may be completing his formal education; in any event, graduation will be the end of a very important part of his educational career. The good high school building helps to meet the spiritual and emotional needs of all students. For them this is a period of dreams and commitments, a period of attachments; it is a period that in no small way sets the course their futures will take and that will long live in their memories. This source of treasured memories, high ideals, and great expectations should inspire the architect and all others responsible to create a truly fine school.

Beauty in all its aspects is a necessary quality of any school building. For every child, the school should feel like his own very special place. He should be able to find there an atmosphere that brings opportunity, self-confidence, and the vision of a bright future. His station in life a few years hence may well depend upon his experiences in the elementary and secondary school. Unfortunately the American scene today, for many children, is bleak. The slums, the monotony of typical subdivisions, the ugly, crowded streets, the conglomerations of signs shouting for attention, the poorly designed buildings, and the careless mutilation of nature are all too evident. These and many other factors make it mandatory that the school for these youngsters become an oasis of all that is fine and good. This may be the only opportunity for many to experience, at a formative age, qualities of aesthetics vital and necessary to the education of every student. If the school fails them at any point—whether it be in stimulating and directing their active minds and bodies, introducing them to a sense of harmony and order in the world about them and in the whole universe, or instilling in them a sense of satisfaction and a feeling of accomplishment through learning—their future has in some degree been impaired.

It seems foolhardy to expect the child to appreciate art, history, civic pride, the beauty of the spoken and written word, and the order and discipline of the sciences and mathematics—in fact, the intricacies and wonderfulness of the entire educational process—in an environment that is drab and void of inspiration. A child needs inspiration, and the school should provide it. A child needs beauty in his life, and the school building should make a major contribution toward fulfilling this need.

A Major Objective

All architectural programs should envision beauty as a major objective of the educational process. The quest for beauty must not be stifled by those who can think only in terms of the mundane. To think, talk, and design merely in terms of the practical, the transitory, the ordinary is easy; it is either yes or no, black or white. To work

in terms of the intangible is much more difficult; it takes the very best efforts of all who want to achieve beauty. It is often hard to explain these intangible aspects to the taxpayers of a community.

Too often, the terms "good architecture" and "expensive buildings" are thought of simultaneously, but they are not synonymous. Good proportions, pleasant massing, a beautiful silhouette against the sky, interest and texture, and the judicious use of simple materials cost no more. Those charged with the responsibility of choosing, however, may select designers who give credence to the thesis that cost, the durability of materials, and the practical aspects of the project are the factors of prime importance. Granted, each is important, but each should be kept in proper perspective.

Beauty need not be expensive. Creativity can produce beauty at no greater cost than the drab or humdrum. This has been proven countless times when a combination of materials, program, and circumstances that might be expected to produce a mediocre school plant have resulted in a structure of beauty when placed in the hands of the skilled, creative, sensitive designer. Too many subscribe to the thesis that beauty is a frill. It is, rather, an inherent quality of every

good piece of architecture. It is not something applied, but the very substance of the structure.

Unfortunately, many designers do not, or are reluctant to, express themselves in terms of that intangible quality that only the fine architect can bestow on a project: beauty —beauty of profile, beauty of silhouette, beauty of composition of masses, beauty of order, beauty of delight, beauty of surprise, beauty of space well organized. They fail to rise to the opportunity that is theirs. It is always easier to talk and design in more practical terms, or to rely on the hackneyed or trite, or to evaluate everything in terms of square foot cost or yearly maintenance. Beauty of design—the architect's greatest contribution—is simply overlooked or treated lightly by too many architects today.

The Ingredients

There are many ways in which beauty and aesthetic value may be expressed in the school building and grounds through creativity, imagination, and invention. Every project should have order, fine proportions, strength, sensitivity, compassion, spiritual values, and courage. Creativity is often correlated with the

new, the different, the exotic, the bizarre. This is far from its true meaning. Certainly, it may be new and different, but creativity in school building design must adhere to certain basic principles: Does it do the job better? Does it solve the problem? Does it give delight? Will it be as handsome in its old age as it is in its infancy? All too often buildings have been planned and designed that were simply the result of a desire to be different. Creativity encompasses soul-searching restraint. Good creative planning is more than problem solving. It is that intricate something that adds strength and meaning. It is that quality that does not diminish with time. It is building for tomorrow as well as for today.

The possibilities for creative design are unlimited. Each new school building need holds possibilities for untapped creativity. When the site, the program, and the child are explored and dreamed over by the creative architect; when he is given full opportunity; and when he accepts the challenge with full recognition of his responsibilities and the potentials of the project of which he is the author, structures of real value will be the reward. For out of dreams, yet unbuilt great buildings are conceived.

37

The Planning Team

Schools are the responsibility of a board of lay people who give their time and talent unselfishly. These citizens are the backbone of American free public education. For this board, the administrative staff labors to implement the board's and its own desire for the finest in education, instruction, and facilities. The board of education, however, often quite jealously guards its prerogative to select the architect; and too often the architect is selected on the basis of his ability to convince the board that he is able to stay within a stipulated budget, that his services should be used because of his participation in local and civic affairs, or that he is a specialist in school design. Each virtue is fine in itself, but hardly enough to qualify an architect for the tremendous task ahead.

The success of any school project lies in the hands of the planning team. This team may be composed of the architect, the board, the superintendent, and often a committee of teachers and lay persons who will use or have special interest in the new school. The superintendent has a vital role to play. When he delegates his leadership position to a person whose background and experience are of only a maintenance or janitorial nature, educational planning is weakened and the completed project suffers. A board composed of conscientious citizens, an experienced superintendent, a representative of the maintenance staff, teachers, and representatives of lay groups, working with a creative architect, is an ideal planning team.

The Torchbearer

Who of the group then will champion the cause of a school building that does more than house the program; that is relatively maintenance free; and that costs neither more nor less than the school just constructed by a neighboring community? Who will be responsible for determining that the teachers' rest room is not too far from the classrooms; that there is enough storage space; that there are no unnecessary frills; that the plans are complete; that the heating system is mechanically perfect; that the lighting is acceptable; that the asphalt playfields are adequate in size; that there is adequate parking close to the school; that there are enough seats in the gymnasium for school activities and community activities; and that there will be no extras on the project? All these aims and objectives are notable and must be met, but they alone are not enough.

The aims and objectives of those planning the school should be as inspirational as the aims and objectives of public education itself, for the school must be planned for the child's spiritual needs as well as his physical needs. Who will carry the torch? A major share, in most cases, must be carried by the architect. The skilled architect, by training and experience, is constantly aware that beauty and function must walk together for the success of any building venture. He should inspire the planning team to envision a great school that not only fulfills the needs of direct educational requirements and goals, but satisfies the emotional and spiritual needs of order and beauty.

Plan Composition and Massing

The educational program of a school building can be expressed in the plan composition and massing of its elements. Elements having a common denominator of size, shape, and height can most often be successfully placed together. Other elements, by their very nature requiring special architectural solutions, may be placed apart. By the balancing and interplay of sizes,

shapes, and volumes, the architect can produce a symphony in form and mass.

Profiles

A school building need not always appear a low, flat factory for learning. Roofs can peak; fascia can undulate; large interior areas requiring height can rise above all, giving a sense of scale and meaning to the building. A varied profile against the sky can be a visual delight.

Architectural Honesty

Like any good piece of architecture, the school building should be completely honest. The building's function is paramount. This does not mean, however, that function should predominate over good proportions, appropriate massing, strength of line and form, and the pleasant play of light and shade. A good school should be devoid of the trite and the tricky. Creative architects with skill and imagination will find architectural solutions that will result in plant forms in which beauty is outwardly expressed in architectural shapes and profiles.

The Site

Every school site should be exploited to its fullest potential for beauty. The school building site need not necessarily be flat. Some of the finest architectural solutions have emerged from the challenge of a rugged site. Trees on the site, outcroppings of interesting rock formations, differences in levels, and existing creeks or streams all add interest to an otherwise ordinary architectural solution. Orientation of the building or buildings for sun, wind, and rain is of utmost importance; the play of light, sun and shade, on the building and on its approaches and courts can bring measures of visual pleasure.

Natural beauty is a quality that exists in unique form and in varying degree in every site. This beauty can be emphasized and made effective in the total school environment through many media—landscaping, color, arrangement, design, and space relationships. Through skillful creativity and appropriate orientation, an otherwise drab, flat, colorless, sterile site may be so blended into the design of a building uniquely adapted to the specific situation that the overall environment is pleasing and inspiring. Such happy relationships of terrain and structure were colorfully described by Kazantzakis on a visit to the famous temple of Apollo:

... It is as though the temple were the cranium of the surrounding landscape, the sacred mound-circle inside whose sheltered precincts the mind of the site keeps ever-vigilant watch. Here the artistry of the ancients, continuing and expressing the landscape to perfection, does not make you gasp with astonishment. It lifts you to the summit along a human pathway, so gently and dexterously that you do not grow short of breath. You might say that the entire mountain had been longing for eons inside its tenebrous bulk to find expression, and that the moment it acquired this temple of Apollo, it felt relieved. Felt relieved—in other words assumed a meaning, its own meaning, and rejoiced.[1]

Nature, Plus Landscaping

Thoughtful planners seek the counsel of a talented landscape architect. Since every building must go on a site, whether it be a piece of rural farmland or an urban city block, the site should be treated in complete harmony with the building and its surroundings. From the very start of schematic drawings, the landscape architect is a vital and necessary collaborator with the designing architect; it is the landscape

---

[1] Kazantzakis, Nikos. *Report to Greco.* New York: Simon and Schuster, 1965. p. 163.

architect who often will humanize, add delight, and solve otherwise unsatisfactory problems of site and terrain. By effective use of paved areas, paths and walks, courts and compounds, pools and fountains, art and sculpture, the architect and the landscape architect can give to the finished school that quality of beauty so vital and necessary to a good school building.

Parking

The great numbers of automobiles driven to school by teachers, students, and citizens of the community must be provided for, but in the most inoffensive possible manner. Large blacktopped parking lots detract from the visual scene. It is far better to have small clusters of randomly placed parking areas, with rows of trees shielding them from view, than large exposed tracts of land that dominate the site. The scale of the problem is vastly reduced and the vista is vastly improved by such cluster areas.

The Approach

As one approaches a school, it should be as inviting as any building in the community. It should say "welcome," and it should say it in such a way as to impart to all who enter a sense of comfort and well-being. It should be impressive, but not ostentatious. It should be in scale with those who use the structure.

One of the most ideal, natural, and logical opportunities the designing architect has for expression of beauty is in the building identification. Free-standing signs, sensitively designed, can add much to the visual experience as one approaches and enters the building.

The Seemingly Useless, But Necessary Element

In addition to the sign bearing its name, a school building may well have a very useless (in the strictest sense of the word), but desirable element that can well serve as a focal point for the whole complex. The education requirements may not specify its inclusion; but this component can become a vital and important facet in the very success of the school and its operation. To illustrate: in one large high school the architect incorporated into the school design a bell tower. After the tower and an accompanying pool were built, the bells were obtained by the community. This tower now dominates the entire school complex. It is visible, and its bells are heard, for miles around. At its base is the reflecting pool with lights that illuminate the tower

at night. High on the tower is the school emblem. In use now for three years, this tower has become a landmark. The students use it as a rallying point; it is a meeting place, an educational symbol, and a source of pride to the community. The school newspaper has been named *The Tower,* and the emblem and its colors have become the letter-sweater insignia of the school. Though perhaps some might describe it as a completely useless piece of architecture, this tower is an essential ingredient in the success of this new school.

The Court and Compound

Creative, skillful, and imaginative plan composition and massing result in the delightful courts and compounds seen in many of today's outstanding new schools. Such spaces and areas add to the quality of the entire project and provide variety and interest to students and teachers. Here students may pause on their way to other areas; here may be placed a seat, a tree, a reflecting pool, a fountain, or a piece of sculpture. It is through such additions that the important ingredient of beauty is honestly—and economically—incorporated.

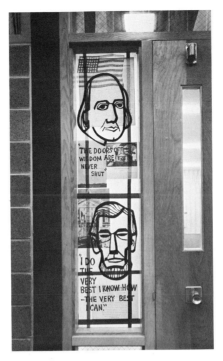

The Role of the Artist Collaborator

A fine school building that is designed with sensitiveness is art in architecture in one of its finest forms. Such a school building has the qualities of a fine painting or of inspirational sculpture with beauty of mass and form. Like the building itself, a well done mural, a decorative frieze, or a free-standing piece of sculpture increases the visual delight so necessary for the educational stimulus of the teaching and learning environment.

Some architects, however, are not artists. As he calls upon the services of the landscape architect, the good school building architect also collaborates with a talented artist. School buildings need and should have art in its pure forms.

The sterile walls and empty spaces of much contemporary school building cry out for the humanizing work of the painter or sculptor. Paintings and frescoes create the mystery of extended space through the use of color. Sculpture moves out into the space of the observer

and binds him to the building. Both arts can assist enormously in giving the building a sense of scale and in dramatizing its function.[2]

Too often, these elements are treated lightly, left until last, or completely ignored. It is the wise architect who solicits the help of the artist collaborator at an early stage of design and uses his help and talent to incorporate visual delight and beauty in the design of the school for which he is responsible.

That Essential Ingredient

Every new school building should satisfy the needs of the educational program in the most efficient possible way. It should be as functional and as practical as is commensurate with today's planning and thinking. The many years the building will be in use should be uppermost in the minds of its planners. Countless numbers of children will pass through its doors and classrooms and remember the building as their school. The student needs beauty; beauty is a constant companion to the learning process. Every new school building should

incorporate beauty and all the aesthetic qualities of good architecture. To achieve these qualities, one has only to give them appropriate priority.

In this day and age, when so many school buildings are being constructed and education has a higher priority than it has ever had before, communities of people can within reasonable limits have nearly any kind of school plant they want. The difference between a plant that is cold, forbidding, repelling, restraining, and depressing and one that is warm, inviting, uplifting, and inspiring is usually not in terms of cost, but in terms of beliefs, commitments, and some degree of creativity.

[2] American Association of School Administrators. *Planning America's School Buildings.* Washington, D.C.: the Association, 1960. p. 85.

Chapter 5/*New Blueprints*

How will educational facilities respond to the challenges of education? How, indeed, will facilities be planned and built so they will not become educationally obsolete long before they become structurally obsolete? It's not unusual for a schoolhouse to be in use for more than fifty years. What will educational needs be a half century from now? It seems certain that children will have far more to learn, that teaching techniques will probably be greatly changed, and that our whole society may be almost entirely different. As education continues to reach out in new directions, to move through a continuing and unending state of transition, new forms of educational facilities must emerge.

A new breed of facilities won't appear overnight, nor should it. Facilities, if they are to serve education, must struggle through the same transitions and growth that educational processes do, and they must change with the times. There will be groping in programing and planning facilities, and mistakes will be made. Error is a natural and inevitable offspring of growth—of reaching out toward something better—but so is improvement, and that is precisely what we seek.

Drawing his thoughts from the "scattered hopes of the American past," President Johnson said, "Onto my desk each day come the problems of 190 million men and women. When we consider these problems, study them, analyze them, evaluate what can be done, the answer almost always comes down to one word: education." [1]

The New Generation

Every school cornerstone laid this year will determine the physical framework of education at the turn of this century. We are building now for the children, grandchildren, and great grandchildren of students in our classrooms today. What will we build for them? Will we turn our faces from an intimidating future, pull the comforting corners of conservatism around us, and snuggle back into safe, conventional ways? If we do, our blueprints will be working specifications for structures little better than cages—places where the talent of coming generations will be stifled, where intellectual vitality will be sapped, and where the student will be left ill-prepared for life in a turbulent era.

Alternatively, we can take up the gauntlet. We might even find ourselves enjoying the stimulation of pitting wits against those social and economic forces which have hurled the challenge. We can discern the shape of the future; its outlines are dim but faintly discernible. Its opportunities are unlimited and challenging. Its problems are stubborn, but provocative, and surely they are not impervious to human ingenuity and mobilized community action.

Our concern here is to examine that future and define its implications for school planning and construction. We know that change for the sake of change is neither realistic nor honest, but we know also that failure to recognize the need for change would be default of responsibility—our responsibility to coming generations.

Some Constants

As change comes, facility design is doing what it must. It is keeping pace with the changing nature of our times. In this dynamic situation, however, there are elements which remain constantly valid and

[1] Celebrezze, Anthony J. *Education and Training: The Bridge Between Man and His Work.* Third Annual Report of the Secretary of Health, Education, and Welfare to the Congress on Training Activities Under the Manpower Development and Training Act. Washington, D.C.: Government Printing Office, 1965.

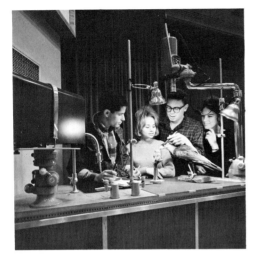 

serve as major bases of consideration:

1. *The educational facility is more, far more, than just a building.* As education becomes more complex and embraces entirely new techniques, educational facilities will be asked to perform more difficult tasks than ever before. The building and its equipment will become more intimately related; in fact, the relationship will require that they become one and the same element. In the school of the future more than ever before, *facility* will refer to the building *and* the equipment it houses.

2. *The educational facility is a servant of the educational program.* As a servant of the educational process, an educational facility must provide a functional environment. It must provide the numbers and sizes of spaces required, all of the elements of human comfort, and spaces that can be reshaped to fit a changing program. It must avoid forcing the educational program to fit the facility and thereby limiting program effectiveness.

3. *The educational facility expresses the spirit of education.* The school is more than a functional environment. It is also a visual environment. It symbolizes to all thinking people the position education occupies in our society. At its best it says to all that education involves more than the production of graduates who are mere containers of knowledge; it pro-

claims the democratic principle of preparing youth to properly meet the various and pressing demands of their future as whole adult people—people with the attributes of knowledge, grace, judgment, and understanding.

A building which is no more than a shelter can hardly serve such a program. The new blueprints must be developed with infinite care by knowledgeable and forward-looking educators and architects.

Education for Everybody

The school plant is not an adjunct to education: it is the living, breathing skin of the creature, the protective covering; it is also the source of intellectual, aesthetic, and emotional nourishment. What sort of skin, then, shall we devise to meet the needs of the next generation? It will be a complex structure, for a schoolhouse expresses in tangible form the psychology of teaching and of learning.

The new breed of building must at once—

—Be relevant to the preschool education of the small child—a happy, welcoming place.

—Stimulate and reassure senior citizens who will come to school to polish unused skills so that they may find a useful,

satisfying place in society as they enter the ever-lengthening retirement period.

—Compensate for dreary home environments and offset the deadening impact of slums and substandard housing, at least until there are no more slums.

—Be a place where the most brilliant scholar and the slowest, least gifted child can be challenged; a place where children who are crippled physically or emotionally can be educated as adequately as normal youngsters.

—Provide efficient, utilitarian facilities for technological training and for the retraining of unemployed workers and provide facilities where the housewife can develop skills for part-time employment or for more effective service in community voluntary agencies.

—Be an educational landmark which commands community respect and instills community pride, but which also may have mobile extensions—classrooms that can be moved swiftly to areas of temporary enrollment concentration and to out-of-the-way spots in sparsely settled rural sections or locations where migratory workers or other groups have special educational needs.

Finally, since public interest in public support will be more urgent than ever before as education is forced into sharp competition for funds, the schoolhouse of tomorrow

must be literally the heart of the community.

Long-Range Planning

In some instances a new breed of building is emerging from the roots of district-wide and sometimes interdistrict planning. This is the result of long-range planning of the very broadest nature. Such far-sighted overviews of the whole scope of educational needs are necessary preludes to any consideration of individual facilities.

Long-range planning is not by any means a new idea to educators. They have been practicing it for years. Some school districts develop carefully thought through and comprehensive long-range plans; others approach planning in a haphazard and often illogical manner. Depending upon conditions within the district, the development of a long-range plan may be extremely difficult or relatively simple. In any event, the plan must be re-evaluated frequently and kept up-to-date with the most current trends affecting education. As a point of departure for long-range planning, it will perhaps be useful to consider three major challenges to education un-der the general categories of *people, knowledge,* and *circumstances.* A long-range plan outline may use a different format, but the ingredients remain about the same. Generally, an adequate district-wide long-range plan should be based upon the answers to the following kinds of questions.

People

—What are present school enrollments? Where do the children live? How old are they? What are their family backgrounds and circumstances? How stable is the population?

—Can we predict future enrollments? What are the educational aspirations of the students? What ranges of experience will they have drawn from travel, early introduction to books, and informative conversations at home? Will they start their education at prekindergarten levels? Will they continue their education beyond high school?

Knowledge

—Is the curriculum properly related to the needs of the people in the community? Its employment opportunities? Its economy? Its unique characteristics such as the presence of military installations or institutions of higher learning?

—How do policy and curriculum relate to the growing urgency of the need for each child to learn more? Is there need for a preschool program? For post high school, technical-vocational, or community college programs?

—Is adult education a part of the program?

—What provisions are made in the curriculum to prepare students for democratic living? For worthy use of ever increasing leisure time? For wise use of natural resources? For living emotionally and physically healthy lives?

—Are community services, transportation, and health services properly related to the long-range plan?

Circumstances

—What special opportunities does the school offer the community? Are the school grounds, the gymnasium, the auditorium, and the resources center available for non-school-related activities?

—What special advantages does the community offer to the school? Are there cultural opportunities such as libraries, museums, civic opera, chorus, and ballet? Sports and recreational events? Opportunities to watch business and industry in action?

—What effect do the schools have on their neighborhoods? Do they enhance or detract from

45

"AUTOMATION EMERGES"

the appearance of their immediate surroundings? Are real estate values affected?

—Are community factors such as history, traditions, culture, geography, economy, and attitudes recognized and properly related to program?

—How will the community grow? Will growth patterns, such as zoning and traffic routes, be properly related to existing and proposed school sites? Is there a master plan for regional and community growth?

—Does the community have private schools which will provide for the educational needs of some of its children?

—How will future deployment of teachers, assistants, and other staff members affect the program?

—Will such aids and tools as educational television, amplified telephone, and programed learning devices be used to improve teaching techniques? Can automation be used as a tool?

—Are some present facilities *educationally* obsolete? Should they be remodeled? Should additions be considered?

—Are some present facilities *structurally* obsolete? Should they be remodeled? Should additions be considered?

—Are existing buildings properly located? Are the schools where the children are, or are transportation problems compounding?

—Do local conditions allow for proper financing of the education of the children of the community?

—What state or federal aid programs are available to the community?

These are but some of the questions; there are undoubtedly many more to be added. The questions are simple enough, but the answers are not! An accurate and comprehensive analysis of past and present conditions is difficult enough; prediction of the future is a real task. The long-range plan is at best an educated guess. If it is to be worth its salt, it must be flexible at the outset. Then it must be subjected to a continuing process of review and alteration so it will reflect each important new trend.

Many well conceived long-range plans are being implemented all across the nation. The new breeds of buildings that are being created from these plans will serve the educational needs of children in exciting new ways.

Like the challenges they are being built to serve, these new building types are not selective to location. They are found in all types of environments—urban, suburban, and rural; in wealthy and poor communities; in warm and chilly climates; in areas of industrial economy, small business, or farms.

What are some of these new building types? What kinds of facilities could emerge to meet educational needs right around the corner?

Automation Emerges

Business and industry have for some time been making extensive use of computers to step up production, to save manpower, and to increase efficiency; and many people are predicting that their use by almost everyone will be commonplace within the next few years. In describing the possible effect of automation in the not too distant future, John Caffrey says:

What will the role of the homemaker be like in the future? Extending present trends, and letting our minds go, consider the problem of feeding the family. Without even assuming major changes in the nature of food, and hoping that science will never replace sirloin with an equally nourishing pill, it is practical to envision the following process. For a given family, the computer has in its memory a mass of information about the dietary needs of its members— their preferences, nutritional requirements, allergies, caloric intake limits, and so on. On Monday morning the housewife asks the computer for a weekly menu and shopping list. She may of course alter it at will

or add the fact that company is coming for dinner so that the computer can adjust accordingly. The shopping list consists, say, of a punched card or disk or strip of punched tape. She goes to market (a custom we preserve in preference to a remote line, because going to market has social and cultural values and for some wives replaces or extends the activities of a club—we don't have to automate everything!) and a clerk inserts the list in the automated system. While the computer-assisted storeroom system is filling the order and automatically packing it, the housewife gossips, has coffee or browses among the displays, which consist of a single exhibit of each item, together with a punched card that can be used to obtain it, or makes a personal choice of fresh fruits or meats, thus preserving the illusion of the human touch.[2]

In a more serious vein, if computer technology reaches the supermarket, it will certainly reach education. Among the general questions which must be answered in the development of any district-wide or interdistrict long-range plan, it has been asked, "Can automation toil for education?" Perhaps that question

[2] Caffrey, John. "The School of Tomorrow." *SDC Magazine* 8:16 ff; Winter 1965-1966. (Santa Monica, Calif.: System Development Corporation.)

should be reworded, "Can we afford *not* to automate some procedures in education?" Very likely the answer will be a simple "No."

It is quite possible that within the next decade a school district with a total enrollment of some fifteen thousand pupils will make extensive use of a computer facility. Smaller districts, of course, could band together in order to assume the financial burden that such an expensive facility would involve. The hypothetical computer-center facility built by the school district might contain a large-scale computer with extensive time-sharing ability and provide functional space for the operating staff and the programing and administrative personnel. Very likely this computer center will be related to the district's administrative offices and a district-wide educational materials center. Access to the computer center will probably be provided by the installation of remote terminals and teletypes in key locations such as satellite educational materials centers, administrative units, counseling units, classrooms, laboratories, and other spaces in buildings throughout the school district. Remote terminals with keyboards and display screens may be placed in pupils' homes; this will free the school buildings themselves of much of the pupil timeload and

allow each building to serve many more children.

Computer networks for school districts will do many things. For administrators, the computer can help forecast enrollments, present and compare budgets, prepare pupil schedules, evaluate curriculum and teaching techniques, forecast building needs, and store records and make them instantly available. The counselor may ask the computer to assist him in interviewing pupils, preparing and presenting testing results, and storing student records related to past performance and future development. The school librarian may find that the computer network contains a memory unit which will store and catalog immense masses of information and retrieve, assemble, and display them simply and quickly. The pupil may be trained to use the computer as a learning tool or perhaps for a vocation.

All of this suggests the emergence of new building types. It is not just the wild dream of visionaries. Every technical development suggested is already an accomplished fact and is available either in the public domain or through commonly accessible vendors. Cost—now a deterrent—will drop substantially in the next decade.

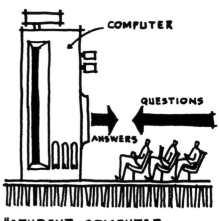

"STUDENT - COMPUTER CONVERSATION"

Beyond the near future, it is interesting to examine the potential of automation and cybernation as forecast by Gordon and Helmer. In everything touching on education, this report stresses the importance of automation and cybernation in affecting the nature of society. Of all the forces bearing on the nature of tomorrow's school, cybernation seems one of the most significant, pointing directions for both content and methodology. It is predicted that by 1975 education will be a socially accepted leisure-time occupation for the many millions whose work life will have been reduced or shortened by automated processes replacing human labor in many areas of work. The classroom may also be profoundly affected if the experts are right in guessing that by 1990 we will have produced computers capable of comprehension, learning, and improved performance. By the year 2000, or shortly thereafter, the remote printing of newspapers and all kinds of documents in inexpensive home receivers will affect the availability of learning materials; under such conditions, home or school libraries as we now know them may become anachronisms.[3]

[3] Gordon, T. J., and Helmer, Olaf. *Report on a Long-Range Forecasting Study.* Santa Monica, Calif.: Rand Corporation, 1964.

The use of computers for the translation of language (not the pidgin translations of existing rudimentary programs, but grammatically correct and readable ones), the use of automatic abstracting programs and automated document file searching will certainly have profound effects on what and how we teach. Projection of what a high school student of 1999 will be taught in a unit entitled "How To Use the Library" is limited only by one's imagination. In the not too distant future, the common use of remote inquiry stations for access to centralized document and data files will probably require learners to know how to use the typewriter and the teletype; but it is apparently not fantastic to predict that the student in the middle of the next century may be able to address his questions to the computer by voice, because there will be automatic conversion of what may be called machine-sensible speech.

The ready accessibility of data, information, and facts and of the calculating capacity of computers may profoundly affect the curriculum. It has often been said of current educational programs that children have to learn a great many facts that they'll never need. Facts that now have to be learned because when needed later they may be difficult to find may—in the future—be retrieved simply by stepping to the home or office console of the computer network. It would seem, therefore, that nearly everyone will have to know how to use computers, whether or not they learn to program or operate the central processors.

The Supplemental Educational Center   *Cleveland Program*

The increasing depth of curriculum content and complexity also has implications for district-wide planning. Since proper in-depth presentation will require complex facilities, it may be far more practical for a school district to provide highly specialized facilities to which students can be transported for special educational experiences than attempt to provide less adequate facilities in each school.

Such a program is under way in Cleveland, where education service centers are being planned. Each center will specialize in a particular area of the curriculum—physical and life sciences, communications, the creative and performing arts, and civic responsibilities.

Along with large lecture halls and smaller classrooms,

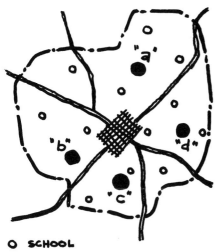

O SCHOOL

● SUPPLEMENTAL EDUC. CENTER
    a. SCIENCE
    b. COMMUNICATIONS
    c. HERITAGE
    d. ARTS

"SUPPLEMENTAL EDUC. CENTERS"

each of the centers would contain libraries, large exhibit areas for permanent and temporary displays, and a wide range of specialized instructional areas.

The science center, for example, would contain laboratories for the physical and life sciences, an aquarium, NASA exhibits of rockets and space travel, and a planetarium specially designed for the center by Spitz Laboratories of Yorklyn, Delaware. The planetarium seats about 500 students and gives the impression of being out in space, rather than using the earth as the center of the universe, as in existing planetariums.

The communications center would naturally concentrate on the many means man has at his disposal to communicate with his fellow man. . . .

While emphasis would be on language study, the center would also house studios for the school system's educational television and radio network and give students on-the-job training in preparing material for these media and in the technical operation of such a system.

Students could publish school system bulletins and newsletters in an actual print shop, and obtain first hand information on the various methods of printing. Such things as a branch post office could be set up in the center to demon-strate the intricacies of mail-handling and make students more familiar with the world around them.

The concept of familiarizing children—especially those from culturally deprived homes —with the world around them is nowhere better illustrated than in the proposed heritage center. [Superintendent of Schools] Briggs' idea here is to thoroughly acquaint students with how a city government functions. Not only would he have municipal officials, judges, and other individuals lecture to classes of students, but he would plan to operate a mock city council chamber and municipal court. Hopefully, he would be able to hold real sessions of city council meetings or jury trials in the center.

Underlying the heritage program would be personal exposure of students to leading figures in all endeavors. "Perhaps local industrialists would come in and give talks on local industry," Briggs explains. Historic tours of the city could be conducted, highlighting its growth and development and the contributions of all ethnic and racial groups comprising the population.

"The result," Briggs explains, "would be students with a better understanding of their city—and as a result, a better understanding of their own role in society."

The fourth center would concentrate on the creative and performing arts. In addition to classrooms and small studios, it would provide facilities for students to perform in music, drama, dance; and adequate space for others interested in painting and sculpture. Workshops for costumes and stage settings would be an important part of the program. "This type of center," Briggs says, "would enable us to bring in guest performers and lecturers and expose the children to a variety of experiences otherwise impossible." [4]

The Educational Plaza

As an alternative to the Cleveland concept of using supplementary educational centers, some district-wide planning is based on the use of educational parks. In this kind of planning, one large site is designed to accommodate a larger pupil population than the typical neighborhood school—in fact, it may include the entire student population from kindergarten through community college. (See Chapter 17 for examples.) Motives for this kind of venture are usually similar—obtaining needed new facilities, curing downtown blight, and eliminat-

[4] American School & University. "Education Service Centers." *American School & University* 37:35, 46; June 1965. (New York: Buttenheim Publishing Corporation.)

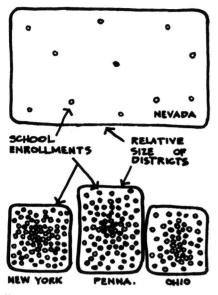

"LARGE AREA - SMALL ENROLLMENT"

NEVADA

SCHOOL ENROLLMENTS

RELATIVE SIZE OF DISTRICTS

NEW YORK   PENNA.   OHIO

"LARGE ENROLLMENTS - SMALL AREA...."

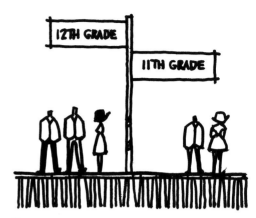

12TH GRADE

11TH GRADE

"..TOO FEW STUDENTS AVAILABLE TO PROVIDE A CHALLENGING ACADEMIC COMPETITION..."

ing areas of de facto segregation. Though the motives are similar, however, the solutions are not. Educational park proposals have included huge campuses to house the complete educational program of the district, more limited facilities for special age groups, and multistoried high rise buildings in the center of a metropolitan area.

Schools and Urban Renewal

With the increasing decay of residential areas in many of our great cities, it is far too common to observe a coinciding decay of neighborhood education facilities. Wedged in the crowded streets in the middle of these cities are inadequate sites containing buildings that are poorly lighted, poorly ventilated, and structurally and educationally defective.

New Haven, Connecticut, among others, has recently decided to do something about its urban problems. New Haven's Conte School and Community Center is a noteworthy example of how a city school can become a key element in urban renewal. According to New Haven's Board of Education, the school and community center is designed to perform four major

functions: (1) to provide the finest education for both children and adults; (2) to serve as a neighborhood recreation center; (3) to be a focal point for all neighborhood social services, including health clinics, family counseling, and legal and job help; and (4), to become the center for all community life—a sort of common ground for all neighbors, not only for recreation, but for consideration of mutual problems. To perform these varied functions, the architects designed a three-part plan: the school itself, an auditorium, and a public library-community house.

In addition to providing city dwellers with a fine educational facility equal to those of their suburban neighbors, Conte in its first summer of use demonstrated its full range of functions. While children from all over the city used its big swimming pool and gymnasium, neighborhood adults enjoyed the library and auditorium, held meetings in its conference rooms, and even had cookouts in the yard. Furthermore, it is serving to lift the entire environmental level of the Wooster Square area which it graces.

Meanwhile, Back at the Ranch

While urban and suburban areas are busy planning and building new facilities, rural areas are

facing up to their own set of changing circumstances in new and exciting ways. Here the problems are different. While urban areas are faced with the necessity of presenting ever-increasing amounts of knowledge to great numbers of children, the rural areas are confronted with the task of offering small numbers of pupils an education of equal quality. If present trends continue as predicted, most rural pupils will seek employment in urban areas, and their quest for knowledge must be much the same as that of their "city cousins." The problems of smallness are large problems indeed.

Definitions of smallness vary considerably and, of course, depend upon a point of comparison. For instance, a 200-pound professional football halfback is small when compared with the 292-pound lineman. Likewise, a 1,000-pupil high school will appear large to a student from a 200-pupil high school. However, in general, small schools may be considered to be those four-year high schools enrolling 200 or fewer students and those elementary schools which send youngsters to the small high school.

There are several approaches to small school improvements, some

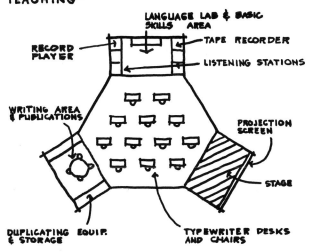

"A SCIENCE ROOM FOR MULTIPLE - CLASS TEACHING"

"A MULTIPLE CLASSROOM FOR ENGLISH, FOREIGN EDUCATION AND BUSINESS EDUCATION"

dealing with district organization, some with administrative and instructional organization, and others with classroom techniques. In nearly every case, these approaches have implications for the types of facilities that are needed. Since there is probably no one best approach to solving the problems, a combination of efforts is needed to provide excellent schools for rural youth. Small school districts, like large ones, are finding that district-wide and interdistrict long-range planning is essential in today's dynamic world of learning.

Modified instructional organization offers possibilities for small school improvement and opportunities that will permit each child to progress through a sequential curriculum free of artificial barriers. The nongraded or continuous progress plan (complete with ungraded curriculum), team teaching, deployment of school aides, shared services and personnel, flexible grouping, multiple classes, flexible high school schedules, personalized instruction, and large-group instruction are all parts of new organizational concepts which may prove useful in the improvement of small schools. Organizational changes, when accompanied by modified teaching activity inside the classroom, could help all schools to treat each student as an individual. Newer educational technology, im-

proved curriculum materials, and increased knowledge of principles of learning offer further opportunities for individual instruction.

Before individual instruction becomes a reality, however, the teacher's job must be redefined and the student must assume a greater responsibility for his own learning. The teacher's job as redefined will be that of resource organizer and coordinator of learning experiences. He may lecture; participate with students in small-group discussions; or be several places at once via tape recorder, television, and film. He may consult with the average learner who has met a roadblock, with the gifted student who has a special experiment under way, or with the low achiever who needs individual help with his reading program. He may supervise programed learning via text, machine, film, or tape. He may coordinate the actions of other teachers for a demonstration unit, or he may assist a school aide in developing materials for resource activities. He may bring in lecturers of national repute via amplified telephone or coordinate the efforts of an adult group in establishing a special evening program. His teaching day is less likely to be a changing of lecture

notes from hour to hour and more likely to be a changing of consultation and organizational responsibility from minute to minute.

When he does give a lecture to a large group, it will be a multi-media lecture with technological devices to assist him in communicating with his listeners. Some of the techniques of instructional procedures within the classroom are tested and proven; others are still in the earliest stages of experiment for small schools. But many of the techniques are ineffective when not accompanied by change in instructional organization.

All of these developments designed to help small schools offer top-quality educational programs must be supported by new kinds of facilities. Multiple-class teaching and flexible scheduling are helping many small high schools to offer comprehensive programs. Multiple classrooms allow schools to schedule different courses with the same teacher in the same room at the same time. Newly developed mobile classroom trailers which may be moved from school to school are offering further opportunities for improved programs and providing the type of complex equipment which, due to smallness, cannot be afforded in each school.

The Flexible Facility

While district-wide planning is having impact on all of a school district's facilities, the individual school and areas within the school also are taking new shapes. A new kind of flexibility is being sought to meet education's changing needs. The trouble with most school buildings is that they represent a long-term commitment not only of funds but of educational methods and program. For many years, thousands of schools have been built containing hundreds of thousands of approximately equal-sized rectangular classrooms, dubbed by their detractors "eggcrates" or "cells and bells." Their owners are restricted to either using space inefficiently—costly in dollars—or forcing equal numbers of children into similar spaces to perform dissimilar tasks—costly in learning!

If there is one point of common agreement among school people—in fact, among all thoughtful people who have an interest in the schools—it is that the educational program is changing and will continue to change. As long as the culture is dynamic and the schools remain sensitive to newly emerging circumstances and learning needs, the educational program will continue to change. Every important development in instructional equipment, every important finding in educational research, and every important shift in occupational needs or the conditions of community life carries implications for modifications in the instructional program. The school program that does not change with the times rapidly recedes into obsolescence. The present rate of change makes it particularly important that the school program at every level be pliable, fluid, and responsive to new needs and new circumstances.

Flexibility is no new development in school plant planning. For the past ten years, at least, architects and administrators have been keenly aware of the necessity for continuous modifications in instructional programs and facilities. Attempts have been made to meet this need through what is commonly called *flexibility*. There is perhaps no one single word in all architectural or educational jargon that has been more overworked or misused than *flexibility*. Flexibility has meant everything from adding a portable building to constructing a large loft-type structure which can be subdivided by partitions and folding doors. All have been sold and installed under the label *flexibility*.

The opinion has often been expressed that architects and administrators have been so overawed by poorly founded concepts of flexibility that the very steps taken to provide flexibility have led to a highly inflexible facility. New and fresh approaches are needed. New insights into this problem are sought by people everywhere. The challenge is to face in a realistic manner the problem of designing school facilities that will make it possible for teachers and administrators to innovate, to make modifications when necessary, and to reshape the educational program as circumstances and the changing character of education require it without undue trouble or expense.

If we wanted the flexible school so badly, why haven't we acquired it? Perhaps it is because building technology has been lagging. Perhaps we have been so rushed to simply provide space that we haven't been adequately concerned about the kind of space. Perhaps we have lacked imagination. And perhaps it is simply because we were not sure what we were talking about when we said "flexible." Certainly an examination of the flexible school is in order.

For the facility built under what might be considered a normal program and on a site not affected by grossly limiting circumstances, the

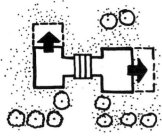

FUTURE GROWTH: BY
ADDITION.

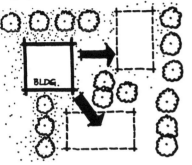

FUTURE GROWTH: AS
A CAMPUS.

following basic areas of flexibility might be examined:

—Flexibility of building perimeter

—Interior change in floor plan

—Use of spaces for several purposes.

Building perimeter. Too bad schools can't be made of rubber, and the superintendent provided with a pump. That way, when enrollment demands exceeded initial construction, he could pump in a little air and the school would grow. When enrollments began to fall, he could deflate his rubber school and never need to fear the problem of empty classrooms. Since it seems fairly improbable that technology will come up with such a school in the near future—there are rubber buildings, of course, but not on this large a scale—other solutions must be found. There are some things that can be done to help reach toward flexibility of building perimeter.

During initial project consideration, a good portion of long-range planning must be accomplished. This type of planning for the individual project may be a natural outgrowth of the well conceived district-wide long-range plan. A detailed summary of probable growth in enrollment and educational offerings or techniques should—in fact, must—be made an important section of the written educational

requirement for any new project. When this knowledge is available, an adequate site may be selected and a facility designed which will accept perimeter modification—or growth—with grace and efficiency.

Like the rubber school, if too much air is pumped into the building, it will burst. Each facility will probably reach a point where further expansion is just too much. Unlike the rubber school, the normal building cannot be deflated without at least some loss, even in the case of so called "portable" facilities. A well and wisely developed district-wide long-range plan should, however, keep most facilities occupied effectively for many years.

Interior change in floor plan. The long-sought abilities to make big rooms out of little ones and vice versa, to open and close acoustically adequate partitions in a matter of seconds, to demount and relocate partitions over the weekend, and to mould interior spaces to fit the educational program are, at last, becoming realities. Industry, assisted and perhaps prodded by educators and architects, has made available vast quantities of all types of systems which help make the

flexible school possible. Some of the components are highly complex, others are relatively simple. Some are prefabricated, but most may be constructed on the job site, using the local labor market.

One way to flexibility is *open space*—open space which can remain open or be divided, redivided, and divided again, at a minimum of time and cost and when the educational program demands it. This concept of space flexibility requires a structural system which provides relatively large and column-free floor areas. Load-bearing walls, if provided at all, are at the perimeter of the open space.

Freed of fixed interior structural elements, this open space can then be divided at random. The variety of flexible dividers available on the market is broad. Prices vary generally in accordance with two basic factors. First, as the degree of acoustical separation (or sound transmission) rises, so does the cost. A rolling divider, such as a chalkboard or cabinet, which provides only a visual barrier is inexpensive and may be needed anyway for purposes other than space separation. On the other hand, an operable partition capable of providing the acoustical separation required when a lecture class occupies the

space next to band practice is a horse of a different color and pretty expensive, too. Second, the cost of the space divider generally increases as the speed and convenience of operating or moving the partition increase.

Other systems within the building are involved, too. Plumbing, electrical, heating-ventilating, ceiling, and lighting systems must be able to adapt themselves to the changing nature of the space division they serve. In general, systems presently evolving are based upon modular units which can be taken from one area and relocated in another, virtually changing places with each other. Utilities are being located, for the most part, between a flexible ceiling system and the roof.

These newly found flexible spaces do not require entirely new visual concepts in school architecture. They can be housed in the most traditional conservative manner or in exciting new ways. The flexibility is in the systems of the building, not necessarily in its aesthetic treatment. Such systems, furthermore, do permit flexibility of change in interior space as education seeks new means to reshape and redefine facilities for forward-looking educational programs.

New Spaces

While the building envelope is changing to provide for the concepts of flexibility, a whole vocabulary-full of new kinds of spaces are being built within school buildings. These spaces are simply facility reactions to developing areas of curriculum, changing teaching techniques, and new kinds of equipment.

To the advent of the space age, the educational response is a program of space sciences and the facility response is the planetarium. The concept of team teaching creates the need for small spaces for individual work and large lecture halls replete with electronic audio-visual equipment to aid the lecturer. Lecture auditoriums are often subdivisable, with acoustically adequate operable partitions to allow size variation to fit the size of lecture groups.

The age of automation has brought educational television, and in turn, one will now find television studios in our schools; television sets in classrooms are no longer novelties. The physical sciences are in such rapid transition that laboratory equipment is now being developed which may be rapidly converted to suit the demands of any physical, chemical, or biological science. The furniture component of such a unit is a basic table with modular cabinets, work tops,

and frames. This will provide a "dry" table which, with the addition of a utility turret and sink, is easily converted for "wet" use. The usual science lecture-laboratory is growing satellite "project laboratories" which may be assigned to an individual student or a small team of students and remains their very own domain until they have completed their complex and advanced experiment without having to tear down their apparatus every time the bell jangles.

New libraries house far more than books. Now, they are centers for such resources as films, tapes, teaching machines—and books, too. There are spaces within them where students may browse, work alone quietly, or work in groups talking or watching films. Classrooms virtually without interior walls allow students to move about from one teacher specialist to another. Space dividers may be no more than cabinets on casters blocking some sight but no sound. Carpet provides for the acoustics and adds to the comfort.

These are but a few of the new breed of spaces created by our new needs. They have one thing in common—they serve today's needs

but will easily change to face up to tomorrow. Our long lost friend flexibility has shown up at last.

Anticipating the shape of the future, especially in times when the culture is rapidly changing, is not an easy task. It is difficult to envision the educational program that the school now being built will be asked to house just a few years from now. Each and every thoughtful school building planner will seek the highest vantage point he can attain, look as far beyond the horizon as his vision will permit, and, ever mindful of the inevitability of change, prepare the new blueprints for the school of tomorrow.

Chapter 6 / *The School Site*

The school site is more than a setting for a building. At its best, it is an integral part of the total educational complex. Where land is plentiful, it may well provide not only the traditional recreational and play space, but an amphitheater or outdoor assembly area and gardens, nature study plots, and wooded areas with great potential for outdoor education. In the midst of a teeming city, it may help to create an overall environment that serves as the educational focal point of the nearby community and sets the tone of the neighborhood in which it is located.

The successful operation of the school plant depends in great measure upon the well planned acquisition, development, and utilization of the site for the school building.

The manner and extent to which a site serves a school district's formal educational needs should be considered as only one aspect of its adequacy. Its adequacy should also be appraised in respect to its potential for contributing to the scope and depth of the development and maintenance of many other basic community cultural patterns.

Site selection and development should proceed from the basic premise that the school is an integral and inseparable part of the total community culture. Since the school is a community institution, it should reflect this relationship physically as well as ideologically. This concept must be accepted and supported in careful site selection and development if the school is to assume a pivotal position in the life of the total community.[1]

Much has already been written about school sites. Efforts are here devoted primarily to identifying school site problems and concerns of special interest to American education in the years immediately ahead.

Long-Range Procurement

A long-range site acquisition program is a most essential ingredient in efficient and economical school plant planning. Experiences of hundreds of school planners have revealed time and time again that a long-range site acquisition program, incorporating thorough site evaluation and coordinated with studies of school population growth and mobility and plant obsolescence, is the only sound procedure for school officials and school boards to follow if they want the pupils of their district to be housed in buildings on school sites which provide maximum educational opportunity, economy of long-range operation, and safe and healthful environment.

Short-term site procurement often leads to the development of headaches for the school planner. Waiting to acquire sites until planning of new facilities is about to start not only complicates the planning but makes successful planning doubtful. Furthermore, short-term site purchasing usually excludes the possibility of undertaking one of the most important steps in the selection of a school site—the making of a comprehensive appraisal of the prospective site in relation to projected school and community programs.

School boards wishing to have successful educational programs must consider long-range site acquisition programs an ongoing responsibility. Four factors contribute, each in a major fashion, to this requirement. Each is becoming increasingly important because of the large amounts of time, effort, money, and education value it represents. The four factors are (1)

[1] American Association of School Administrators. *Planning America's School Buildings.* Washington, D.C.: the Association, 1960. p. 128.

a major increase in the number and complexity of difficulties which today can be involved in the acquisition of land for both new and expanded school sites, (2) an increase in school site costs, (3) an increasing public desire to implement the school-community concept, and (4) the necessity to evaluate potential sites in terms of projected educational programs.

Site Size

In 1962 a U.S. Office of Education survey revealed that 93,000 public school plants in the United States were comprised of 97,000 buildings on 729,000 acres of land and housed 42 million pupils. The study also revealed that school sites on the average were increasing in size at all levels of elementary and secondary education. The increase was most notable at the secondary level: The median secondary plant site, which had been only 3 acres before 1920, reached 27 acres by 1962.[2]

The standards for minimum site size set by the National Council on Schoolhouse Construction are

[2] Collins, George. *National Inventory of School Facilities and Personnel.* U.S. Department of Health, Education, and Welfare, Office of Education. Washington, D.C.: Government Printing Office, 1964. pp. 45-52.

rather generally accepted by school planners and architects. In its 1964 publication, the Council recommended the following minimum sizes for sites:

> Elementary schools—10 acres plus 1 acre for each 100 pupils
> Junior high schools—20 acres plus 1 acre for each 100 pupils
> Senior high schools—30 acres plus 1 acre for each 100 pupils

Thus, the minimum size of a site for a 600-pupil elementary school is 16 acres, and for a 3,000-pupil senior high school, 60 acres.[3]

The Council emphasizes that its recommended guidelines are minimum standards only and that many school systems will find it highly desirable to exceed these suggested levels. Indeed, many American school systems are increasingly buying 40- to 100-acre sites for schools with 1,000 to 3,000 enrollments.

Procurement Problems

The competition for land in America is keen. School boards purchasing new school sites or expansion property are encountering previously unexperienced difficulties. There is every reason to believe that the competition will get more intense in the years ahead. Often the land most suitable for

[3] National Council on Schoolhouse Construction. *Guide for Planning School Plants.* East Lansing, Mich.: the Council, 1964. p. 27.

school sites is in demand by industrial and commercial interests. Many potential school sites are being purchased by the developers of shopping centers, industrial parks, suburban offices, and laboratories. Thus, not only are school sites getting bigger but the availability of satisfactory sites in present and future population centers is decreasing.

Contributing to problems of site procurement is the factor of complexity of ownership. Because larger sites are required for modern schools, it frequently becomes necessary to acquire the property of several owners in amassing a satisfactory tract of land. Often the parcels of property are not vacant, are being used for a variety of purposes, and are not similarly zoned. A store may be located on one parcel, a service building on another, and houses or apartment buildings on others. Trying to arrive at a fair value for each piece of such a wide variety of properties is far more difficult than buying an open piece of farmland or unoccupied or noncommercial property. In the process of acquiring the total

piece of desired property, many hours must be devoted to consultation with realtors, owners, zoning boards, and business and community groups, and also to maintaining good community relationships for the school system throughout the entire property-purchasing process. When multiple ownership and commercial and private interests are involved, a great deal of time, effort, and skill is devoted to estimating property values, eliminating entangling leasing agreements, and sometimes to just ascertaining true ownership.

Some school districts located in heavily populated areas are establishing educational parks. People in these districts believe that very large school sites on which may be housed pupils from preschool through the secondary or even college levels will provide the solution to some current educational problems and more adequate educational opportunity. The proponents of this type of planning also believe that over the years less money will have to be spent for sites, that facility conversions will be more effectively accomplished, and that the time, energy, and expense involved in buying new sites will be reduced. The establishment of edu-

cational parks is one approach to long-range site procurement.

Other school systems are engaged in long-range school site procurement programs conforming to more typical school plant location patterns. However, regardless of the plan being pursued, it is not difficult for even the casual observer to see that it is becoming vastly more difficult each year to surmount the problems encountered in securing school sites and that the amount of time consumed is becoming far more extensive. If school property is to be acquired at the lowest possible price and without recourse to condemnation proceedings any more frequently than is absolutely necessary, as much as several years may be necessary for the acquisition of unencumbered properties. These factors should make evident to school boards, school administrators, and school planners the importance of long-range school site procurement programs.

Site Costs

Another sound reason for long-range school site acquisition programs is the upward spiraling of property values. In urban areas today, prices of $10,000 to $40,000 per acre are not uncommon, and in areas of high density it can cost millions of dollars to consolidate

a few acres into a school site. Here and there the problem of increasing property values has been relieved somewhat by federal, state, and city urban renewal projects. Where these opportunities are available, school planners should take advantage of programs that assist in the acquisition of school sites. At the present time, however, there is not a sufficient volume of funds to alleviate materially the growing concern of local school planners.

The local school board and its administrator will find increasingly larger percentages of their district's money being consumed by the cost of new sites and site expansion properties. There are hundreds of examples that clearly demonstrate the advantages to the school system which implements a long-range site acquisition program. Not having such a program is folly and only puts off until tomorrow a problem which can become increasingly difficult to resolve in the future.

Implementing the School-Community Concept

Many citizens, educators, architects, urban planners, and sociologists believe that schools operate more effectively and the educational

program is more productive when they are closely related to and used by all the people of a community. This is not a new concept, but it has a new adaptation. School boards for generations have been making it possible for pupils to walk to school by locating school buildings centrally within natural school districts. When the entire nation was engaged in a massive school district consolidation program, the school-community concept was in evidence. A group of school districts consolidating their several small buildings into one or more large buildings generally found it advisable to place the new structures centrally in the entire new school community.

Today the centralized location of schools within the community, in addition to being convenient, is necessary for the development of a widely used and strongly supported educational and activity center for the people of all age groups within the community. No longer does the custodian turn out the lights and lock the building at the end of the traditional school day.

More and more today we have the "lighted schoolhouse"—its gymnasium in use by community recreation programs for persons of all ages; its classrooms in use by adult, manpower retraining, or continuing education programs; and its auditorium used by the little theater group or for a meeting of a group of citizens of the community.

Planning the school as a community center is another important aspect of long-range school site procurement. If schools are to be most suitably located in their communities, a long-term view must be taken of the cultural and sociological, as well as the educational needs in each area. This long-range site acquisition approach with concern for the school-community concept is profitable not only in the attainment of school sites, but also in taking cognizance of other community problems. Education is not the only high-priority community function. Urban planners must seek to achieve reasonable balance in the use of community land, not only for the needs of the schools, but also for highways, parking, and the other needs of individuals and groups. Involving citizens and educators in the decision-making process of allocating and making the best use of community land can produce better, more satisfying, and more productive results.

Site and Program Evaluation

Another major reason for school districts to maintain a long-range site acquisition program is the time required for comprehensive evaluation of prospective sites. In the two preceding sections consideration was given to site evaluation in terms of monetary value and with concern for location and function as a community center. Of equal importance is evaluation in terms of the architectural considerations of building placements, vehicular and pedestrian traffic controls both on and around the site, busing and servicing access, community impact, long-term operating and maintenance cost, and relationship to other community institutional activities. Most important of all, however, the site needs to be evaluated in terms of educational considerations.

Administrators, teachers, and curriculum experts in the school system will need to consider the kind of educational program to be housed on the site. For example,

will the school-within-a-school plan be used in order that individual pupils not lose their identity in a mass enrollment? Will a combination large group-small group plan of instruction be used, requiring maximum flexibility which can best be achieved in a one-story rather than a multistory building? These and other decisions will enter into the evaluation of prospective sites. The long-range site program must assure local districts that their educational programs will not have to fit into prospective sites but that, whenever possible, the site will enhance the maximum attainment of the curriculum objectives.

Time-Consuming Steps

The increasing complexity of legal involvements, the continued rise in school site costs, recognition of the school-community concept, and the need for evaluation of school site potentials are four good reasons why school systems—rural, suburban, and urban—should have continuous long-range site acquisition programs. Carefully selected sites are essential components of educational facilities and should overshadow all procurement cost discussions. It takes a great deal of time to find what appears to be suitable property; analyze its

economical, sociological, psychological, and educational values; prepare purchase and development analyses; negotiate purchase; secure boundary and topographical surveys; plan utilization, utility connections, personnel relocations, and possible demolition. All are time-consuming steps. Every school system should have a long-range site procurement program; selecting, procuring, and developing good school sites in most cases takes years to accomplish.

School Site Development

The same purposes which control the selection and acquisition of a school site should guide its development. In determining how a school site should be developed, the responsible people—school board members, administrators, teaching staff, community planners, and local citizens—should develop a statement of the purposes that the school and its site should serve to meet the needs of both the school and the community. This statement of purposes should be a part of the educational specifications in a thoughtfully conceived school building program and become the written guide used by architects, engineers, and educators in site development proposals.

Even after such carefully conceived plans are carried out, site

development activity is not finished. It is a continuous process which gets its initial impetus at the time construction plans are being completed, but which continues throughout the life of the school plant. The development which takes place at the beginning of and during the life of a building is a combination of two factors: (1) the adaptation of the site to meet the educational and community needs of the time and (2) the maintenance and continued improvement of the site.

The development of the school site has a direct bearing on learning. It can open up new vistas for outdoor education. It invites new teaching techniques. It calls for special areas designed to meet the unique needs of different types of learners. Young children need grounds specifically designed for them, and the physical education and athletic programs require special consideration. The limited urban site presents special problems of its own and is a challenge which must increasingly be anticipated. Vocational and technical schools and junior colleges also have unique site development needs. Site devel-

opment plans have many implications for plant management and affect costs of maintenance. Though a comprehensive site development program is an involved and time-consuming part of school building planning and management, it brings rich rewards for the efforts put into it.

Initial Development

Planning begins when consideration is being given to the location of a school site and continues into the plant planning stage with increasing intensity as architects, engineers, and educators begin to function as agents of the school board to translate purpose into plans. At this point the site should undergo further analysis. Topographical surveys must be made to guide the architect in building placement, the engineer in site utility planning, and the landscape architect in land development. The finished site development plan will be a consolidation of such factors as existing site characteristics, purposes and program, building masses, utility requirements, and pedestrian and vehicular traffic.

Sometimes, because of the cost involved, site development is postponed until after buildings have been completed and it is hoped that school-employed labor can be used to finish the job at a later date. Occasionally this approach has proven to be successful, but more often than not it has failed miserably in making the best and most economical educational and generalized use of the site.

Continued Development

Regardless of whether the school site is completely or only partially developed, there are two major factors which must be incorporated in every well conceived plant management program:

1. *Maintenance and completion of partially developed improvements.* When the work on a school site is completed, the school district's buildings and ground maintenance department determines what maintenance is required daily and periodically and what site development, only partially completed, needs to be included in annual work projects. The maintenance program calls for assignment of responsibilities; in-service education; maintenance equipment and supplies; related storage space; and work schedules varying with weather conditions, plant growth, and soil characteristics.

Proper performance of the maintenance function is necessary to the successful and efficient use of school facilities and grounds. It requires capable personnel, possessing knowledge of and concern for planting; nurturing; and caring for a variety of plant growth, parking lots, sidewalks, driveways, bus loading zones, and other service facilities to meet the needs of students, school employees, and patrons. When site development has been poorly planned or when initial work has been limited by budget or other considerations, the maintenance department is left with a sizable job for which they may well be unprepared and which they may be incapable of handling successfully. This serves to emphasize the need for planning and executing site development under expert guidance as a part of the general building program.

2. *Adaptation to changing requirements.* School site requirements change with the passing of time. Even the most beautiful and complete existing school site can encounter newly emerging development problems. Changes in curricular offerings may require the addition of night school parking, or

changes in community interests or the adoption of a board policy to commingle school and park lands might alter materially the school site requirements. In other words, school site development does not necessarily cease with the completion of the original project.

School Site Information and Assistance Resources

In addition to formerly cited information on site acquisition and development, there is available to school administrators, architects, and others engaged in school planning a wealth of information from other sources. Most of this information can be obtained free of charge or at small cost.

Public agencies. There are dozens of public agencies which publish books, brochures, and other media giving information of value to persons acquiring and developing sites for educational facilities. Among them are the U.S. Department of Agriculture and its testing stations, college research and development programs, and county agents; local, regional, and national parks departments; and county, state, and municipal sanitation and highway departments. All of these

agencies have experts who can be very helpful in seeking solutions to problems in the acquisition, development, and utilization of school sites. Even a visit to a nearby arboretum or botanical facility can be helpful in site planning.

Local zoning and planning agencies are important public bodies that should be involved in site selection and development. The planners of school buildings are rightfully much concerned with highway locations, industrial and commercial developments, and community relationships, and mutual benefits are realized through this team approach.

State departments of education publish guides, studies, and codes on school plant planning; and the U.S. Office of Education has a number of publications of particular interest to school plant planners.[4]

Professional organizations and universities. School planners can look to a number of professional education associations for information on the selection and development of school sites. A list, by no means all-inclusive, would include—

American Association for Health, Physical Education, and Recreation

American Association of Junior Colleges

American Association of School Administrators

American Vocational Association

Association of School Business Officials of the United States and Canada

National Association of Physical Plant Administrators of Universities and Colleges

National Council on Schoolhouse Construction

National Rifle Association

Outdoor Education Association

In the architectural and engineering fields there are—

The American Institute of Architects[5]

[4] School Sites—Selection, Development, and Utilization, 1958. Functional Schools for Young Children, 1961. Problems in Planning Urban School Facilities, 1964. The Secondary School Plant, 1965. Basic Planning Guide for Vocational and Technical Education Facilities, 1965. Washington, D.C.: Government Printing Office.

[5] See especially:
BT 1-58 "School Site Selection and Utilization" by William W. Chase
BT 1-45 "Budget for School Site Development" by Robert F. White
BT 1-22 "Landscaping the School Site" by a committee of the Association of Landscape Architects
BT 1-50 "Mind, Body, and Stimuli" by Gyo Obato
BT 1-21 "Environment and Education" by Victor Lowenfeld
BT 1-29 "Outdoor Education in the Secondary School" by G. W. Donaldson
One copy of each reprint is available free; additional copies are 10¢ each from the American Institute of Architects, 1735 New York Avenue, N.W., Washington, D.C.

American Society of Heating, Refrigeration and Air Conditioning Engineers

American Society of Landscape Architects

American Society of Planning Officials

American Standards Association

Building Research Institute of the National Academy of Sciences

Educational Facilities Laboratories, a nonprofit organization, disseminates materials on site development and utilization. Recently, quasi-public type authorities have been developed, through legislative action, to oversee the financing and construction of billions of dollars' worth of educational construction; these authorities naturally are interested in campus grounds. There is little doubt that they will be valuable resource organizations for educational site planners.

Many colleges and universities have long been interested in school plant planning. They conduct site and plant surveys, and their findings have been published in a variety of forms. The schools of education in several institutions have permanent faculty and staff members actively working on site-related problems on a professional education level.

Commerce and industry. There are many private firms and individuals available as school plant resources for dealing with the specific problems related to school sites. The manufacturers of outdoor recreational, educational, and grounds protection equipment are a valuable source of information. The assistance of manufacturers of fences, playground equipment, outdoor lighting, plant growth control, and servicing materials are often helpful, and their knowledge and experience can be had for the asking. Naturally, school planners will have to make allowance for the vested interest aspect of their advice.

A Worthy Goal

The acquisition and development of a school site to serve a school district's educational needs and to make the school an integral and inseparable part of the total community culture is a goal worthy of much time, effort, and money. Though it is far too vast a subject to be undertaken comprehensively in a single chapter of a publication, an effort has been made here to highlight major school site problems that will have to be faced in the years immediately ahead and to provide references to other sources. The purpose has been to provide information and to stimulate thinking and action that will lead to the best possible solution of problems in terms of present and future educational and community needs in any given situation.

Chapter 7 / *Schools in the City*

What of the city?

Most school administrators grew up in small communities and had their early professional experience in small towns or suburbs where "new school" meant new small-town or suburban school. During the thirties there was widespread belief that cities had matured. Ten years ago there was little interest expressed in city school building planning. Seminars on urban schools were rarely held, few articles were written, and only a few city schools were built. Many of these were commonplace, dull, and ugly.

But things have changed. The city and its problems, and the schools it builds and supports, are of keen interest. Rarely do we pick up a current magazine, turn on our television set, or scan the daily newspaper that we do not encounter predictions of more and more people moving into urban areas. The poor have gone to the city seeking a better life for their families, some of the rich have gone back to the city for the advantages of urban living, and those in between surround the city in booming suburbs. City schools—long ignored—are getting increased attention, and a new breed of urban school has emerged.

What Is an Urban School?

An urban school is a school serving an area that is densely populated, where many people live in multifamily dwellings—whether garden apartments, row houses, flats, brownstones, public housing projects, or skyscraper apartment towers—and where land costs are high and building sites small.

Unique Characteristics

What characteristics distinguish the urban school? Are the students different from those in the town or suburban school? Is the educational program different? Is school administration different? What about the environment of the city neighborhood and the distinctness of urban land? And why do city schools take new forms? Analyses of the needs of city pupils, the educational programs, the administrative procedures, the existing and planned-for conditions of neighborhoods, and the uniqueness and characteristics of urban land might serve as useful points of departure in the consideration of urban school building design.

The students are often different. This may not always be true, but today city areas where new schools are most conspicuously needed tend to be "one class" neighborhoods, lacking a full spectrum of people. Students in the high schools serving a town of 10,000 people include the rich and the poor, the white and the colored, the disadvantaged and the privileged, the Christians and the Jews; and nearly all of them are in "the middle class" since the good Lord made so many of them.

The city school is usually located in a neighborhood having a limited mixture of people—a slum in which only the poor and culturally deprived dwell; a neighborhood of identical units of public or private housing; an interesting community of old houses identified with a particular ethnic or national group; or a pleasant area of both old and new structures popular with artists, professional people, young people just out of college, and well-to-do families returned from the suburbs. In each instance, the pupils attending any one particular school tend to be of a kind. The needs of these pupils and the educational program developed for them are unique. Consequently, if we respond to the unique needs of urban youth, the school designed for them must be unique.

Educational programs specifically designed to meet the widely varying needs of urban pupils must themselves vary widely. Technical and vocational education may be more important in one urban school

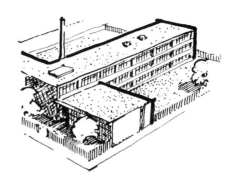

than in another. A high school with a strong vocational program will attract students from all parts of the city. New York City has many special schools—the Fashion Trades High School, the Bronx Science High School, an aviation trades school, and a maritime trades school aboard a ship tied up at an East River pier; Miami has a special hotel and tourist-business -school; and Chicago has a new commercial high school located downtown which will grow vertically into an urban tower. Paramedical studies may well be offered at the high school level, particularly when the school is related to a junior college or to a hospital or medical center. The urban school system appears to have a definite advantage over the town or suburban school in being able to offer such a wide variety of highly specialized programs. The structures built specifically for these special programs will understandably have forms quite different from those of comprehensive schools outside the city.

Administrative organization is different in city schools. Systems are large, with hundreds, even thousands, of schools run by a central administration. Within such school systems, the establishment of a great number of standards has been

necessary. Many standards are imposed on building design and operation which sometimes seem to disregard local variations in need. A desire for maximum economy in purchasing, operations, and maintenance generates standards. It can be argued that a high level of population mobility makes standards more appropriate in the city, but many of the advantages of independent schools are sacrificed when central control is excessive. Innovation is difficult; in most instances changes in needs are reflected but slowly in the educational program and facilities. The city school, if designed to satisfy standards, can rarely be designed in response to the ideas of individuals—the principal and the teachers who will use the building. The architect responsible for the design of a new urban school may work with administrators at the central office; but this is quite different from direct contact with faculty members when the architect designs a town or suburban school.

The character of a neighborhood can more strongly influence the city school than it does its country cousin, because the school on a large landscaped property tends to create its own environment. There are exceptions, of course; a few urban schools are frankly designed as "islands," inward-looking and walled-off from' surrounding

areas. More often, and perhaps more appropriately, the school is a part of the total environment, contributing to and gaining from the street scene and enriching the neighborhood and making it a part of its "campus." There is another difference: good town or suburban schools usually reflect their natural surroundings; city schools seldom have natural, but more often man-made environs. Geometric land patterns and the cubistic building shapes of neighbors create a "hard" environment. This is not necessarily bad—urban forms can be interesting, and some animated urban areas enjoy the excitement of city architecture. The potential advantages of urban neighborhoods certainly should help create new forms for urban schools.

Land in the city is expensive. While the rural site can cost hundreds of dollars an acre, the city site can cost hundreds of thousands of dollars an acre. It is inevitable, therefore, that the city school site be smaller. This is consistent with the tradition and existing pattern of any city. Where land is available at reasonable cost, the 600-pupil elementary school can reasonably expect to utilize sixteen or more acres; but the site for a 600-pupil school

in a medium-density residential area of the city is often only half a city block, or about two acres, one of which is playground, hopefully adjacent to a larger park district playground. The high cost of land and the resulting small sites are strong influences on school design.

Urban school land and building design are subject to many controls and regulations—zoning ordinances, building codes, and sanitary and fire codes—and design must be coordinated with city plans, traffic plans, and complex utility networks. Civic aesthetic controls also must be considered in some cities, as for example in Washington, D.C., or in New Orleans' Vieux Carre. The expansive, low buildings appropriate in the country are not appropriate in the city, and the urban school takes on a distinctive shape. It is more compact, multilevel, and designed to satisfy many controls. It is a *city* building.

City Building Habits

Urban attitudes toward building are interesting. In the city, building forms have evolved that are unlike rural and town forms. The city exists for convenience—whether it be convenience for trade, for production, for administration, or for culture and education—which is achieved through compactness and high density. These conditions create high land values. The most convenient locations are the most valuable. As urban land increases in value, it is no longer thought of as a two-dimensional plane, as is land in the country. In the city, property is three-dimensional; it extends from the earth's center all the way up to heaven.

In prime city locations, tower structures of 20 to 40 floors are common. Multifloor loft-type buildings provide huge flexible floor areas. Rows of buildings such as the row houses of Baltimore, the brownstones and tenement houses of New York, and the continuous rows of houses marching up and down the hills of San Francisco stand side-by-side sharing "party walls." Such areas do have character—a character often established during the nineteenth century. High density provides the convenience to inhabitants of walking to and from their places of employment, shops, restaurants, and theaters. Some of the new urban schools will be built in these well established areas. Other schools will be built in redeveloped urban areas which have tended to introduce more open space and planting, expressways and parking facilities, and the construction of large, independent, freestanding buildings. Still other schools will be built in the less

densely populated city residential areas where individual houses, two-family houses, and multifamily apartment buildings provide homes for city dwellers. Regardless of the character of the area, the urban school at its best should have a spirit and form that is in harmony with its own special city neighborhood.

Examples of Urban Schools

Some specific schools in urban areas are cited here. In most instances, an attempt has been made to relate the design of the school to the urban environment, to respect the building habits of the city, to use appropriate city materials, to accept the limited amount of land available, and to serve a particular student body and educational program. New York's P. S. 199 is located in an urban renewal area on Manhattan Island near the Lincoln Center for the Performing Arts. The plan and building form are very formal. It is a monolithic structure—a freestanding rectangular prism, surrounded by regular rows of brick piers. This elementary school for 1,090 pupils, on a 2½ acre site, is in harmony with its redeveloped neighborhood, which includes new 30-story slab-like apartment buildings and the formal buildings of Lincoln Center.

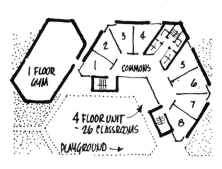

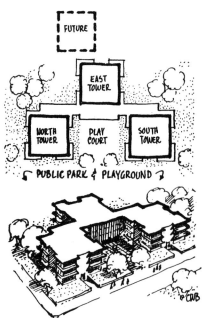

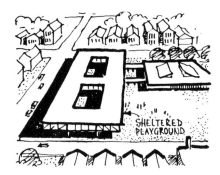

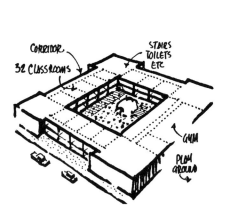

In contrast to outward-looking P. S. 199, Chicago's Doolittle Elementary School is built around an interior courtyard and is completely inward-looking. The building is a two-story hollow square with all classrooms facing the courtyard and windowless exterior walls. Doolittle serves the redeveloped Lake Meadows area south of Chicago's Loop where huge apartment slabs are set on spacious lawns.

Anthony Overton Elementary School, also on Chicago's South Side, attempts to bring some of the amenities of good suburban schools to an area of old apartment buildings and new public housing towers. Every classroom in this school located on a park-like site is in a corner of the structure and has a view of the surrounding neighborhood. Four such rooms are clustered and three floors are stacked in each of three classroom units. Bridges connect these three units and a gymnasium-auditorium unit.

The unique form of James Johnson School at the north edge of Douglas Park in Chicago was developed in response to a program based on team teaching. The four-floor classroom unit has pie-shaped classrooms opening onto commons areas. The building is oriented toward the park, with upper floors enjoying a lake view. This is an agreeable improvement in a neighborhood of old houses and apartment buildings.

Acknowledging a limited site and New Orleans' plentiful rainfall, the classrooms in Phillis Wheatley School are supported by steel trusses on stilts, creating a sheltered playspace. In an old neighborhood of small houses, this city school is lower in height than the previous examples cited. It is a good neighbor and the important focal point in its community.

Not a new building but a 50-year-old structure, New York's old Commercial High School on East 42nd Street provides a good example of a unique urban school designed for a specific environment and for a specific purpose. Built on a tiny site in the heart of a congested commercial area, this school adopted the contemporary custom of building, with party walls joining it to neighboring structures. Classrooms look into a small central court.

Probably the most dramatic urban school is New York's Maritime Trades School, which, with beautiful logic, is aboard a ship tied up at an East River pier near the lower end of Manhattan Island. This city school has a perfect location for its program—the technical aspects of maritime trade commerce —and a most appropriate form— the ship.

Though many city schools are faceless, these few examples suggest the tremendous diversity in urban schools and provide some insight into possibilities for the future. Each school cited owes any success in design to a conscious attempt to create facilities to serve its particular student body and educational program well and to acknowledge its neighborhood and bring to it new usefulness and beauty.

The Loft

The compact loft building has long been a standard city building type. Large unobstructed floor areas are created which can be subdivided according to needs and changed as needs change. Chicago's Merchandise Mart is an excellent example. This multistory structure with approximately 200,000 square feet per floor was built in the late twenties, and its large areas originally used for light manufacturing. After World War II, when demands for office space were increasing, floors were redesigned to accommodate offices and display spaces and air conditioning was added. This principle of convertibility can be applied to educational facilities.

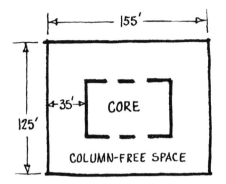

TYPICAL FLOOR — CBS BUILDING

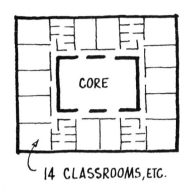

14 CLASSROOMS, ETC.

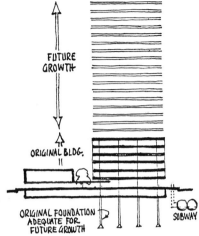

In a loft-plan school, a long-term investment is made in the basic structural frame and in the mechanical-electrical system. Partitions and equipment, on the other hand, are short-term investments to satisfy the needs of the current educational program. As population and program of the school change, part or all of the interior space can be remodeled to accommodate new programs—the equivalent of new tenants in an office building. No good urban school examples of loft planning can be cited, but one can visualize a multifloor adaptation of the well-known Hillsdale High School in San Mateo, California, with each floor enjoying the flexibility inherent in a building design incorporating widely spaced structural columns, movable partitions, and an adaptable mechanical-electrical system.

The Tower

The modern office building offers similar flexibility. An excellent plan has evolved in which a central service core for elevators, stairs, toilets, and mechanical-electrical services is surrounded by a column-free office area. Examples are the John Hancock Building in San Francisco, the Brunswick Building in Chicago, the IBM Building in Seattle, and the CBS Building in New York. The 38-floor CBS Building has an 85' x 55' core serving each 155' x 125' floor and provides a continuous column-free band of usable space 35' wide all around the core. One floor of the CBS Building would efficiently provide space for fourteen 750-square-foot classrooms, plus 4,200 square feet for office, seminar, and conference rooms. The implications for urban schools are obvious. Where land is very expensive, the high-rise office building may suggest an economical form for the city school.

The new Jones Commercial High School in Chicago adopts this idea. The school is located downtown on South State Street. A central location is mandatory; students attend classes at the new school and work in downtown offices. The site is small—1.2 acres—of which 0.4 acre is reserved for a physical education unit and minimum parking space. The 0.8 acre along State Street accommodates an auditorium and cafeteria unit, a garden courtyard, and a 108-foot-square academic unit. The academic unit has a central core surrounded by column-free space for classrooms, laboratories, library, and offices, in the spirit of the modern office building. This seven-floor unit was constructed with foundations and structural frame to accommodate future growth to a total height of 24 floors, thus planning for future vertical expansion rather than the usual horizontal expansion common in the towns and suburbs.

The tower has always been an urban landmark. In the past, the tower has identified the church, the government, or the commercial center. In an age which is increasingly recognizing the growing importance of education, the tower seems an appropriate form for the urban school. Some university examples, such as the University of Pittsburgh, the University of Illinois Chicago Circle Campus, and the new towers for Boston University, MIT, and Harvard already exist. Secondary school examples other than the one cited do not yet exist, but some interesting studies for the future have been made. In 1960 students at the Harvard Graduate School of Design studied the possibility of combining, in a single high-rise structure, a high school and a commercial office building. A design study published in 1962 proposed a high school and community college on a 2-acre city site with six four-floor schools stacked vertically to create a single tower structure with common and community facilities located underground and a bridge-like structure spanning a street. Such ideas are worthy of additional research.

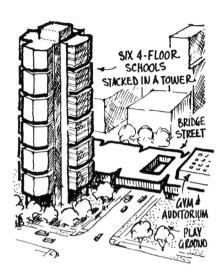

SIX 4-FLOOR SCHOOLS STACKED IN A TOWER

BRIDGE STREET

GYM & AUDITORIUM

PLAY GROUND

FRIENDS' SELECT SCHOOL PHILADELPHIA-

OFFICE BUILDING-SCHOOL WITH ROOFTOP PLAYING FIELD

Sharing Land

Land need not necessarily be used for one single purpose. There are many excellent examples of combinations of many separate related or unrelated functions on a single site. In Rochester, New York, for example, the Midtown Plaza stacks an underground parking garage, shops, restaurants, an office building, a hotel, and a rooftop restaurant in a single complex.

In most cities, apartments rise above shops and professional offices, and offices rise above theaters and shops. High land costs generate such combinations, and much convenience is often gained. Schools, too, might benefit from such multiple-function combinations. In the 1960 Harvard study, possibilities were explored for combining in a single tower a large comprehensive high school near ground level and a tall apartment structure rising above it or a commercial high school and a commercial office building. Since then, in both New York and Chicago, elementary schools have been located within public housing structures. Not only are such schools convenient for pupils, but the facilities serve as valuable community centers to be used after school hours for adult education, community meetings,

and social affairs. Since land cost is such a major factor, one must conclude that the school can often benefit from sharing land with other facilities, especially when positive advantages are achieved.

Air Rights

Air rights present another opportunity for imaginative solutions to the problem of finding adequate sites for new schools. Again, other types of urban buildings point the way. Many office buildings have been built over railroad properties, using air rights. These rights are purchased, along with small plots of land between the tracks to accommodate foundations for the structures above. Restaurants bridge Chicago's expressways, apartment towers rise above the Manhattan approach to the George Washington Bridge, and a number of university buildings span city streets. The concept is valid; the space above railroad tracks and yards, expressways, and canals is otherwise wasted; and much of this space can be regained for use by utilizing air rights. Schools, too, can benefit. The Harvard study proposed a 2,500-pupil high school bridging an expressway. This bridge school, furthermore, tied back together a neighborhood which the expressway had cut apart.

The bridge concept suggests another direction for urban design

which we now see emerging in some of our cities—the multilevel neighborhood, with vehicular traffic, services, and parking at lower levels and pedestrian circulation at upper levels. Baltimore's Charles Center and Chicago's riverfront contain multilevel areas; Cleveland planners would like to unite various educational and cultural institutions in the University Circle area with a great pedestrian plaza built over the boulevards; and citizens of Grand Rapids, Michigan, will create a plaza relating its community college and cultural center above an expressway feeder and garage. Public school building planners should not assume that all entrances to future school buildings must be at ground level; pupils may well arrive at an upper level over busy traffic arteries by elevator or escalator. Bridging also permits the use of noncontiguous parcels of land in adjacent blocks. A new pattern of growth may evolve that will be in strong contrast to the formal rectangular properties traditionally associated with educational facilities.

Underground

Can some schools be partially underground? Yes, if ground and water conditions permit, if air conditioning is properly designed, and

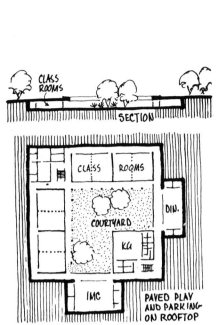

CLASS ROOMS

SECTION

CLASS ROOMS

DIN.

COURTYARD

KU

IMC

PAVED PLAY AND PARKING ON ROOFTOP

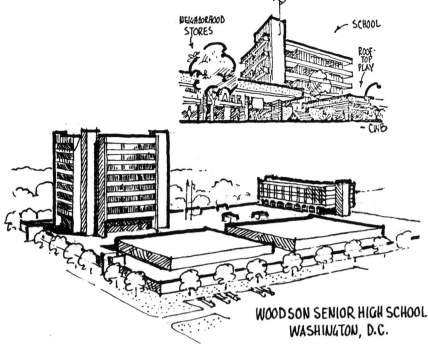

NEIGHBORHOOD STORES

SCHOOL

ROOF-TOP PLAY

- CWB

WOODSON SENIOR HIGH SCHOOL
WASHINGTON, D.C.

if safe exiting is provided. Gymnasiums, auditoriums, laboratories, and mechanical equipment spaces are often windowless, and an underground location for such spaces could save above-ground space for classrooms, offices, and other facilities for which window space is ordinarily provided. Such underground space can have a dual use. Underground or partially underground space can use earth and concrete efficiently to provide fallout radiation protection. Total protection is usually impossible, but one increases safety factors by scientifically designing a reasonable amount of protection at little, if any, more cost than that of the school facilities provided.

Community Ties

Effective cooperation between park officials and school officials in the selection of park and school sites can be most beneficial to the urban community. If park and school sites are adjacent, teachers and pupils can make good use of parks and playgrounds during school hours—the hours parks are ordinarily little used.

A neighborhood includes not only housing, recreation facilities, and a school, but also retail stores. Traditionally, the school has been separated from stores. Could they be combined to advantage? The rooftops of neighborhood stores might well provide spacious play spaces—still another opportunity for vertical stacking of functions.

If the school itself contains, or is combined with, community cultural and adult education and social facilities and makes good use of these facilities, then the school becomes the single most important community center and is used by a large number of citizens. These citizens have a special, personal interest in the school and will tend to support it, assist with its program, and take pride in it. This kind of interest is often lacking in city neighborhoods.

The function of the school is changing in the city. Its program is being extended to serve not only children but adult citizens as well. As a community center, the school complex includes meeting rooms, an expanded library, a swimming pool, athletic and game spaces, a theater, and exhibition space for the whole community. In other words, the urban school is becoming the center of neighborhood life, the rallying place, the cultural center for people of all ages. This concept of a community school should inspire broad changes in the scope of building; in the administration, operation, and financing of schools; and in relationships between citizen

groups, their school board, and the city government.

Bigness

Since by their very nature urban schools are located where many people live, some of them inevitably will be big. Enrollment in Chicago's school system has increased in recent years by 25,000 pupils per year, and it has been predicted that by 1970, it will reach 750,000 pupils. New York City several years ago passed the 1-million mark. When large numbers of children are enrolled in school, administrative decisions of necessity must favor large schools. But some are too large. The inherent weaknesses are apparent—the feeling of being lost in the crowd and the difficulty of merely coping with an environment of bigness, with too long corridors and too overpowering building complexes. The "institutional feeling" which Walter McQuade defined as "large numbers plus sameness" can be deadly to the individual. In designing the urban school, the sensitive school planner strives to achieve variety in building forms and a scale which is compatible with human reactions.

If thousands of pupils must be accommodated on a single school site, it is still possible to achieve

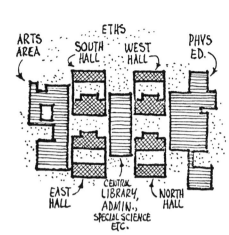

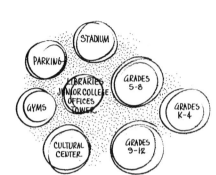

many of the advantages of smaller schools by subdividing the pupils, teachers, and facilities. Suburban Evanston Township High School has for decades operated not as a single school, but as a cluster of smaller "halls" or "houses," each with its own faculty and student body. In Detroit, the new Eastern Senior High School follows this same general plan. Each of four "houses" in this secondary school accommodates 650 students, with common facilities such as gymnasiums and auditorium shared by students from all four houses. Thus, each of the 2,600 students enjoys not only the advantages of a small school but the broader facilities usually provided in only a large school.

Consolidated Campus

In consolidated campus or educational park facilities, school children of all ages share a common site. The East Orange, New Jersey, educational plaza scheme proposes on a single 16-acre campus a primary school, middle school, high school, and junior college, with common facilities for physical education, the arts, and building services. The new plaza is designed for 9,800 children, to replace 10 elementary schools, a junior high school,

and 2 senior high schools—all aging structures.

In Syracuse, N.Y. . . . the school board has approved a $30 million proposal for four large elementary-school parks located at the edge of the city. "We build racetracks out where there are trees and green grass," says superintendent Franklyn Barry. "Children should have the same thing."

In Pittsburgh, Pa. . . . the school board is considering a comprehensive city-wide system of parks as part of an extensive urban-renewal blueprint. John T. Mauro, director of the city planning department, describes each park as "a campus threaded throughout an entire community." The plans call for the city to be divided into five sub-cores, each one served by a major transportation artery like a railroad or highway. The sub-cores would have high schools and technical institutes. On the same site would be shops, offices, and hospitals. The goal, says architect David Lewis, is to make neighborhoods "start looking outward, rather than inward, toward a shared center."[1]

If such large single acreages could be found in the city, the educational park might solve some of the problems in urban school planning. Such large sites, however, are seldom available. Even if they were,

one may well question the advisability of mixing large numbers of 6-year-old and 19-year-old pupils on the same campus. Furthermore, the transportation problems and inconveniences in bringing so many thousands of students to one location must be recognized.

Nucleus and Satellites

Small urban schools, each conveniently located on its own site, may conceivably be linked electronically and by bus or other means of transit to a central education nucleus where expensive special facilities are located. In such a center one might find the master instructional materials center, special education facilities, computers, television and film studios, specialized shops and laboratories, an exhibition swimming pool and large spectator athletic facilities, special theaters, the auditorium, and the concert hall, along with faculty specialists and administrators. It may be that some of the disadvantages of bigness can be overcome more effectively in such a system.

Individual satellite schools would be built on a relatively small scale. Students would travel, in ac-

---

[1] Newsweek. "The Park Way." *Newsweek* 68:48; July 18, 1966.

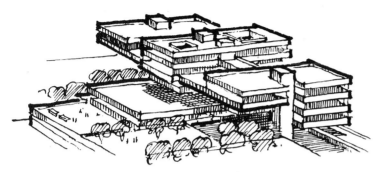

UNITED NATIONS INTERNATIONAL SCHOOL
CANTILEVERED OVER THE EAST RIVER
NEW YORK CITY

cordance with their needs, to the city's educational nucleus to use specialized facilities not duplicated at each school and to enjoy the variety and excitement this unique center provides. Most of the time, however, students would walk to their own neighborhood school where they and their parents would know and be known by the faculty and other students. Electronic links to the nucleus would make available to each student many of the resources of the nucleus, such as closed-circuit television and other specialized educational programs planned and presented by highly skilled members of the instructional staff.

Mobility

In recognition of population mobility in the city, should some school facilities be mobile? There have been many attempts to create mobile facilities, using many methods and a great variety of materials —wood, concrete, steel, aluminum, and plastics. A few of these units have been attractive, but many have offended citizens. Different degrees of portability must be recognized. The pioneering British system, called "Clasp," incorporates factory-made metal parts assembled at the site to create a school structure that is relatively permanent, although the building can be disassembled and moved. American manufacturers have produced trailer-size units which are set on foundations at the site. These generally have been used to serve a temporary need. Some units are truly portable; they arrive on their own wheels and can easily be towed away. In most cases, however, these trailer-type units have been mere makeshift additions to old schools.

There are opportunities for future development and a growing need for new concepts in design of mobile units. In changing neighborhoods, perhaps a permanent core containing utilities and basic facilities could be established so that a varying number of mobile units could be added or subtracted as change takes place. This kind of school would have a unique character; the challenge lies in making it agreeable.

Mind and Spirit

In the city, as in the town and suburb, the school and its neighborhood fail if beauty is missing. Beauty around the country school and the suburban school is easier to define; it is that quality of agreeable relationships between architecture and natural environment which gives pleasure to the senses. However, even when this natural environment is lacking, the city, too, can have beauty. The senses can respond favorably to a quiet city street, to the complex geometric forms of a visually stimulating urban neighborhood, and to the drama and excitement of the city center. To achieve beauty, the urban school must reflect its neighborhood, enhance what is good, and help change what is bad. Its form and design, generated by program and the needs of pupils, must exalt the mind and the spirit.

Chapter 8 / *The Exceptional Learner*

School districts throughout the country are recognizing to an increasing degree their responsibilities to all the citizens in their communities—the bright and the dull, the old and the young, and the exceptional as well as the so-called average student. The nation as a whole is committed to making the best use of the talents of all its citizens. Indeed, its strength lies in the full development of the capabilities of all the people, in opening the doors of opportunity to the handicapped as well as to the more fortunate.

During the pre-Christian era, handicapped human beings were persecuted, mistreated, and neglected. As Christianity spread, they were pitied and protected. In the last 150 years they have gradually become accepted and integrated into the mainstream of life. The past 10 years have witnessed a dramatic psychological shift in the public from viewing them as deficient to emphasizing their actual potentialities for self-fulfillment.

The term *handicapped* has been difficult to define because of the varying degrees of impairment which afflict people and because something new is learned about such problems every day. Consequently, statistics concerning the handicapped are difficult to collect and to compare with reliability. A term used more frequently is *exceptional.* This term is more inclusive, since it also covers the gifted child. Here the terms *handicapped* and *exceptional* are used interchangeably and do not include the gifted.

Six broad categories and eleven types of handicapped children are commonly identified—

—*Pupils with intellectual limitations:* (1) the educable or the slow learners and (2) the trainable mentally retarded.

—*Pupils with impaired vision:* (3) the blind and (4) the partially blind.

—*Pupils with impaired hearing:* (5) the deaf and (6) the hard-of-hearing.

—*Pupils with neurological and nonsensory physical impairments:* (7) the crippled and (8) the chronic cases.

—*Pupils with speech problems:* (9)

—*Pupils with behavior problems:* (10) the emotionally disturbed and (11) the socially maladjusted.

Unfortunately, along with many of the blessings of the sixties, the number of children with handicaps is rising. According to Kathryn Dice Reier of the Pennsylvania State Department of Public Instruction:

At the 1950 White House Conference we were told that the proportion of handicapped-to-normal children in the United States was one in ten; by 1960 the ratio had risen to one in eight. It is now one in five. In other words, 20 percent of the children in this country have some kind of handicap that requires special attention from a medical and environmental, as well as educational, standpoint.

I do not say that one child in five needs a special class. I'm talking about the incidence of handicapping—many "handicapped" children do not need a full-time special class, or even a part-time one. Some need even more than full-time classes; they require residential care. But when you lump together the incidence of handicapping in children in the various types, this is an overall statistic, verifiable by census figures.[1]

Although concern for the care of exceptional children has grown in recent years, only a relatively small percentage of all school-age children who need special education are provided with its opportunities.

In eleven states fewer than 10 percent are enrolled; in fourteen states, between 10 and 20 percent; fourteen have

---

[1] Quoted by Ludwig, Marilyn E. "Educating the Exceptions." *AIA Journal* 44:52; September 1965.

between 20 and 30 percent; five between 30 and 40 percent; and in only six states are as many as 40 to 50 percent enrolled.[2]

A significant force behind the recent development of opportunities for the education of exceptional children has been state legislation. By 1948 a total of 41 states and the District of Columbia had enacted legislation for special education in local school districts. Only 34 had made provisions for financial participation on the part of the state in the maintenance of these programs. Today all 50 states have such legislation.

Large cities have often pioneered in educational programs for handicapped children. New York, Detroit, Cleveland, and Chicago had relatively extensive programs by 1914. All have continued the development and improvement of their special education offerings. How such action has accelerated in recent years is revealed by the example of additions to the services of the Chicago schools since 1953.[3]

[2] Prouty, Winston L. "Exceptional Children—The Neglected Legion." *NEA Journal* 55:25; March 1966.

[3] Willis, Benjamin C. *Special Education in Chicago.* Annual Report of the General Superintendent of Schools, 1964. Chicago: Board of Education, 1964. p. 13.

Classes for the trainable mentally handicapped / *initiated 1953*

Secondary school classes for the educable mentally handicapped / *initiated 1953*

Classes for young maladjusted children in regular schools / *initiated 1953*

Girls' Branch of Chicago Parental School / *opened 1953*

Classes for multiply handicapped blind and multiply handicapped deaf / *initiated 1955*

Reorganization of educational program and rehabilitation of residential facilities of the Chicago Parental School / *effected 1956*

New building for the physically handicapped (Jane A. Neil) / *erected 1956*

New buildings for socially maladjusted boys (Flavel Moseley and Moses Montefiore) / *erected 1958, 1960*

Research project on the mentally handicapped / *conducted 1958-1961*

Class for the brain injured / *initiated 1959*

Summer school for the physically handicapped / *initiated 1960*

Itinerant teacher plan for the partially seeing / *initiated 1960*

Social centers for the physically handicapped / *initiated 1961*

Manual language class for the slow learning deaf / *initiated 1962*

After-school speech clinics / *initiated 1962*

After-school hearing clinics / *initiated 1963*

New curriculum for the mentally handicapped / *developed 1963*

Secondary school class for the partially seeing with crippling conditions / *initiated 1963*

A valuable guide to the development of programs and facilities for exceptional children is proposed by Dunn. He states:

It is impossible to formulate a set of universal axioms that hold for all exceptional children in all communities. Nevertheless, an attempt has been made to outline those which seem to come closest to accomplishing it.

1. Each exceptional child is primarily a child with the same rights to acceptance, understanding, and education as other children.

2. Wide individual differences exist among children in each area of exceptionality.

3. Early screening, identification, and placement in a special education program are generally necessary if exceptional children are to make optimal progress in school.

4. The team approach to comprehensive case study involves medical, social, and psychological as well as educational specialists, but educational diagnosis and placement are central responsibilities of the education authority in charge.

5. The success of a particular type of special education service will depend on well developed criteria for placement so that pupils with other types of problems and needs are not inappropriately enrolled in it.

6. Programs should not be initiated or continued unless well-trained, competent personnel are available.

7. Specialized curriculum, materials and equipment are needed, though the quantity and type will vary from area to area.

8. Since the general objective of "developing personal, social, and economic effectiveness" is too broad to permit careful curriculum development or appraisal of teaching and learning effectiveness, specific goals need to be developed for all special education programs with an emphasis on both scholastic and social learning, on the national purposes of education, and on the aptitudes and potentials of the pupils concerned.

9. A mental health approach in terms of accepting each pupil and providing a warm classroom climate is a profitable entree for assisting a student to self-acceptance, self-evaluation, and the development of realistic goals.

10. Clinical-education instruction is needed for exceptional children which involves individualized teaching procedures based upon careful appraisal of each pupil's abilities and disabilities.

11. Education for exceptional children should be an integral part of a total education program when possible and practical.

12. Continuous re-assessment of exceptional children and re-evaluation of school programs are essential to progress.

13. Follow-up of each student after he leaves school, and placement assistance where needed, are responsibilities of the school.

14. Community-wide cooperation among educational and non-educational services for exceptional children will broaden the comprehensiveness and avoid gaps and duplications.

15. Special education programs are strengthened by frequent interpretation of them to educators, parents, legislators, and the public.

16. The promotion of educational research, teacher preparation, and instructional services in education for exceptional children are the joint responsibilities of national, state, and local agencies.[4]

One factor which affects the nature of the facilities required is the administrative arrangements by which the services of special education are provided. The most common types of educational services are provided through—

—The residental school

—Hospital instruction

—Homebound instruction

—Itinerent plans

—Special schools

—Special classes within the regular schools

—Cooperative programs in which the varied needs of individuals are met by specialists working both with the pupil and with his regular classroom teacher

—Resource rooms where specialized equipment and services for a variety of needs are provided

—Specialist consultants who are central office personnel

—Boarding homes for day pupils

—Interdistrict plans.

A second factor involved in the planning of facilities is class size. The Chicago policy is quoted here:[5]

[4] Dunn, Lloyd M. *Exceptional Children in the Schools.* New York: Holt, Rinehart and Winston, 1963. pp. 36-39.

[5] Willis, Benjamin C. *Special Education in Chicago.* Annual Report of the General Superintendent of Schools, 1964. Chicago: Board of Education, 1964. p. 32.

Program	1963 Authorized Class Size
Physically handicapped schools	8-14
Hospital instruction	1- 4
Home instruction	1
Physical therapy	1
Deaf: Elementary	6- 8
Hard of hearing: Elementary	8-12
Impaired hearing: Secondary	10-16
Blind: Elementary	5- 9
Blind: Secondary	8-12
Partially seeing: Elementary	8-14
Partially seeing: Secondary	10-16
Educable mentally handicapped: Elementary	10-15
Educable mentally handicapped: Secondary	15-18
Trainable mentally handicapped	8-10
Socially maladjusted: Elementary	10-15
Socially maladjusted: Advanced	12-18

Multiple handicapped: Class size smaller than for either handicap separately.

Specialized plant facilities and/or equipment are needed for virtually each type of impairment. Some suggestions follow:

Educable Mentally Retarded

Classroom area of 900 square feet

Ample storage area for large variety of materials, some movable storage equipment

Sink

Folding stage

Drinking fountain

Variety of simple musical instruments

Telephones

Tools and work table

Art center

Science center

Aquarium, terrarium

Adjoining and easily accessible toilet areas for boys and girls

Full-length mirror

Screens for separating functional areas

One-way vision windows or television monitors for observation

Access to gymnasium and outdoor play area

Selected audiovisual equipment

Equipment for teaching safety

Trainable Mentally Retarded

Same as foregoing, with provisions for security and safety

Partially Sighted

(Most of the time these pupils are found in a regular classroom)

Sight teachers room equipped with taped lessons, recorders, and reproducers

Books in primer or larger type

Pupil desks in regular classrooms and in a resource room adjustable

in height and vertical angles, with light but dull finish

Chalkboards gray or green, not black

Typewriters with primer type

Dictaphones

Magnifying glasses

Pencils with heavy thick lead and cream-colored paper.

Blind

(Part of the time in regular classrooms)

Braille reading and writing materials

Typewriters

Many models of familiar objects for tactile recognition and identification

Talking books

Calculators

Embossed and relief maps and pictures

Impaired Hearing and Deafness

Hearing aids

Visible speech machines

Amplifiers

Programed materials

Visual aids

Crippled Children and Chronic Impairments

A special facility for children in this classification is located in Racine, Wisconsin. Because of the thoroughness of planning and study which preceded construction, a detailed account is quoted here. "In

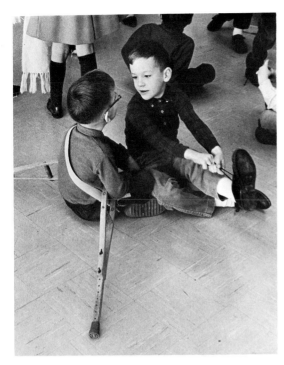

planning the special education facilities for the school, the Racine board of education agreed on these principles—

1. Orthopedic pupils were to share a wing of a complete elementary school building (near both a junior and a senior high school) to permit easy use of special facilities in the orthopedic school for all students full-time or part-time, elementary or advanced in training.

2. Water therapy was accepted as being more desirable than heat treatment for the major share of our orthopedic charges, though heat treatment was to be included in the program.

3. Rest was considered as an essential part of the treatment program and special facilities were to be provided.

4. Occupational and physical therapy seemed equally important to the program; both were to be provided with adequate space.

5. Special lunch and transportation facilities were to be planned, suited to the special needs of the orthopedic students and to the rigors of a Wisconsin climate.

6. The use of special hall railings and similar artificial aids, not available in the home, were to be avoided.

7. Scrupulous attention, however, was to be given to providing floor materials and floor conditions suited to pupils who are often impaired in their ambulatory movements.

8. All medical care was to be directly under the family physician, but school clinics were to be sponsored by a panel of competent specialists. Referrals were made to the school by the family physician.

9. Psychological and speech services were to be provided in special areas planned for the use of all students served by the school." [6]

Facilities provided for the 200 children enrolled in the orthopedic wing of the Racine, Wisconsin, school include—

Four regular classrooms—

—Each room has 50 percent more floor area than standard classrooms in order that children in wheelchairs or with crutches can move freely.

—Extra-large tables are provided with special cutouts to assure the children of proper body support and of more room for supplies and materials with less possibility of pushing them to the floor.

—Grab bars are located near each chalkboard for support.

—Several chalkboards in each room are low enough for use by children in wheelchairs.

[6] Lake, Ernest G., and Williams, Malcolm. "Facilities for a Pilot Orthopedic Program." *American School Board Journal* 141:15-16; December 1960.

—Each classroom has its own ramped exit.

—Each classroom has its own lavatory facilities.

—One-way vision mirrors enable staff, parents, and visitors to observe the children in each classroom without disturbing them. The mirrors are placed in conference rooms adjacent to the classroom and accessible from the hallway.

—Extra-wide doors are provided to admit children in wheelchairs.

—Rubber tile flooring is provided for secure footing.

—A spacious workroom is found next to each classroom for committee work, small-group instruction, or for giving the distractible child a quiet working space.

—Optimal light intensity is provided.

Speech correction and testing room—

—A spacious room with an adjoining observation room with a one-way mirror and a two-way communication system is provided.

—Best of acoustical treatment is supplied.

—Individual testing booths also are available.

Dining room—

—The special training dining room is separated from the main dining room by folding doors.

—A large mirror in one corner allows children to observe themselves for training purposes.

—An enclosed and sheltered court is located next to the special dining room especially for use by the younger children.

—A greenhouse and planting area is included in this court since gardening is a hobby which is or can be pursued by many handicapped children.

Taxi area—

—All handicapped children are transported by special arrangement with the taxicab company.

—Children are driven inside where overhead doors protect them from the elements.

—A small multipurpose room adjoins the unloading platform to prevent chilling of the rest of the building during the unloading procedure.

—A wheelchair storage room adjoins the loading platform.

Physical therapy room—

—Various kinds of heat, light, water, electricity, and massage equipment are provided.

—Also contains much movable equipment such as curbs, ramps, foot placement ladders, footboards, stall bars, steps, and an overhead track · for strengthening and restoring diseased muscles, nerves, and joints.

—A soundproof treatment room with a one-way mirror.

—Space for several children to exercise simultaneously.

—Office space for recording and keeping the medical treatment records.

—A conference room for the therapy team.

—The hydrotherapy room contains a Hubbard Tank and whirlpool.

—An electrical hoist with an overhead track makes it possible for a child to be lifted from the treatment table and placed in the tank.

—Swimming pool

—Gymnasium

—Occupational therapy room

—Activities of the occupational therapist are carried on under a physician's direction.

—Foot-powered jig-saws and looms are a part of the equipment.

—Food and clothing area provides practical training under the conditions of a normal home environment.[7]

Speech

Corrective work done by individual therapy

Large mirror

Cupboard space

Soundproof rooms for audiological testing

Books, games, and toys

---

[7] Gleaned from *Ibid.*

Two-way communication system

Individual testing and learning booths.

Emotionally Disturbed and Socially Maladjusted

Individual work space

Isolation rooms or partitions

Acoustically treated space

Viewing windows

Provisions for teacher aides.

Special Rooms. An important factor sometimes overlooked is the necessity for a team approach to work with the handicapped. Such an approach requires a good and instantaneous communication system, offices, testing rooms, counseling rooms, conference rooms, library, record-keeping facilities, and a fireproof place for the storage of records. The electronic age is of great assistance in this connection.

At the AIA Workshop on Educational Facilities for Exceptional Children, one general point of agreement on such facilities concerned size and that old familiar friend, flexibility. A frequent complaint of teachers, Kathryn Dice Reier reported, was the size of classrooms—they tend to be too small—and the need for flexibility. She explained:

What I mean by flexibility is lots of room in which to move around. I'm thinking about people being flexible in freedom of movement, both the child and the teacher. I'm thinking about having as little [equipment] fastened down in a permanent place as possible. I realize that there are some things that have to be fixed, like doors and windows and outlets and so on. But I'm particularly interested in having things movable and changeable so that they can be turned around or faced in a different direction or used in different ways by different age groups and for different activities.

. . . .

Suppose you have a class in which all the children are in wheelchairs. Now, is it going to be easier to move the wheelchairs or to move the library bookcases? This is a real problem to a teacher. This is what I mean by flexibility.[8]

There are many unsolved problems in relation to the education of handicapped children. Teacher training, curriculum strategies and materials, rural dispersion of children, cost, and needed research are some of them. Yet great strides forward are being made. The psychological shift from deficiency motivation to growth motivation as a fundamental view of the exceptional child is one. The devoted and fruitful work of many people who believe in growth motivation is another. Recognition that cognitive

development of the kind allowed by their limitations opens up to the handicapped a world for exploration, a world traditionally denied them, is a third. And, finally, there is the realization that our knowledge of individual variability applies to these children too and that application of this knowledge leads to development likely to take a child as far as he can go.

What about the future?

—Biochemistry will enable mankind to eradicate many of the ills which now afflict the educationally exceptional child.

—Trends indicate that the provision of needed educational opportunities and facilities will rise sharply during the next decade. Possibly every child will have the advantages of going to a school where he, too, can be a part of an active, satisfying experience of growth.

—Ways will be devised for using a wide variety of media, some of which are not yet available, for a great extension of the eyes, ears, minds, and muscles of these children.

—The very necessary steps will be taken to identify and, to ameliorate children's impairments at an earlier age. This is especially true of sight, emotional and social adjustment, and aphasic, perceptual, and cognitive problems.

—Provision will also be made for

older youth and adults as opportunities are extended for continued development.

—Possibly new modes of travel and communication, like air-cushioned vehicles and the new communications systems described by David Sarnoff and others, will make possible the school attendance or the provision of home services to children in the most remote locations.

—If wise political-economic-social decisions continue to raise the level of the abundant life, facilities and opportunities resulting from research and development will appear for which there are no present dreams.

The exceptional child must be a part of the great American dream of equal educational opportunity for all. In summing up his annual report for 1964, Superintendent Willis of Chicago declares:

Special Education in Chicago is the story of a journey out of retreat from life into the light of undiscovered abilities. It is the contentment, and then the confidence, and then the courage, that comes with accepting that we do not all begin at the same place. It is the inner challenge to each to begin with his own today as he builds for his own tomorrow.[9]

[8] Dice, Kathryn. Quoted in *Workshop on Educational Facilities for Exceptional Children, May 14-15, 1965.* Washington, D.C.: The American Institute of Architects, 1965. p. 15.

[9] Willis, Benjamin C. *Special Education in Chicago.* Annual Report of the General Superintendent of Schools, 1964. Chicago: Board of Education, 1964. p. 31.

Chapter 9 / *The Young Child*

As the intensity of the spotlight on education increases in the sixties, early childhood education is receiving its share of the focus. Throughout the country, many young children are experiencing educational opportunities that were for the most part not readily available to their older brothers and sisters. The reasons for the development of special programs for young children are many. Day care centers are needed for the children of the growing number of working mothers, suburban housewives are seeking respite from the persistent attention demanded by small children, and anxious parents want to give their youngsters a head start on the college admissions race track. Many people are also feeling an urgency for action to combat the serious social consequences of poverty and cultural deprivation.

The most significant reason for placing strong emphasis on early childhood education, however, is not among those previously mentioned. Experience with experimental programs and recent research have emphasized the need for this downward extension of educational programs. Early in 1966, the Educational Policies Commission declared:

> The development of intellectual ability and of intellectual interest is fundamental to the achievement of all the goals of American education. Yet these qualities are greatly affected by what happens to children before they reach school. A growing body of research and experience demonstrates that by the age of six most children have already developed a considerable part of the intellectual ability they will possess as adults. Six is now generally accepted as the normal age of entrance to school. We believe that this practice is obsolete. All children should have the opportunity to go to school at public expense beginning at the age of four.[1]

If mankind is to succeed in coping with the opportunities and challenges of future existence, the great hidden potential of the human mind and personality must be tapped in a manner and to a degree beyond all precedent. Sufficient evidence exists to indicate that productive research and development in early childhood education is now possible and deserves top priority in the effort to bring this about. Historical and research evidence supports the validity of the old saying, "As the twig is bent, so is the tree inclined." Yet in educational practice in the past we have failed to take into account sufficiently the degree and significance of five years of directional growth,

---

[1] National Education Association and American Association of School Administrators, Educational Policies Commission. *Universal Opportunity for Early Childhood Education.* Washington, D.C.: the Commission, 1966. p. 1.

or lack of it, in the children entering our kindergartens.

This conclusion does not assume that all is lost unless early, preschool, educational experience is provided. It is also true that a twig can be staked and its growth redirected. Nothing said in this chapter should be interpreted as negating the importance of remedial and supplementary educational programs. It is true, however, in some developmental aspects that the direction of the twig is irrevocably determined by the time the child reaches the school. Although no valid reason exists to consider early childhood education a panacea for all problems of education, it is one of the powerful factors for the improvement of the educational process, albeit a long-neglected one.

Developing Potential

A most significant study reported in 1964 by Benjamin S. Bloom emphasized the conclusion that early environment and experience are far more critical in human development and learning than was previously acknowledged. Bloom underscores the following reasons why this conclusion has been largely neglected in the past:

> The prolongation of the period of dependency for youth

in the Western cultures has undoubtedly been a factor in desensitizing parents, school workers, and behavioral scientists to the full importance of the very early environmental and experiential influences. . . . There appears to be an implicit assumption running through the culture that change in behavior and personality can take place at any age or stage in development and that the developments at one age or stage are no more significant than those which take place at another.

A central finding in this work is that for selected characteristics there is a negatively accelerated curve of development which reaches its midpoint before age 5. We have reasoned that the environment would have its greatest effect on a characteristic during the period of its most rapid development.[2]

Bloom made a thorough study of all the research available through longitudinal studies on the development of selected human characteristics from the earliest age for which data are available to ages 18 to 20. By correlating the findings of this research, he reached the conclusion that by the age of 5, a person has already attained 50 percent of the de-

velopment he will exhibit at ages 18 to 20 in the following selected characteristics:

Characteristic	Age in years of 50 percent attainment
Height	2½
General intelligence	4
Intellectual interests	4
Aggressiveness in males	3
Dependence in females	4

He also discovered that by grade 3, a student has attained one-half of the general school achievement he will have in grade 12.[3]

These conclusions, although admittedly in need of further research, are substantiated sufficiently to influence decisions that need to be made in curriculum revision and in school organization. Early childhood education becomes a necessary concern, especially for the culturally deprived, when so much of human development occurs in the early years and when so much of it is a function of the environment and of experience. The corollary to this concern is found in Bloom's point that to produce a given amount of change in human characteristics requires more and more powerful environments and increased amounts of effort and attention as the indi-

vidual grows older and his characteristics become increasingly stabilized.

Bloom draws additional significant implications for education from the research concerning the effect of environmental factors on the development of intelligence, particularly in the early years. He states:

A conservative estimate of the effect of extreme environments on intelligence is about 20 I.Q. points. This could mean the difference between a life in an institution for the feeble-minded or a productive life in society. It could mean the difference between a professional career and an occupation which is at the semi-skilled or unskilled level. A society which places great emphasis on verbal learning and rational problem solving and which greatly needs highly skilled and well-trained individuals to carry on political-social-economic functions in an increasingly complex world cannot ignore the enormous consequences of deprivation as it affects the development of general intelligence. . . . Where significantly lower intelligence can be clearly attributed to the effects of environmental deprivations, steps must be taken to ameliorate these conditions as early in the individual's development as education and other social forces can be utilized.[4]

[2] Bloom, Benjamin S. *Stability and Change in Human Characteristics*. New York: John Wiley & Sons, 1964. p. 214.

[4] *Ibid.*, p. 89.

[3] *Ibid*, p. 205.

Head Start

The development in early childhood education which currently supersedes all others in scope and national attention is the Head Start program. During the summer of 1966 the program enrolled 573,000 four- and five-year-old children throughout the nation. In a number of large cities like New York, Pittsburgh, Los Angeles, and Baltimore, the Head Start program became an enlargement of early childhood programs already under way.

Operation Head Start is still too young to be evaluated with any degree of accuracy.

At this point, however, Head Start does have a number of accomplishments on the credit side. Most teachers conclude that the children who experienced the program and then entered the kindergarten made a much better and quicker adjustment to school. Parents who previously showed little interest in schools have become active workers and participants in the life of the school community. The need to do some hard planning in relation to the Head Start program has stimulated thought in the direction of improvement and change in the total structure of education. Finally and importantly, Operation Head Start resulted in an increased or a new

awareness of the importance of early childhood education.

Head Start, as is to be expected, has its difficulties and its continuing problems. These problems are shared by all programs for the preschool child. The research required for knowing what specific kinds of environment and experiences should be provided has not been done. The problem of follow-through to provide that the first advantages of compensatory education are maintained in succeeding grades is far from solved. Trained teachers are nonexistent, and inservice training becomes a necessity. The problem of enrolling the children most in need of the program is often fraught with the difficulty of dealing with disinterested parents, although some parents do become interested and involved in the program and make notable contributions to it. The cost of a well planned program is far above the ordinary per pupil expenditure. Just to get space for the program, without even considering the desirability or adequacy of the space, is a task of great difficulty in many communities.

In spite of the problems it presents, the values seen in early childhood education appear to keep enthusiasm at a high level. Possibly this statement best describes the present status of the movement. It is predicted by many educators that the importance, knowledge, and

practice of early childhood education will increase. As this occurs, it will look to research findings for validation of its necessity and significance.

Objectives of Early Childhood Education

Many people consider the purposes of nursery schools to be the provision of child care and of socializing experiences. Some schools have extended their programs into the cognitive domain, but they are exceptional. In the light of research findings, however, the tendency to disregard the significance of cognition in the early years is being reversed.

The following objectives of early childhood education clearly indicate an extensive program:

1. To provide the basic needs of physical comfort when necessary: food, clothing, personal cleanliness, rest

2. To provide medical attention for diagnosis and, if necessary, treatment of chronic or passing physical and health problems

3. To provide opportunity for large- and small-muscle coordinated activity

4. To provide an environment and experiences which open the eyes to see not merely objects but relationships,

uses, beauty, function, size, configuration, conformation, color, texture, balance, movement, shadows—the entire gamut of things, but things with exciting and interesting characteristics and properties

5. To train the hands to feel the texture of things, to take apart, to put together, to mold and shape, to communicate, to balance, to push, and most of all to know because the hands and muscles say so

6. To help the ear discover the world of sound, its beauty, its annoyance, its uses, its sources

7. To cultivate the sense of smell by experiences in differentiation, classification, and identification, and to learn the importance of olfactory conditions in home, school, and community as they relate to the quality and satisfactions derived from one's surroundings

8. To explore the range of taste sensation by differentiation, classification, description, and identification

9. To teach the names and other words by which identifications and meanings are established and communicated and to encourage participation in much communication

10. To develop the ability to talk about and to think about things and events in the abstract without direct and immediate sensory involvement

11. To establish patterns of thought about significant aspects of the child's environment such as wheels, buildings, safety, people, danger, caring, belonging, me, teacher, you

12. To provide experiences of successful accomplishment

13. To provide opportunities for the development of positive self-concepts

14. To provide experience of the beginnings of sharing in the common experiences of joy, sadness, peace, and conflict

15. To assist the parent in becoming more knowledgeable about his child's development

16. To enable parents to assume greater responsibility for the education of their children

17. To coordinate the family and school experience of the child.

A statement of the objectives of a school program leads to a spelling-out of its details in terms of the people involved; the nature of the teaching, learning, and community activities and the characteristics of the space and facilities needed; the spatial relations of these facilities to others; the types of materials and equipment involved; and similar considerations.

The suggestions for needed facilities are based on the present meager body of knowledge concerning an optimum program. In some school systems the likelihood of providing even these suggested facilities is remote. With federal and state resources that have become available, the effort to establish programs may take the direction suggested by Martin Deutsch:

> . . . I also very strongly recommend that programs not be established on an instant basis, but that large communities establish two or three programs with adequate possibilities for monitoring what's happening, and use the first year or the first two years, for training, for curriculum development, for familiarization with materials, and then move into programming on a large scale basis.[5]

[5] Deutsch, Martin. "Some Aspects of Early Childhood Programs." *First Steps Toward the Great Society.* Washington, D.C.: National Education Association, 1965. pp. 16-17.

Since vast experience is being accumulated rapidly and since much evaluation and research is involved in current programs, the knowledge available about curriculum; the development of materials; and the training of teachers, parents, and volunteers may make the suggestions which follow quite outdated in the seventies.

People Involved

The predominant tendency is to plan facilities for three- to five-year-old children, although Operation Head Start concentrated on ages four and five. The total number of preschool children assigned to one school location is a moot question, since buildings can be so constructed, if the site allows, that the preprimary group is isolated from other groups. Some good reasons have been proposed for thinking in terms of a three- through seven-year-old organization and facility. Class groups should be limited to 15 children.

The regular staff should number at least one for five children or three for each class group of fifteen. At least one of the three should be experienced and trained. Semiprofessionals, volunteers, or parents with some orientation and

training assist the professional staff member. In addition, the services of the speech therapist, school physician, psychologist, nurse, social service worker, cook, custodian, bus driver, and secretary should be provided.

Activities, Space, and Facilities

General building and site considerations. The early learning center should be either a separate building for three-year-olds through grade 2 on the same site as the community elementary school or so attached to the elementary building that it forms a separate wing. The building should possess expandability, convertibility, and versatility. Access to school buses should be provided in such a way that a guarded, covered gangplank eliminates stair climbing at the building or at the bus.

A separate playground area for the early learning center should provide at least one hundred square feet per child. The area should be completely fenced in. If possible, it should provide different levels with at least one small hill for rolling, sliding, and crawling. Some trees for climbing and some shrubbery for aesthetics and study are advisable. There should be areas for experience with texture and for different kinds of exploration: sand, grass,

dirt, hard top. In addition, the following may be provided:

Fenced area for animals	Tent
Stream or wading pool	Wheel toys
Nature area for planting	Tunnels
Outdoor Franklin stove	Bridges
Climbing apparatus	Hill slide
Boards and large blocks	

A desirable arrangement is a continuous indoor-outdoor play area which enables children to play in both areas simultaneously. The teacher can supervise both groups by means of either sliding doors or a continuous window area.

The general design of the building should be simple yet attractive. An effort should be made to scale all aspects of the building to child dimensions without forgetting accommodations for the adults. Since animals, planes, cars, and trains are well within the center of a child's interest, they may have appeal value in the exterior and interior decorations of the building and grounds. Within the building, long corridors, cul-de-sacs, steps of poor design, ramps, and projections of any sort along the corridor walls are to be avoided.

Classrooms. The following listing is not all-inclusive and is intended to be only suggestive. A classroom for young children should include—

—An unobstructed area of at least nine hundred square feet

—Ample storage space provided by wall closets, movable storage bins, and a walk-in storage closet (as large as possible in view of the stress on exploratory activities and on sensory experience)

—Half of the floor covered with carpeting, the other half with vinyl

—A collapsible platform for dramatics

—A low sink with access from all sides in the vinyl floor area

—A variety of wall texture—brick, wood, linoleum, wallboard

—Space planned for supervision of entire area simultaneously

—Wide windowsills at child's elbow level

—Heating, cooling, and ventilation control

—Natural and artificial light under intensity control

—Ceiling and upper walls treated acoustically

—Equipment: pupil furniture designed for multiple use (painting; play with puzzles, pegs, beads, and clay; carpentry; experiment with gears, motors, and batteries; play with many educational toys requiring the manipulations mentioned in the objectives); large blocks and small blocks; doll house, fire house, post office, and the like; animal cages; work benches and tools; piano and rhythm instruments

—A science corner with much equipment and apparatus, aquarium and terrarium

—A reading corner with comfortable chairs and book storage and display facilities

—Audiovisual aids—phonograph; filmstrip, overhead, and opaque projectors; tape recorder; necessary drapes and storage; closed-circuit TV

—A home center with small kitchen equipment, clothes for "dressing up," and full-length mirror

—A chalkboard and tackboard at eye level of child

—Toilet facilities adjacent to classroom—equipment scaled to child

—A one-way mirror window in the storage room for parent observation of children

—A child-height drinking fountain.

Other Rooms. Needless to say, supportive space such as the following is necessary—

—A combination conference and staff room of sufficient size to hold meetings of about twelve people is often recommended.

—Another room is needed for the use of special service staff members and as a "quiet room" for children who may need sleep while other children are busy.

—A covered outdoor play area also is desirable.

—A readily available kitchen is recommended for food preparation and cooking experience.

Value

At first glance, the cost of early childhood education seems prohibitive. To build the facilities just described will virtually double the usual per pupil cost. Current expenditures also are high due to the small number of children per staff member. What must be remembered, however, is that if the research findings are proven valid and if, through further research, the optimum time for the development of certain abilities and characteristics can be determined, the ultimate result will be smaller rather than larger educational expenditures. The high cost of remedial education and in some cases of dealing with criminal or

antisocial behaviors will be avoided. The greatest gain, however, will appear in the fuller development of the potential of all students and, in some cases, the transformation of people from potential dregs of society to productive, successful citizens.

The Future

Early childhood education can be one and only one significant factor in man's perennial effort to find better ways of releasing the untapped potential of the human mind and personality. At the same time, it can be a way of eliminating much human waste and degradation. Yet our knowledge of the parts of the process is very meager. Much more research is needed. The present is a time when the interest and support of the American people is making possible widespread theoretical and applied research.

Much research is still needed about the most desirable kinds of facilities needed to house the educational program for the young child, but the importance of early childhood education is receiving increasing attention. The Educational Policies Commission in its recent report concludes that "exposure to a wide variety of activities and of social and mental interactions with children and adults greatly enhances a child's ability to learn." [6]

The best preparation for the teachers, the optimum length of the school day, the best class size, the contributions which parents can make, and the ways in which teachers can elicit those contributions—these are some of the only partly answered questions. Each school will give its tentative answers. But some of the needs are known already. The teachers should have an understanding of children, a knowledge of human development, a strong curiosity about the world, and an acquaintance with various theories and practices of early childhood education. They should work closely with the parents of the children. The classes should be small enough to permit individualized attention. And the goal should be to promote each child's intellectual, social, emotional, and physical development. [7]

[6] National Education Association and American Association of School Administrators, Educational Policies Commission. *Op. cit.*, p. 3.

[7] *Ibid.*, p. 11.

91

Chapter 10/*Planning the Community Junior College*

From very modest beginnings in the early part of this century, the junior college has emerged as an important part of higher education in this nation. During its early years of development, the typical junior college was a relatively small institution located in one building or utilizing space in a high school building. It was, for the most part, a two-year liberal arts college and, more often than not, independently supported. Today the typical junior college is a relatively large institution, occupying a large campus with a beautiful and strikingly functional physical plant and enrolling thousands of students. A number of junior colleges today have multiple campuses, each of which is larger than some well-known universities were 25 years ago. Most of these larger junior colleges are publicly supported.

Dramatic changes in the junior college during the past half century have not been limited to physical plant. Changes in the instructional program have been even more striking. The term "community junior college" is now commonly used to identify this two-year institution. During its years of growth, the junior college has become more closely related to the characteristics and needs of the communities from which the majority of its students come. Programs are planned and developed to meet their particular needs. During its long history of growth and development, no attempt was made to develop a universally recognized and accepted "junior college program." Diversity in offerings and flexibility in organization rather than a rigidly defined universal curriculum have characterized the junior college program. There are, of course, similarities. For example, junior colleges generally attempt to meet the requirements of universities and senior colleges so that work can be readily transferred. But community needs and the interests of the student body have led to the development of programs uniquely adapted to the locality served by the junior college.

Most community junior colleges have programs growing out of three clearly identified areas:

1. The parallel with general education, usually following the requirements and the curriculums of the universities and four-year colleges to which some students will transfer. In this respect, the junior college has retained its early characteristics of a liberal arts institution.

2. The two-year terminal or occupational program developed to meet community or area needs. The junior college early recognized that many young people who did not seek baccalaureate degrees needed and wanted post high school education to equip them for occupations or semiprofessions. Two-year programs were developed to meet the needs of these students, and such offerings now form a large and important part of the total work of the junior college.

3. Community service programs uniquely adapted to the locality. The junior college early recognized its relationship to the community in which it was located and from which it drew its main support. Community service programs, including adult education, have consequently become by far the most important junior college offering. Recognizing the eagerness of many Americans to upgrade their education, to learn new skills, or to acquire new information, the junior college designed curriculums to meet the needs of older citizens and set up schedules whereby they could attend classes without disrupting their work or other activities. In addition, most junior colleges have developed other types of activities and services to meet educational needs in the community.

Role of the Junior College

The place of the junior college in the hierarchy of educational institutions has received much consideration during recent decades. To illustrate, the junior college frequently has been identified as the thirteenth and fourteenth grades of secondary education, with an umbilical tie to the high school. It has also been identified as a "little" university with a sort of "step" relationship to the four-year institution. Today, however, the community junior college is emerging as a separate and distinct institution, related to both the high school and the senior college and university, but existing and operating as an entirely separate and unique entity and serving a whole new area of educational needs.

In its true concept, the junior college is a *community* institution. It emerges from local needs and local demands; it gathers to itself the character and qualities of the community it serves; it develops its programs to serve community needs; and it listens attentively to community reaction. Exemplifying the characteristics of a commuter institution, it generally does not provide dormitory facilities. Its offerings are diversified and its administration flexible; it changes its programs as community needs and requirements change.

The junior college recognizes no typical student or age group. Its students come from the high school graduating class, from commerce and industry, from special interest groups, and from the retired citizens group. Ages range from the late adolescent to the senior citizen, for the junior college fosters the growing concept of "continuing education," is responsive to changing social needs, and adapts its program to shifts in occupational requirements. It extends opportunities for post high school education to that large part of the population denied this opportunity because of economic conditions or selective admission.

Guide to Planning

The physical facilities required for meeting the varied and unique objectives of the junior college must be carefully and individually planned. This chapter is not a "do it yourself" manual. Its main purpose is to suggest to community junior college administrators and planners procedures that will aid them in planning and developing a physical plant that will provide the best possible environment and climate for successful operation of junior college programs and the flexibility necessary for continual and rapid growth. The general objective is to aid in providing a superior setting for teaching and learning in the community junior colleges.

The suggestions made here are based on the assumption that community junior colleges are not slightly modified high schools nor miniature universities, but institutions of higher learning uniquely organized to offer programs leading to objectives, goals, and purposes not found in the same degree in other institutions. Hence, emphasis is placed on a learning environment that will be most effective in reaching these objectives, purposes, and goals.

While many suggestions made here may be applicable to boarding and residential junior colleges, this chapter and the one that follows are directed primarily to institutions that have no dormitories or residential facilities. It should be emphasized again that this is a guide. It is not intended to be definitive; rather, it is intended to help each responsible individual in formulating his own planning instruments.

The key to planning and developing community junior colleges is *curriculum* and *program of services.* In the development of education specifications for physical facilities, almost everything that is done is related to the curriculum and the work of the college. Administrators with experience in this kind of developmental planning are fully aware that their most important task is not poring over blueprints; there is much to be done before detailed facility planning. The site must be selected, if the building is to be located on an entirely new campus; enrollment projections must be made; detailed curriculum must be developed; and this curriculum must be translated into space requirements—the kind and amount needed, the arrangement of space into specific areas (rooms, laboratories, teaching auditoriums, offices, and activity and service areas) —in terms of predetermined patterns of student distribution and enrollment.

Some Principles for Planning

To begin planning and developing a new institution or an institution on an established campus is not to sit down with pencil poised and say, "Let's begin planning." There are many explorations through the byways of curriculum and academic objectives, many false starts, and many abrupt halts at the dead end of ideas. There is much reading, much conferring, much searching, and no little dreaming. There are numerous rushes of enthusiasm as new concepts are pursued. There is writing and exchange of ideas. But finally, the glimmerings of an idea begin to emerge. Something begins to take shape—the first vague, indefinite outline of a new college campus or a new college building. Constructive, tangible planning is under way.

There are a number of guiding principles in planning that may open new viewpoints and support creative endeavors.

1. There is only one certainty in planning—that certainty is *change.* The only recourse is to plan in terms of flexibility to meet change, rather than attempt to predict exact needs at all times. Flexibility, however, is not an easy concept to understand, and much poor planning has been done in its name. Flexibility is not merely the sliding partition, the divisible auditorium, the multipurpose space, the pie-shaped building, or any other of a multitude of designs and devices calculated to house any and all programs, class sizes, or activities, although any one of these features may contribute some degree of flexibility. Flexibility is something much deeper, more philosophical, more intellectual than design, arrangement, or gadget. It has to do with the scope and character of programs, teaching procedures, scheduling, teaching aids and their uses, sizes of groups and classes, instructors' schedules, deployment of personnel, and functional hours on the campus. Out of a study of flexibility based upon these factors may very well come need for new design, convertible space, folding partitions, and all the rest; but real flexibility must start with a dynamic, progressive, forward-looking program.

2. Planning must include provisions for expansion. No matter how large buildings now are and no matter how completely the campus has been planned, they will be inadequate by 1975.

3. All planners must be fully aware that the junior college campus of tomorrow will be used full time—day and night, summer and winter, in fair weather and foul—and will be used by people of all ages and at all levels of sophistication.

4. Careful consideration must be given in the planning process to the size and needs of the staff. Facilities should be designed to make it easy for the full potential of total staff to be developed and used effectively.

5. If there is any truth to laments that the modern age has failed to develop taste, this failure undoubtedly comes partly from 95

aesthetic impoverishment in the classroom. The fundamental problem in planning insofar as this purpose is concerned is to translate sensitivity, values, and ideals into activities and physical form.

6. The architectural design should frankly say, "This is a college." Too many colleges look like factories, undifferentiated; they have plenty of light and air and some clever geometry, but they don't say, "This is a college, a seat of learning, a place of intellectual achievement."

7. Wise facility planning can come only after serious and thoughtful consideration of distribution of classes, lectures, and laboratories throughout the day—the afternoon and evening as well as the morning. The theory that students are more alert and learn better in the morning than in the afternoon or evening is not supported by objective research or experience. Such scheduling is impracticable and uneconomical.

8. New materials, new methods of construction, and up-to-date efficient mechanical equipment and methods of communication should be taken into consideration in planning and developing new physical facilities.

9. The campus must be planned for beauty and for function as related to the student on the campus. Orientation should be inward toward campus life, not outward. The "cattle pasture" approach to planning that scatters buildings too thinly over a large acreage with too much space between buildings adds to neither the beauty nor the functionality of the campus. There are physical and psychological advantages in locating buildings fairly close to each other—not huddled, but adjacent. Space should not be squandered in sweeping campus vistas or expensive building setbacks to provide pretty pictures to passers-by.

10. The interrelationship of academic departments should be considered in the placement of academic buildings. Location should be determined by student and faculty schedules rather than the philosophical or intellectual kinship of disciplines.

11. The space most frequently slighted in planning is the faculty office. Administrative and business offices, faculty offices, clerical offices, and miscellaneous desk space take up about one fourth of the total space in a junior college plant. The salaries of staff members is by far the largest single item in the junior college budget. Failure to provide facilities in which staff members can work to the best possible advantage is false economy and impairs the quality of the program.

12. Efficient utilization of space should be given serious consideration in planning junior college facilities, but prime consideration in deciding how space is used must be given to the educational program—the the purpose for which the space exists. Complete utilization of space in a well-rounded junior college program is impossible. To work toward this end without regard for the needs and interests of students and faculty members and for flexibility in the program could be destructive.

Site Selection

Selection of the site for a community junior college is one of the most important decisions made in the entire planning and developmental process. The site will characterize and "flavor" the institution and its student body for as long as it is used for a college campus. The design of buildings and the layout of the campus—the master plan—will be determined by the topography of the site and its relationship to streets and entrances and exits. Even student policy will be influenced by opportunities for recreation on the site and landscaping. Thus, the importance of wise selection of the place to establish the campus of the junior college cannot be overemphasized.

What are some of the considerations in site selection?

1. The size of the junior college site must be examined in view of—

   (a) *Probable ultimate size of the*

college. Site selection may very well come before enrollment projections can be made. However, general estimates can be made from knowledge of the population of the area to be served by the junior college. If the college is in a growing metropolitan area, it is safe to assume that it will ultimately be a large institution enrolling 5,000 to 15,000 students or more.

If the college is in an area of smaller, more stable, or more slowly growing communities, it may be assumed that its ultimate enrollment will be 1,000 to 5,000 students. If the college is in a rural area of small towns and villages, its ultimate enrollment may be 400 to 1,000 students.

(b) *Comprehensiveness of the program and curriculum.* (Obviously, the more activities, programs, and diversity of curriculums on the campus, the more space is needed.) It is suggested that a minimum of 80 acres be secured for a small junior college campus, that a minimum of 150 acres be secured for a medium-sized junior college, and that a minimum of 200 acres be secured for a large junior college. These recommendations are *minimum* only; a community junior college with minimum acreage and no way to acquire additional land for expansion will be seriously handicapped in-

deed. Analysis of space requirements will indicate that these suggested site sizes are perhaps conservative. To illustrate, 10 acres will be required for parking areas and traffic lines on a campus of 1,000 students, 80 acres on a campus of 15,000 students.

2. The topography is important. The site must function as a campus. It is a place to build buildings, to put down streets and sidewalks, and to develop a good environment through the allocation of space and landscaping. Very attractive junior colleges are built on rolling, wooded sites. Such topography lends opportunity for interesting campus layout and architectural features, but it should be pointed out that parts of such campuses are lost for building or recreational purposes and that master plans are dictated in part by the location of ravines, ponds, and sharp slopes. Planning is easier and may be more conventional on level sites where the placement of buildings is uninhibited by topography and land utilization is almost 100 percent.

3. The relation of the site to the community, to streets and highways, to power lines and sewerage lines is an important consideration. Unfortunately, the site selected is not always ideal. The costs of many parcels of land that would make wonderful college campuses are prohibitive. However, even

if the junior college cannot occupy the most desirable tract of land, wisdom and care should still be exercised in the selection of sites available to the junior college. A site with access through a semiabandoned part of the city or through crowded industrial streets, or one far from good access highways or surrounded by unzoned third-rate commercial property should not be considered. The junior college campus should be a showplace in the community. This priority should be kept in mind in site selection.

4. Land drainage is another important factor which some junior college planners give too little consideration. Sites should be studied carefully for drainage *after* construction. Many tracts of land with apparently no drainage problems in their natural state develop problems when excavations are made, dirt is pushed around, buildings go up, and sidewalks and streets are built. Extensive study of the whole problem before construction starts may well save many later headaches.

5. The cost of preparing the land for construction may be an important item. Many sites do not pose any problems of this kind; others—rocky, hilly, sandy, or thickly forested—could make

preconstruction preparation costly.

6. Future growth trends of the community or city in which the junior college is located should be studied. Will the city move away from the college? Or will it grow toward the college? Will it ultimately envelop the college site? If so, in what way? Where will new highways be built? Will any new highway or street development change the "front" of the campus to a new direction? Who or what will be "neighbors" to the junior college?

There is considerable disagreement about the kind of zoning regulations needed to protect the campus of an educational institution, but nearly everybody agrees on the most desirable neighbors. The most ideal neighbor for the junior college is a city or state park well landscaped and protected. The second preference is a residential neighborhood with better-class homes. Residential areas with less expensive homes, garden apartments, and high-rise apartments also are regarded as good neighbors for a junior college plant. Less satisfactory are large shopping centers, professional buildings, and miscellaneous commercial office areas. And much less satisfactory—to be avoided if at all possible—are airports, railway yards, filling stations, garages, factories, and drive-in restaurants and stands. A separate word may be said for

churches. They are high on the list of desirable neighbors for colleges, but unfortunately, churches in the past have not regarded educational institutions as their most desirable neighbors.

7. Those who have responsibility for selecting junior college sites should also give careful consideration to—

(a) *Parking areas.* Academic and student service areas should be protected from vehicular traffic; therefore perimeter campus parking is preferable. If at all possible, parking areas should be located on several sides of the campus, not too far from buildings. Large expanses of asphalt parking areas should be avoided. For safety and convenience it is better to have several smaller parking areas than one big one. With imaginative planning and but little additional cost, parking areas can be made attractive, with landscaped islands, walkways, or other features that contribute to the attractiveness of the entire campus.

(b) *Aesthetics.* Planning walkways, placement of buildings, and landscaping should not be afterthoughts or secondary considerations. Certainly the location of walkways is determined in part by natural traffic flow, but total campus aesthetics are important, too. The place-

ment of buildings on a master plan will of course follow a functional pattern, taking into account soil and rock formations and relationships in the total complex. The location and orientation of the various units should be such that the campus visually unfolds and each building forms a complementary vista for another. There are on many campuses natural features—a clump of trees, a gentle slope, a small brook, a rocky crag, or an overlook— that are particularly pleasing to the eye. Some contractors, if not restrained, will ruthlessly destroy such features to facilitate the use of heavy equipment and to get uniformity. If at all possible, such natural features of the site should be incorporated into the overall campus plan to enhance the attractiveness of the campus.

(c) *Atmosphere.* There is an elusive quality to every campus that is sometimes called atmosphere. Atmosphere is the intangible quality created by the design of the buildings, the size of the campus, the quality and kind of landscaping, and the care and attention given to grounds and surroundings. It is that extra dimension of a total plan that expresses the unique and distinct character of the junior college and the underlying philosophy of an institution that is introducing students to a new world of maturity and responsibility. It is building forms, design, relationships, and texture. It is spaces—gardens and grassy plots, gentle slopes, trees and shrubs, traffic lanes and parking lanes, sweeping vistas and secluded nooks—all blended together into a pleasing harmonious whole.[1]

The Planning Process

Planning and developing a new junior college campus should be an orderly procedure that follows a well developed schedule, that establishes sequence and sets realistic dates for the completion of the various planning functions. It is only common sense to assume that even the most carefully planned timetable or schedule may have to be modified due to unforeseen circumstances that may arise, but the fact that there is an established schedule with dates for completion of each phase of planning and construction keeps the process moving in orderly fashion and minimizes disappointment.

There is, of course, no one best order of priorities or time schedule

[1] For further information on site selection, see Chapter 8 and—
Lopez, Frank G. "The Problems of School Sites: Building Types Study 242." *Architectural Record* 121:189-218; January 1957.
Patterson, Dow. "Planning the Junior College Site." *American School Board Journal* 142: 30-31; April 1961.

that is fully applicable to every situation. Each planning group must develop its own schedule; but in developing this schedule, pitfalls may be avoided if consideration is given to the following aspects of the total planning and development process:

1. *General Exploration of Basic Assumptions*

(a) Make basic assumptions concerning the junior college, its curriculum, its program, its procedures, and its philosophy of administration and instruction at the beginning of the planning period. These basic assumptions will become guidelines and support for the entire planing procedure.

(b) Explore basic assumptions through individual discussion, group conference, and study of basic policies for community junior colleges.

(c) Develop and reach common agreement on a body of basic knowledge and understandings that will support policy formation and decision making.

2. *Reference Materials for Planning*

(a) Develop a set of reliable reference materials through consultation with universities, state departments of education, local libraries, the American Association of Junior Colleges, and the U.S. Office of Education and by checking back issues of the *Junior College Journal*

and other professional periodicals and current studies in curriculum planning.

(b) Digest these materials and develop a concise statement of general recommendations that can be readily used as points of reference.

3. *Enrollment Projection*

Projections of enrollments over a significant period of time should be made in an early stage of the planning process. Throughout the period of planning and afterward, these projections should be continually restudied, re-evaluated, and revised as necessary.

4. *Development of the Curriculum*

The broad outlines of the basic curriculum will be developed by study of the requirements in lower division work at the state universities and senior colleges; study of any curriculum requirements for junior colleges that have been established by state legislation; study of the experience of institutions in developing a core of general education courses; examination of the catalogs of other junior colleges; consultation with curriculum consultants, local lay committees, and the faculty; and the development of sensitivity to the expressed and implied needs of the community or area served

99

by the institution. This study and exploration should lead to a well balanced program for the community junior college, with courses delineated, departments or divisions formed, and number of instructors determined.

5. *The Master Plan*

   With the advice and assistance of consultants on campus planning, and following state or regional policies and regulations that must be recognized and complied with, develop a short-range and a long-range total campus plan based on student needs, program requirements, growth patterns, and available resources.

6. *Detailed Planning*

   With the information at hand, the viewpoints that have been established, and the decisions that have been made in the preliminary planning procedures briefly mentioned above, the architect is ready to begin developing firm specifications and working drawings for the units to be constructed in the order established by the planning committee.

Enrollment Projections

It is difficult to project accurately enrollments for any community junior college, but when the population is fluid and the locality shows signs of spectacular and dynamic growth, even more caution should be exercised in projecting enrollments. Those making the study can underestimate the junior college enrollment by using only known and provable factors or overestimate growth by placing too much credence on unknown factors.

Where does one start in making enrollment projections? What are the steps involved in developing projections?

1. A projection of the general population of the area served by the junior college is needed. Some sources of information are more reliable than others. Studies made by utility companies—light and power, telephone, gas, and water; by banks and finance corporations—especially savings and loan institutions; and by the area's major industries are usually well prepared, conservative, and reliable. These agencies and institutions that must rely on their population projections for future operation and capital outlay expenditures cannot afford large margins of error. Other sources of information, such as chambers of commerce, boards of trade, industrial commissions, and private industry or commerce may be less reliable, but they are useful in validating or cross-checking other studies. What generally do all these studies indicate? Is the population growing? How much? Is a leveling off or a population plateau in sight? What is the growth curve over the next ten years? Fifteen years? Are there indications of growth in particular age or sociological groups?

2. A projection of the school population in grades 1 through 12 is needed. The best and most reliable source for this information is, of course, the district or county school board office. How do the data on school population relate to data on general population? Are the growth patterns consistent? What is the dropout rate between grades? Is is consistent or is it changing? Is there any foreseen change in the birthrate that could alter the projections in any year or sequence of years? At this point, a reconciliation chart, showing general population estimates and their relationships and percentages will be helpful.

3. An estimate of potential junior college students—young adults, graduates of the high schools, and others—must be made. This step, of course, calls for considerable "educated guessing." Local school board offices can supply information on the number of high school graduates now going on to college, but this figure can be very misleading to a junior college official. How

100

many more will go on to college when a community junior college program is available? Will any of those now going away to college plan instead to attend the junior college, thus increasing the percentage of high school graduates coming into the local institution?

The high school counseling staff can be very helpful in obtaining information through a questionnaire circulated among high school students indicating the number considering attendance at the community junior college. From these figures, percentages can be calculated and applied to high school senior class enrollments for any year. This will provide a conservative estimate; students are inclined to indicate a preference for going away to college. Such estimates, however, may be further checked by obtaining similar percentages from already established junior colleges and making comparisons.

4. Certain unknown factors also should be considered. High school graduates of former years may now take advantage of the opportunity and enter the junior college as freshmen. These students, of course, would not have been included in other estimates. How many will there be? No one knows, but this is a factor. Another unknown factor will be students in their freshman year at a four-year college or university who may elect to stay home for

their sophomore year and attend the junior college. How many? Again, no one knows.

Other factors to be considered are the support or lack of support given the junior college by high school counselors, the geographic distance to the nearest four-year institution and whether it is public or private, the economy of the area, and whether or not this is a good crop year for farmers. All these factors will affect enrollment at the community junior college, but none can be measured or calculated with complete accuracy or reliability. Nevertheless, they must be considered. Even though they may not affect final estimates, to fail to take these factors into consideration would be foolhardy.

5. The holding power of the junior college will be an important factor in projecting the total enrollment from year to year. If a new institution is being established, this factor cannot be very accurately weighed until after the institution has been in operation for a year or two.

Even when the best available sources are used, enrollment projections are largely guesswork, no matter how "educated" or "professional." Continual checks of validity

and accuracy with annual revisions based upon actual figures are therefore necessary. It should be emphasized once more that these procedures are recommended for community junior colleges only.

Curriculum Development

The proposed program and curriculum of the new community junior college should be the point of departure in planning. All physical facilities on a junior college campus should serve curriculum and program needs.

The curriculum and program of any community junior college is necessarily established by—

1. Course requirements for receiving degrees at the four-year colleges and universities to which students will transfer.

2. Expressed and known needs of the community served by the junior college.

3. Broadly based educational needs and cultural forces with educational implications that directly or indirectly apply to the local community.

It is fairly easy to develop curriculums to meet transfer requirements; analysis of catalogs of four-year colleges and universities or visits with deans and registrars of these institutions will provide this information. Interpreting the needs of the community, however, is not

so easy. We are prone to base judgments on external factors that are found to be invalid when a more thorough analysis is made. For example, a community junior college in a farming area may anticipate need for an agricultural curriculum, only to find that this is not a real need; or it may lose its drawing power through student indifference because it misinterpreted its large number of co-eds as indicating a real need for strong home economics programs.

Many fine texts on the development of curriculums in the junior college are readily available. For this reason, no attempt will be made here to reiterate what has already been stated. Some general suggestions concerning curriculum as it relates to facilities planning, however, may be helpful:

1. The general education core of the curriculum with preprofessional curriculums related to it should be developed first. Electives in each field should be given thorough study. In a growing institution, it is better to have related curriculums than a series of separate and unrelated programs offering a diversity of courses. The general education core in the college curriculum has been described in many ways by many people. For our purpose here it will be defined as that part of the curriculum which aids in the development of the whole person.

Man in the decades ahead must be competent, skilled, and able. He must be well trained, but more than merely trained to perform a given set of tasks; he must be resourceful, adaptable, flexible, knowledgeable of his times and earlier times, concerned with his government, and able to make intelligent decisions, and have reasonable understanding of other people of the world who are now his near neighbors. The general education core should develop these essentials of good citizenship. Since all people have responsibilities for good citizenship, occupational curriculums should have a general education core along with the specialized course work required.

2. Highly specialized, terminal curriculums should be developed slowly, through thorough and continuing study of needs and initiatory costs.

3. Art and music offerings should be general at first; development of complete curriculums should be delayed until needs can be based upon something more specific than a fleeting desire to learn cartooning, take up painting as a hobby, or sing in the glee club. When the interests of students in art and music are more clearly defined, curriculum development can really begin.

4. The subjects required for graduation or completion of a particular program should be determined as soon as possible, for the requirements established will have a direct influence on the physical plant. For example, if political science is required of all students, the need for instructional space for political science will be much greater than if it is an elective course. If requirements are different for some programs than for others, enrollment will be affected and demands for space will be different. There will be some courses, such as freshman English and courses in the humanities, the social sciences, mathematics, the natural sciences, and health education, which all students should be required to take. These and other decisions affecting curriculum should be made, insofar as possible, prior to facility planning and space allocation.

5. Before facility planning is initiated, some basic policy decisions about the physical education program, athletics, and recreation must be made. What interscholastic sports will be sponsored by the college? Will there be a program of competitive sports? What physical education and recreational facilities—swimming pools, for example—will be available to all students and to the public?

6. Detailed and complete course descriptions—perhaps more detailed than will eventually appear in the college catalog —should be prepared prior to facility planning. These course descriptions, dealing in brief form with the materials taught and the manner in which presentations will be made, make facility planning much easier. With such information at hand, architects and administrators who must make decisions will know the kind of instructional area needed and the type of equipment that will go into it and will even be able to make some decisions about class size and schedules.

7. The importance of defining curriculum relationships in the early stages of planning cannot be overemphasized. The relation of one instructional field to another and the interrelationships of all college activities will not only determine the kind of planning that will be done for the physical plant, the placement of buildings, and the size of instructional areas, but also set a pattern for future program growth and development. The establishment of curriculum relationships in the entire area of communications represents one of the many decisions that must be made in planning facilities and allocating space.

Will facilities for foreign language instruction, English, and speech be located in a language, arts, or communication unit, or do they more properly belong with the humanities, where there are relationships between art, music, philosophy, design, and drama? Is religion a social science or a humanities course? Is business writing related to communications more closely than to commerce and business? Is engineering drawing related to art as well as to mathematics and to what degree?

It is vitally important to determine what the curriculum relationships on a new junior college campus are going to be, for these relationships determine the extent to which different disciplines share or use instructional areas and what courses will be taught in what buildings. Good campus planning and good facilities planning demand that decisions be made concerning such relationships before a campus master plan is drawn up or detailed facility planning begins.

Chapter 11 / *Facilities for the Community Junior College*

Many years ago Walt Whitman wrote, "The genius of the United States is not best or most in its executives or legislators, nor in its ambassadors or authors, or colleges or churches or parlors, nor even in its newspapers or inventors—but always most in the common people." [1] This observation by a thoughtful man has relevance to planning the junior college plant, for the community junior college in its organization, its program, and its purposes is an educational institution for the common people. Its doors are open to everyone who has completed a high school education. Its students come from all economic levels, all social classes, and all age groups. Admission standards are not a barrier to enrollment, and tuition charges are nonexistent or so modest that they do not exclude students from low income families. It is the post high school institution that reaches deeply into all population groups and shapes its program to their needs, interests, and aspirations. With full recognition that the community junior college is preparing people for future roles in life—

---

[1] Whitman, Walt. *Leaves of Grass.* From preface to 1882 edition.

where they will vote, sit on councils and boards, be part of a community that expresses opinion on common affairs, serve as productive members of a labor force, build homes, rear children, and shape institutions —and that their experience on the campus is life itself, its facilities have a personal touch and human scale.

Teaching and learning are the main business on the college campus, but there are—as every teacher, administrator, and student knows — a multiplicity of ways through which teaching and learning take place. The timid youngster from the farm may profit much from his associations in the dining hall and the student center or as a participant in student activities. The troubled teen-ager's most profitable experience may be in personal conferences with a faculty member in a quiet office. The musically talented youth may move a little closer to his highest aspirations by participation in an orchestra or regular work in practice rooms. The older and more mature part-time student may turn to the science laboratory, the machine shop, or the language laboratory to acquire the skills and understandings needed to improve his competencies and increase his earning powers. Each learns in his own way. The diversity in the student body requires diversity in program and facilities.

The human response to architecture on the junior college campus should not be awe and admiration that leads one to tread lightly and speak softly. Rather, it should be a response that inspires, stirs initiative, and kindles aspirations. The gifted teacher and the inquiring student should not feel compelled to push admirable architecture aside to do their work. Architecture should be supportive rather than restraining. Its avenues to community life should be free and open, so that the campus shop and the backyard garage in the neighborhood, the economics department and the treasurer's office in the city hall, and the department of sociology and the League of Women Voters have an affinity.

Architects, administrators, instructors, and everyone involved in the planning process must be fully aware that the focal point of attention in shaping all facilities is the landscape of human experience rather than sweeping campus vistas; that learning is more important than parking; that barriers to free and

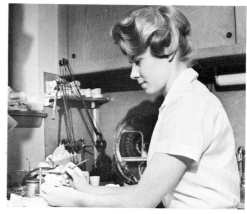

easy learning must be removed; that freedom of movement and freedom of thought are more important than arbitrary standards and controls; that new materials and new instructional techniques will come into use; and that the college will inevitably grow—grow outward from the campus—until it absorbs the whole of community life.

Translation of Curriculum into Space Requirements

The translation of a proposed instructional program into specific classrooms, laboratories, and complementary areas is no simple task. There are pitfalls to be avoided as planners move from imaginative and creative thinking to the prosaic realities of square feet of floor space, movable partitions, load-bearing walls, equipment, acoustics, environment, building size, and cost. In every translation of curriculum into physical facilities, judgments will be made and interpretations given that later experience will modify, but the prime functions of planning are to keep these modifications from being too numerous and to develop an overall facility that will provide for a good teaching and learning environment.

In translating the educational program into space needs and attempting to achieve maximum facility usage, planners must first develop a basic core of information on the number and distribution of students, the number and distribution of faculty and supporting personnel, the distribution of students 10 and 15 years from now, and the attrition rate of students. This, of course, is brought together through study of enrollment projections. Estimates must be made of the number of students who will register for the different course offerings. When the planners know how many students, generally speaking, will enroll in freshman English and how many will enroll in general chemistry, they will then know how many freshman English instructors and how many chemistry instructors to employ.

After enrollments in the various courses and the optimum section size have been determined, good estimates of the number of classrooms needed to teach these subjects, of faculty distribution, and of department size can be made. Such estimates vary from institution to institution depending upon whether the junior college is serving a rural area or a metropolitan area and upon the character and makeup of the student body. It is suggested that those planning completely new junior colleges study distribution

patterns in similar junior colleges that are well established. Their own enrollment records will constitute the best source of information for planning additions or for expansion of well established junior colleges. Information on the distribution of students by courses should be taken from enrollments early in the first semester. The number of dropouts or second semester enrollments are of little significance in planning because facilities must be provided for maximum enrollments. The number of students expected to leave the institution at the end of the first year must be carefully estimated so that course distribution in the sophomore year can be estimated with some accuracy. The distribution of students by courses 10 or 15 years in the future should be estimated in the same way, using the rate of growth found in overall enrollment projections.

Those with responsibility for planning facilities must also determine the amount and the size of faculty office spaces needed, the contact hours of faculty with students, the optimum size of sections, and the hours available for teaching.

The length of the college daily schedule is a very important factor in determining the facilities needed. Obviously an institution that schedules its classes between the hours of 9:00 in the morning and 4:00 in the afternoon for five days a week will need more instructional space than an institution with classes scheduled from 8:00 in the morning until 5:00 in the afternoon for five and a half days a week.

With a rapidly expanding student body in most institutions and a growing shortage of quality college teachers, innovative teaching and learning procedures must be devised to serve larger numbers of young people *effectively.* Deliberately restricting classroom size to ensure small classes at all times is a luxury that the growing junior college cannot afford. Spaces for large lectures, small discussion groups, closed-circuit television, team teaching, mechanical teaching devices, individual study, and instructor-directed projects, along with some traditional-type classrooms, are essential for a flexible program. If new techniques of teaching are to be used, classrooms and laboratories must be devised to make the most effective and efficient use of these techniques.

The effectiveness of the seminar, small class, or tutorial approach seems to be no greater, at least in some fields, than large-group instruction. This does not mean that spaces of varying sizes—large, medium, and small—should not be provided; but these smaller spaces can be provided in considerable degree by the use of movable partitioning and partial partitions in large loft-type structures. If the junior college is to retain its place as a high quality educational institution, emphasis must continue to be placed on excellence of teaching and on an environment that encourages learning. There will be large-group instruction, and there will be seminar situations in which rather intimate relationships between students and instructors are maintained. The size of groups will be determined by the kind of subject matter presented and the technique of instruction most conducive to superior achievement. Opportunity for frequent conferences between students and instructors should be provided in appropriate offices or conference rooms. Time for these conferences must be provided in the schedules of students as well as their instructors.

Study of junior college facilities in several sections of the country reveals that offices, work spaces, and conference rooms for the instructional staff have been too casu-ally planned. In some instances it seems as if leftover space has been allocated to these purposes. With the high priority given to personal contacts with students in out-of-class situations and the increased preparation and research time demanded by the new techniques of instruction, serious thought must be given to planning offices and work space for faculty members.

Generally speaking, there are three kinds of space needed on a junior college campus: general instructional, service and auxiliary, and special instructional areas. General instructional space includes not only classrooms and teaching and demonstration auditoriums, but also faculty offices and small meeting rooms. Administrative offices, conference rooms, reception lobbies, student service centers, food service and health facilities, student government offices, the bookstore, student and faculty lounges, and service buildings for maintenance—custodial service centers, repair garages, heating and cooling plants, and other utilities—may be classified as service and auxiliary space. The library or learning resources center, the audiovisual center, teaching museums, planetariums, science laboratories, workrooms and supply rooms, art and music studios, electronic (language) laboratories, and the like are usually regarded as special instructional spaces. But providing space per se does not meet the requirements of good planning. What really matters is the kind and quality of space; provision for multiple use of space; relationships of one kind of space to another; optimum sizes of any given space; and the relation of all space to the philosophy, objectives, and goals of the college.

Faculty Offices

The arrangement of offices, the number of faculty members occupying an office, and the sizes of faculty offices have become points of controversy among junior college administrators in recent years. The increasing attention given to such facilities is due, in large part, to the growing importance of the instructor's availability to students for consultation and guidance and the trend toward independent study. It is our belief that faculty office space on a junior college campus is as much a necessity as classroom space or laboratory space.

The junior college faculty office is not an escape room for the faculty member, nor is it a place to while away time between classes. It is a *work room* for a faculty member—an instructional area, a place where faculty-student conferences are held, a place where instructional sessions may be scheduled with one or two persons, a center for the preparation of instructional presentations, and a place for evaluating work and keeping records. It would be ideal if a sizable room could be assigned to each junior college instructor, but realistic considerations of total space requirements and economic cost, here as elsewhere, usually make some compromises necessary; seldom if ever are ideals fully reached.

Many boards question the amount of space allotted for faculty offices and sometimes suggest the construction of large common areas where a number of faculty members share the same office space, comparable to clerical office space in business establishments. The junior college administrator should reject such proposals. Never should a large common room with a number of desks be planned for or assigned to this purpose. The function of a faculty member in conferring, working, and planning with students is not of a clerical nature. If the situation does not provide the dignity of confidentiality and a reasonable degree of privacy, this important part of the junior college instructional program will be seriously impaired. Because of the normal variations in schedules, two faculty members may occupy a single office without serious loss of effectiveness, but if the number of faculty members assigned to a particular office is greater, the price of inadequate and inappropriate space is paid in terms of unanswered questions, unresolved problems, and unmet needs of students.

The offices of department and division chairmen are focal points of department or division business. To allow for conferences among several people and for display of instructional materials used in the department, it is recommended that they be at least twice the size of a faculty member's office. A reception room and a secretarial area with a small work space for a mimeograph machine and storage room should be a part of the chairman's office suite. In junior colleges where a minimum of secretarial help is employed, the chairman's secretary may serve as the departmental secretary. A small conference room where about a dozen people can be

comfortably seated around a conference table is another very important part of the chairman's office suite. Not only will departmental meetings be held in this conference room, but it can also be scheduled for group instruction.

Administrative Space

The administrative area may be as large and complex or as small and compact as the ultimate enrollment of the junior college will demand and as the administration feels necessary. In most junior colleges the administration area will contain the general administrative offices, the finance office, the admissions or records office, and the facilities for student personnel services. The size and number of administrative offices must be determined by the organization of the junior college and by the desires of the administration. The amount of space needed for the finance office and the admissions and records office have been underestimated in most junior colleges planned during the last 10 or 15 years. Both of these areas demand a great deal of storage space and work space. Because they are concerned with many kinds of records, room is needed to spread out. Even with the advent of microfilming, a great deal of storage space and work space will continue

to be needed for records. Ample fire and security vault storage should be provided for both the finance office and the admissions and records office. If microfilming and data processing are being considered for the future, space for these should be provided.

Space should be planned so that registration may take place in the administration building. At registration time, many institutions move the entire operation to a field house, gymnasium, or some other building where there are wide corridors or large open spaces where temporary desks can be set up and a heavy flow of student traffic handled. Careful and sensible planning of the administration building in terms of student traffic· flow may very well allow all registration to be carried on in the administration building.

The student personnel services area, whether in the administration building or at some other location, should provide facilities for counseling and guidance. Special rooms for small-group testing, conference rooms, and a small vocational guidance and counseling library are needed.

The Library or Learning Resources Center

Library areas, including seating, stack spaces, work areas, desk space, and audiovisual and conference rooms, require a minimum of 35 square feet per student for at least 25 percent of the peak period attendance. This is, indeed, a minimum. Unless the design provides for easy and rapid expansion when needed, libraries based on this formula will have some limitations. A more practical and realistic formula for determining the ultimate size of the library space needed is 40 square feet per student for 30 percent of the peak period of campus attendance.

It is difficult to compute the amount of stack space needed. Every library has its own policy for placing materials on library shelves. Methods of counting library holdings are not uniform. Some libraries contain numerous unbound or unprocessed items that are not counted; some collections of books have many oversized volumes in such fields as music and fine arts. A practical working formula for planning might be 125 volumes per standard stack section, or 12 volumes per square foot. A standard section of stack is 3 feet wide by 7½ feet tall, and, as has been indicated, will house approximately 125 books, thus leaving space for reasonable 109

future expansion. The amount of floor space needed for this standard section is approximately 11 square feet.

It should be remembered that a "filled" stack section is one in which there is always space left for future growth. In most college libraries books are arranged on the shelves by subject and author, and therefore space must be left for expansion. Furthermore, growth is not uniform. There inevitably will be overcrowding in some areas, while there is still some vacant space in other areas. Examination of the book collection in an existing junior college library will provide information that will be useful in estimating the number of standard sections needed.

Junior college libraries on the average grow 7 percent annually. Plans for the junior college library should provide for such increase. Rather than attempting to estimate space requirements on the basis of a 7 percent annual increase, some administrators consider the ultimate size of the library collection as 30,000 to 50,000 volumes and base plans for stacks, storage space, and expansion upon this general estimate.

As the use of a wide variety of teaching and learning aids and equipment increases, the concept of a learning resources center or an education materials center as contrasted with the conventional or traditional library is becoming more widely recognized. The manner and extent to which the learning resources center differs from the book-oriented library depends upon the philosophy of the institution, its approach to student learning, and the ingenuity and creativeness of administrators and architects.

In its simplest form, the learning resources center may have the book-oriented, reference, research, and study library as a core; facilities for audiovisual materials storage, maintenance, and use; and display space for art, sculpture, and drawings. Such centers are usually equipped with electronic devices for full and effective use of equipment and materials.

The most sophisticated learning resources center or educational materials center may include all of the above and in addition have more highly specialized student learning spaces; provisions for independent study, machine programed learning, and computerized educational experiences; faculty offices and workrooms; and individual projection and listening booths where students may work independently. The big chal-

lenge to administrators and architects is to make the wide variety of newly developing instructional materials and equipment readily available for use by both students and faculty members.

In some junior colleges library materials have been separated by disciplines, with learning centers for science and mathematics in one place, the humanities in another, and the social sciences in still another. Each part of the library thus becomes in effect a self-contained unit for a particular discipline. Through imaginative planning the parts are tied together into a functional whole.

The basic underlying principles in planning library facilities, whether they be traditional or forward-looking, should be action; prime learning opportunity; and communication—visual, oral, and audio. Gone is the museum of books, the library keeper, the sacrosanct silence of passivity. In the library there should be beauty, airiness, comfort, light, movement, communication, and sound — controlled and subdued, to be sure, but sound that indicates things happening in a natural and unforced way.

Sound is not the distracting factor it was once believed to be—and with new acoustical materials, carpeting, and good internal design, the hum of activity can be reassuring, friendly, and acceptable.

A Place for Students To Be Themselves

There are some unique characteristics of the junior college student body that are relevant to the student center. Unlike most senior colleges and universities, the junior college is usually a commuter institution. Students live at home and come to the campus for a full day or perhaps for only a few hours in the late evening. Most of the full-time students are young, only one step removed from secondary schools where they were under the direct supervision of teachers and administrators. Now for the first time they are more nearly on their own. They must learn to discipline themselves and to take responsibility for their personal behavior, independent study, and classroom work. They are sensing the excitement of growing up and the headiness of independence, and yet they feel need for the guidance and stability provided by adult supervision.

The need for a home base—a place where they can mingle with their associates; where they can relax, read and study, and keep their belongings—is perhaps greater for young people on a junior college campus than for students in a residential college, whose dormitory rooms serve as a home base. For these students, the activities center has a personal development function as well as a service function. Lounges, recreation areas, patios, courtyards, reading alcoves, browsing libraries, and food service areas provide opportunities for students to learn from each other, to develop self-discipline, and to acquire a sense of identity with the institution as a whole. The student center may well be the focal point of junior college life. It is the gathering place, the communications center, the unifying agent for the whole campus.

The part-time student, who is usually older and more mature, may regard the junior college campus as a place to which he goes for an hour or two of instruction or to make use of shops and library facilities. Campus atmosphere or college tradition is not important to him. He regards the junior college as a service institution. But he, too, needs services of a personal nature—a place to eat, a center for obtaining general information, and a place to secure supplies.

The service function of the student activities center is closely related to the personal development function, yet its purposes can be more sharply delineated. If students are to remain on the campus throughout the day and have the benefit of unobtrusive supervision, some food service facility must be provided. There is also need for a health clinic, a bookstore, telephone service, and a place to rest. Frequently the student center is a separate building with lounges, game rooms, a bookstore, student government offices, student personnel offices, and snack bars.

Many junior college planners today are turning from complex cafeteria-type food service to snack bars and to batteries of soft drink, milk, and sandwich dispensers. With this less formal and simpler type of food service, big kitchens, large work areas, and extensive storage space are eliminated. On some campuses a series of snack bars has been provided, breaking up large concentrations of students. The obvious disadvantages to this type of service are the necessity for multiple deliveries and the existence of a number of places on the campus where refuse and discarded materials accumulate.

Student activities are an important part of the total educational program on the junior college cam- 111

pus, and facilities for them should be planned with as much care and as much sensitivity to the needs, purposes, and behavior patterns of students and the objectives of the college as facilities for any other part of the program. On some junior college campuses, food service facilities and recreation areas are separated from the quieter lounge areas, browsing libraries, student activity offices, health clinic, and bookstore. These two areas may be separated by a patio, a covered walkway, a landscaped terrace, or an outdoor dining and lounging court. This type of planning relieves congestion, reduces noise, and adds important touches of informality and atmosphere in keeping with the character of the institution.

Occupational Education

Occupational education is rapidly becoming one of the most important parts of the entire community junior college program. Technological change has created new jobs and new careers and has uprooted people from long-established occupations. Many people are now employed in jobs that didn't exist a few years or even a few months ago. No longer is the major focus of

attention in the labor market on the day laborer, the handyman, and the office worker. Demands and opportunities are greatest for the technician and the semiprofessional. This new type of worker not only needs and must have a high degree of skills and competencies but must know the why of performance. Because of its closeness to the community, its many opportunities for developing cooperative occupational education programs with business and industry, its flexible program, and its policies for admission, the community junior college is uniquely fitted to offer programs of occupational education. It serves not only the younger person who has just completed high school but the older person whose occupation has been disrupted by technological change or who is employed but wants to improve his competencies through part-time college work.

Loosely defined, there are three general areas of junior college occupational education: the science-engineering technologies, the health and paramedical technologies, and the business and commercial technologies. Many junior college administrators identify and plan for a fourth area of a miscellaneous nature which includes preparation programs for such occupations as agricultural technician, library assistant, teaching aide, police science

technician, urban planning technician, and others.

Space limitations will not permit a detailed analysis of facilities for occupational education, but two points should be strongly emphasized. First, whatever these facilities are and however they are developed, they should not be located in out-of-the-way places or otherwise treated as step-child endeavors. Occupational education is as important and should be as well recognized as any other program on the campus. Second, these facilities should be planned for as much multiple use as possible. There are many possibilities for several occupational training groups to use the same facilities, and there is some opportunity for using them for general education—for example, science laboratories, audiovisual rooms, and teaching auditoriums. Special facilities for many occupational programs are expensive to build and to equip. The wise campus planner will look for ways to use these facilities for more than one program. He may discover, too, that there are occupational education programs that do not need facilities other than those already on the campus.

Administrators should consider the use of the extended campus for many occupational education programs, especially in the health-related and paramedical fields. There is no particular magic, other than personal convenience and easier supervision, in having all programs on a single plot of ground called the campus. A college campus may include the hospital with its laboratories and opportunities for clinical experience, nursing homes, blood banks, medical laboratories, clinics, business places, stores, shops, and factories. It is effective learning experience rather than location that is important. The community junior college campus may encompass the whole community.

Space for Physical Education

The youthful vigor and abundant energy of junior college students and the emphasis on physical well-being in the total program make the athletic areas and physical education facilities important parts of the campus plant. There are some junior colleges where physical education and athletic activities have been so strongly emphasized that a massive gymnasium or well equipped field house seems to dominate the campus. But more often better balance in facilities is maintained. It is our contention that the gymnasium or field house should not

be the first building constructed on the campus and should not be overly emphasized in the master plan. But on the other hand, this part of the program should not be treated too lightly, and these facilities certainly should not be the last to be constructed.

Intermural activities and physical education—essential parts of the program—require that shower, locker, and dressing room facilities for both men and women be planned early with ample provision for expansion. To a considerable degree, particularly in milder climates, outdoor spaces can be utilized in the physical education program. Well planned softball diamonds, tennis courts, and a track lend themselves especially well to intermural programs and can be provided if space is available at much less cost than the gymnasium.

It should be pointed out that it is not necessary to locate showers, locker room space, dressing rooms, and other auxiliary spaces for physical education in the gymnasium. On many junior college campuses, these facilities are located in separate buildings joined to the field

house or gymnasium by a covered walkway or a protected corridor. This approach to planning physical education facilities permits the development and operation of a program before the gymnasium or field house is constructed.

The size and character of the field house or gymnasium will be influenced by the extent to which the facility is open to the general public and the emphasis placed on competitive sports. In any event, the main emphasis should be on physical education rather than on accommodating spectators at athletic events.

Service Space

Maintenance workers and custodians are an important part of the junior college staff. To a considerable degree the care and upkeep of the large capital investment in the plant is entrusted to them. The general appearance of the campus and the operation of complex mechanical systems — heating, ventilation, plumbing, air conditioning, communications—and the increasing number of electronic devices depend upon the quality of their work. They are largely responsible for safety, for cleanliness, for health, for effect-

 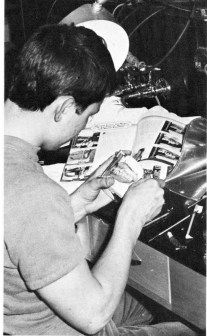

ing economies in the use of supplies and materials, and for reducing unnecessary waste.

Unless there are appropriate shops, adequate supply centers, and the necessary garages and headquarters facilities, the work of the maintenance staff will be impaired. As the college plant becomes more highly mechanized and the number of parts and variety of materials used increases, storage space becomes more and more important. This space should be located so that deliveries can be made easily, without intruding upon or disrupting teaching and learning activities. With the trend toward central utilities—heating and air conditioning—the service units may well be planned as a part of the campus utility plant rather than be located in a special service building.

Some Disciplines

In community junior college campus planning, an overall perspective must be maintained which keeps sight of the interests, needs, and wants of students; the potential of faculty members; diversity in curriculum; variations in instructional patterns; flow of traffic on and about the campus; special services that must be provided—all in appropriate balance; and relationships to the general purposes of the institution. But there are some segments of the instructional program —some disciplines—which, by their very nature and because of their extreme importance in the instructional program, claim special attention. Science and the humanities are but two examples.

Science. One may loosely designate three areas or types of facilities required in science instruction. They are the laboratory areas, formalized teaching areas (classrooms and auditoriums), and individual study and work areas (faculty offices, conference rooms, small instructional areas, and preparation and stock rooms). The challenge to the architect lies in the possibility of relating these areas to each other in a manner that constitutes a functional cohesive unit.

The science building with its surroundings should symbolize a vigorous, inquiring, dynamic spirit. There should be something arresting about the facilities that suggests the hidden power of science and the long look ahead. This building should have an appearance of solidity and permanence that inspires confidence. It should stimulate the curious, creative, experimental minds of students. It should say through its appointments, its design, and its orientation, "Here is a place where important things are happening, where important discoveries are on the threshold or already being made."

The science building should be located so that it commands its part of the campus. Every person who is in its vicinity should be conscious of this building and what it stands for. It should claim respect but not dominate nor overshadow. It should be inviting rather than forbidding. It should reach out through its terraces, patios, courts, wide approaches, running planters, and wings to other areas of the campus as if to underscore its articulation with them and their programs.

Humanities. No educational term in common use has more definitions than the term *humanities.* Some define it rather narrowly. For others, the term encompasses nearly everything not considered science, mathematics, occupational training, or physical education. For the purpose of planning facilities for this field of instruction on the community junior college campus, we refer to the *humanities* as art, music, and the performing arts integrated with literature, history, and philosophy.

Those who are planning this type of facility may take away or add whatever they want, but the importance of the humanities in a junior college program and the variety of materials and instructional methods used demand that these facilities be given careful attention. In some manner and to some degree the humanities reach every student and leave lasting impressions on the concepts to which he adheres, the values which guide his action, and the purposes to which he aspires.

Teaching procedures in the humanities involve audiovisual presentations; use of specialized motor-driven machines; displays of pictures; and use of posters, mobiles, and sculpture. It calls for special lighting, soundproof music practice rooms, seminar rooms, and large teaching auditoriums for general lectures and large group meetings. Students paint, sing, act, declaim, debate, and perform. They look, study, feel, sense, grow, mature, and develop sensitivity, depending upon the character and quality of their experiences. In the well conceived and adequately planned humanities unit or units there are art galleries, places for individual practice work, and places for independent study. There is an auditorium for drama and music where the public as well as students can go to see, to experience, and to participate.

The humanities building will fall short of its highest purposes if it is nothing more than a delineation of spaces for a variety of activities. In its dimensions, proportions, arrangement of space, design, and overall character it should suggest the highest aspirations, the deepest emotions, and the finest sentiments of civilization. From the very beginning of planning, this facility should be visualized as a teaching implement that will help young people grasp and understand the passions that have moved people in all ages, the purposes to which they have aspired, and the ideals that have motivated and guided their actions as they have moved along the road from primitive life to a technological age. The facility must not have the appearance of a fortress to hoard and safeguard the treasures of the ages. Rather, it should have an open-ended quality that inspires young people as they look toward the future to draw upon the experiences recorded in music, art, literature, history, and philosophy to meet and resolve problems now but dimly appearing on the horizon.

The challenge to the administrator is to visualize the potential that lies in the humanities for motivating student efforts, stirring imaginations, and directing the maturing of their minds and to transmit his concepts and ideas to the architect. The challenge to the architect is to shape facilities through the handling of space, color, design, and relationships that invite and hold the interests and attention of people, stimulate their creativity, and encourage them to explore the cultural experiences of the ages.

Chapter 12 / *Vocational and Technical Schools*

In America we have traditionally believed that opportunities for success in a chosen field of work are limited only by one's own capacities. We have believed that everyone is endowed with inherent rights to choose a career and prepare for it to the best of his ability. The public schools of this country have been looked upon as the foundation of this ideal. Today more than ever before, the school stands squarely between an individual and the job to which he aspires. Technological change and increased demands for skills of a high order call for corresponding increases in the quantity and quality of vocational and technical training.

In this age of change in practically all areas of living, expectations from vocational-technical education have taken on new proportions. Educational leaders in this country recognize what might well be considered a renaissance and expansion of technical and vocational courses and programs to provide needed educational experiences related to the world of work. Leaders in this field believe that vocational education has again become a respected member of the educational family. They believe that the increased recognition of the importance of education in reaching national goals and the demands being made upon the schools to prepare young people for their places in a rapidly changing world of work will bring new interest, new life, and new emphasis to vocational-technical education.

Manpower Needs

Many factors have influenced the heightened concern for more effective vocational programs and facilities. The high school has generally been considered responsible for providing programs to help prepare students for further education, job responsibility, the armed services, and home and family life. It has been estimated that this nation spends 80 percent of its education dollar on about 20 percent of its students. The college-bound, academic student receives the lion's share. Today only 6 of 10 students who enter elementary school graduate from high school, and approximately 8 of 10 students now in school will not complete a four-year college program. Educational programs must be provided for these students. Generally speaking, this need is not being met as well as it should be.

Training for skilled work seems to have been neglected or taken for granted in many instances. It has been predicted that 87 million people will be working full time by 1970, representing an expansion in the labor force of about 1.1 million workers per year. The program of vocational and technical education must be expanded and improved to meet the needs of these new workers.

Regardless of his race, intelligence, or place of birth, the human being is the greatest resource any nation can possess. Maximum development of human resources must become a major national objective. The large numbers of youth in schools and colleges represent an opportunity to invest in the only resource which can in the long run bring the promise of a productive and useful life to everyone. Each time this precious resource is wasted, to whatever degree, it represents a grave loss to the nation and the world.[1]

Occupations are being disrupted by technological change and new occupations are constantly appearing. This is an age of almost

---

[1] Venn, Grant. *Man, Education, and Work.* Washington, D.C.: American Council on Education, 1964. p. 157.

unlimited career opportunities for young people—an age of great challenge to the schools in preparing students for the world of work. Unfortunately, many able young people have not had the training opportunities and the job counseling needed to prepare them adequately for openings requiring highly specialized skills. Without greater efforts to develop better educational programs and train more workers, there will be a critical shortage of all kinds of technical workers by 1975. Laboratory assistants, electronic technicians, data-processing specialists, construction estimators, marketing specialists, technical secretaries, draftsmen, supervisors of production control, technical photographers, practical nurses, food service managers, and safety inspectors are already in short supply. There are indications that this decade will experience an annual shortage of nearly half a million skilled craftsmen, carpenters, bricklayers, plumbers, electricians, mechanics, lathe operators, and machinists; that the demand will grow for sales and office workers, typists, secretaries, stenographers, tele-

phone operators, office clerks, and retail and wholesale sales personnel; and that there will be steady openings for service workers such as cooks, waitresses, barbers, policemen, firemen, and beauticians.

The United States, boundless in its material wealth, unmatched in its standard of living, and justly proud of its rich heritage, can ill afford to allow the great bulk of its children to reach young adulthood poorly prepared to maintain and extend the heritage for those who will follow. In transmitting his manpower report to the Congress in 1964, President Johnson said:

> We must raise our sights—and strive to realize each person's highest productive and earning capability. We must seek to develop more completely our people's talents and to employ those talents fully—to fulfill the rich promise of technological advance and to enable all to share in its benefits.[2]

Place in the Educational Scene

There was a time when the people of this country debated whether vocational education properly belonged under the aegis of public support. No longer. Today vocational and technical education

has a secure and important place in the domain of public education. There is less certainty about where it should be located in the sequential and institutional divisions of educational experiences. The December 1965 NEA Journal carried a series of three short articles on the location of job preparatory education in specific types of institutions. One held that the comprehensive high school is the proper place for this type of education; another, that special vocational-technical high schools serve this function best; and a third, that the two-year community college is best suited to job training.[3]

There are signs that differences of opinion about the rightful place of vocational-technical education are of less significance than they previously were. In fact, the controversy of the comprehensive high school versus the vocational-technical high school versus the community college is now moot. These conflicting opinions, often resulting from lack of information,

[3] Zack, Jacob B.; Coe, Burr D.; Urich, Ted; and Mauck, Joe. "The Best Place for Vocational Education . . ." NEA Journal 55: 48-52; December 1965.

[2] Johnson, Lyndon Baines. Manpower Report of the President. Transmitted to the Congress March 1964. Washington, D.C.: Government Printing Office, 1964. p. xi.

understanding, and interest, are gradually fading, and broader understandings are emerging. There is a growing realization that all three types of educational institutions have their places in American education as it relates to vocational-technical training. As needs increase, educational programs designed for the vocational development of youth and adults will be strengthened and improved in both comprehensive and specialized vocational-technical high schools throughout the nation and will be continued and expanded in good community colleges. Many people look for a trend toward the vocational-technical center, because small high schools cannot meet the needs of the times for specialized training and because certain types of training require highly specialized and expensive equipment which it is not practical to duplicate in other educational units.

Vocational-technical education must be an integral part of good planning for today's schools. At a time when the needs of society are so clearly identified; when the national interest in well-trained manpower is at an unparalleled level; and when expressions of need are being voiced loudly by business, industry, and citizens, there is no other choice. If local school systems fail to meet these needs and to develop programs and facilities with the capacity to train and retrain members of society in the continual development of the salable skills needed in the world of work, some other agency or force will step in to undertake the job. Our stakes are high—too high to risk delay while we dispute such trivial arguments as those related to centralization of training versus comprehensive high schools, general education versus vocational education, specialized programs versus service-type training, or cost versus investment in people. This job must be done now, and it must be done better than ever before.

The role of the high school has been changing. The pace of change accelerates and becomes more challenging with each passing day. A review of major national policy statements on education reveals that occupational preparation is now recognized as a major objective of the high school. There is growing concern because young people not preparing for further education in college need specialized education to prepare them for employment. This has always been true from a relative point of view, but this decade's changes and the challenge of the decades to follow have sharpened the focus in this direction.

The Challenge

Change is taking place at an increasingly fast pace because of improvements in communications, production, and transportation. The "educational lag" has been reduced. Leaders in education can and must plan and project ahead from ten to twenty years with public support and acceptance. A school building or facility that is planned for today only is obsolete when ready for use three years hence. There was a time when courses of study were generally considered to need revising every five years; now, some technical courses, such as those related to some phases of electronics, need revising every three months in industrial practice. The problem is further compounded by the fact that many communities are faced with the problems of very rapid growth. Small country stores are being replaced with massive shopping centers, large cities are overflowing into the suburbs, and industries are diversifying and decentralizing. These changes result in growing pains for all government agencies—especially for the public schools. 119

Wenrich points out that "technological advances emphasize the need for trained manpower." It would be foolhardy to overlook the tremendous explosion in the field of technology and its impact on the world of work in the tomorrows immediately ahead. We can expect increasing specialization in the labor force. Parents and children themselves are deeply and increasingly concerned about their preparation for the world of work. Psychological studies have indicated that a majority of eleventh- and twelfth-grade students listed job preparation as a primary concern, Wenrich reports, and opinion polls from parents indicate that they, too, give job training for their children high priority.[4]

The Students

Experts predict that productive citizens in the next decades will have to be retrained in at least four to six vocations in a lifetime. Vocational education, therefore, is a challenge to provide programs not for youth alone but for stu-

[4] Wenrich, Ralph C. *NEA Journal* 50: 16-18; February 1961.

dents of all ages. The vocational education program and the facilities designed to serve it will be called upon for constant manpower retraining and retreading. Thoughtful planners will design facilities with the flexibility required to meet these considerable and diverse needs.

Employment practices favoring the high school graduate with a salable skill have an impact on programing and school design. The dropout problem is not new and is far from being solved. Many believe, however, that the establishment of innovative programs and schools or centers with multilevel vocational programs will help to retain many students. Unmet vocational needs may be responsible for many students' lack of interest in their school work. Slow learners, lacking the aptitude for highly technical training and the ability to enter college, need help. They too must live, they too must work, they too must enjoy the image of a self-respecting citizen in a productive society. Vocational-technical education, however, should not be considered merely a program for the slow learner or potential dropout. The program should be designed to meet the abilities and needs of each individual student—whether he be dull or bright—and the demands of an ever-expanding labor market.

Young people are planning their careers earlier than ever be-

fore; to be sure, their plans may be tentative, but they are giving serious thought to their futures. Schools all across the nation are expanding vocational guidance services to help students to identify their interests, their aptitudes, their strengths, and their weaknesses. Sights must be realistically set to avoid frustration and failure. With the wide range of abilities, interests, and aptitudes represented in a true sampling of large school systems, the scope of training, both academic and vocational, is limited only by one's imagination.

Facility Needs

What implications and what challenges does all this have for the structure and design of physical facilities for vocational-technical education in today's world? Of course, many of the concepts of good educational design for any school program must be incorporated into planning for vocational-technical education. Pleasing appearance, functional design, comfortable thermal environment, flexibility, and proper lighting, as well as adequate spaces for administration, guidance, and health services should be comparable to those designed for any good educational

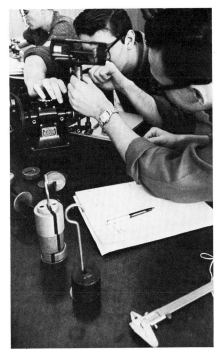

facility. Consideration must be given to ample parking spaces for full-time and part-time students. If it is planned as an area vocational-technical center, the location of the building in terms of easy access to population centers is of prime importance.

Like the design of any other school facility, that of a good technical-vocational center must depend in large measure on at least two major factors: (1) the business structure of the community and the socioeconomic characteristics of its people and (2) the greater needs of society in terms of job training requirements in the state and nation. A vocational center—whether a part of a large comprehensive high school or a more specialized institution—should not be planned to meet merely the needs of a single community. In these times of great population mobility there is little, if any, justification for such provincial planning. Within these two factors and with the effective use of survey techniques, it is possible to determine with fair accuracy the existing and future needs for vocational training. It is possible to project quite accurately, through occupational survey techniques, both the needs that exist and the opportunities in society for specific job training. At the same time, some guidance techniques have been de-veloped which have proven reasonably successful in identifying youth who might benefit from specific training skills. Careful planning of such surveys and analysis of results should be the base upon which more specific planning of the educational facility will rest.

School districts need to be alert, both in planning and in financing, to the assistance available to them at state and federal government levels. The federal government, realizing the broad implications of effective job training in a mobile society, has placed itself in a cooperative role in this respect. State governments, to a lesser but increasing degree, also are assuming responsibilities for planning and financing.

The demand for technicians in our society today has been quoted to be as high as 250,000 to 275,000 per year. The fact that we train and graduate something less than 25,000 technicians per year should cause even the casual observer of this trend to be alarmed. We have neglected this phase of our educational training too long already, and unless immediate steps are taken to step up the training of technicians, there is little doubt that our society will suffer in the years ahead.

Vocational education offerings may be housed in a comprehensive high school, an educational center, a community college, a technical institute, or an area self-contained vocational-technical school. In any one of these institutions valuable educational opportunities can be offered successfully if careful planning is done to provide the facilities and features required by current demands in this special field of education. All planning and design should revolve around the basic concept that the center's purpose is preparing students for employment opportunities—preparing students with salable skills for the current labor market and developing attitudes in students conducive to productive service and the inevitability of change.

Geared to Reality

Facilities should in general reflect the training demands of occupations, of the employers of the ultimate worker, rather than merely the wishes of educators or architects. If these groups agree on facility design, a happy family of planners may be the result.

The vocational center may well operate over a considerably longer day than most schools. It certainly should operate during the regular school day, in the late afternoon, during evening hours, possibly on Saturdays, and certainly during the summer months. The multiplicity of demands on this facility by both youth and adults calls for this continuity of operation. Vocational-technical students generally carry a full course of study, with no study halls provided. There are usually fewer electives than are found in a general high school. Many of the students will hold part-time jobs and will therefore attend school on an irregular schedule. Flexibility of program planning and scheduling will be required.

Consideration of these factors might well mean that the vocational-technical center will be called upon to accommodate a somewhat more limited extracurricular activity program than the typical high school. It will probably have only a limited or a different emphasis on sports, but physical education facilities and health education and services should not be neglected. It will require a different kind of library. The guidance program in this center will emphasize student identification, identification of job opportuni-ties, and student placement and constant follow-up activities. This activity will be an important part of the program and should have facilities carefully planned and well suited to its function.

Scope of the Program

An area vocational center might have the following types of course offerings in skilled trades and service occupations. This listing is only suggestive; it is not all-inclusive, and no implication is intended that these are required offerings or that all of them might be found in any one center.

Automotive Mechanics
Aviation Mechanics
Machine Shop
Carpentry
Industrial Electricity
Industrial Electronics
Mechanical and Architectural
    Drafting
Printing and Publishing
Maintenance Mechanics
Food Preparation and Service
Cosmetology
Laboratory Technology
Police Technology
Nursing
Data Processing
Masonry Work
Sheet Metal Work
Plumbing
Computer Technology
Power Machine Operations
Business Education
Office Practice
Medical Technology
Dental Technology
Refrigeration
Agriculture
Baking
Needle Trades
Fire Fighting
Tool and Die Making
Dry Cleaning
Forest Technology
Industrial Hydraulics
Barbering
Accounting
Commercial Art
Conservation
Fashion Merchandising
Photography
Metallurgy

It must also be borne in mind that in a self-contained vocational-technical unit or center there are academic requirements and cultural and recreational needs to be met. A balanced general and related education program should be offered, at least in the following subjects, with applications relating to the vocation as required.

English
Social Studies
Related Science

Related Mathematics
Health Education
Physical Education
Related Drawing
Music
Art

Vocational facilities built as part of a comprehensive high school might be somewhat more limited in the number and type of vocational offerings. They would already have available the necessary balanced academic offerings. The major problems in this instance are the acquisition of adequate primary space and the proper status of vocational-technical education in competition with other space and program demands. The status of the vocational student should clearly be that of a first-class citizen. The facilities should be so designed and so located as to enhance the dignity of work.

The Planning Team

To attempt here to define the specific planning requirements in each of the occupational training areas would be folly and actually would be an improper approach to sensible planning. Much has been said already in this publication about the need for flexibility, and

vocational-technical facilities are certainly no different from other educational facilities in this respect. One cannot be sure that any one type of shop will serve a useful purpose for too long a period of time; even within its own span of usefulness, it may change its face. A vocational center, possibly even more than the typical educational facility, must be adaptable to change.

The planning team in any locality must pool its own resources when specific facilities are being planned. The voices of trades, occupations, the professions, and services must be heard. The counsel and experience of the educator in combination with the talents of the best available architect must be called upon. Full advantage must be taken of resources at state and national levels. It is probably wishful thinking to assume that all elements of the planning group will begin planning with unanimity of thought. However, somewhere between the points of divergence—between the occupations' yearning for permanence, the architects' desire to build

design into function, and the educators' realization of the inevitability of change in program—the facility will take form. Each community will iron this out in terms of need and purpose in its own area. This is not to suggest that an overall master plan for vocational-technical education is impossible, but rather that under ordinary circumstances each educational community can do a better job in terms of its own local needs. To the extent that this facility can be designed and built with maximum immediate functional purpose and at the same time provide for change and flexibility, the planning team will have achieved its end.

There is no reason in today's thinking to regard the vocational-technical center as anything less than essential in a total program of education. It is hoped that the day of regarding trade training as suitable only for the less able or the slow learner is a thing of the past. The nation's commitment must be sufficiently strong to provide the resources needed for forward-looking facilities for vocational-technical education. They need not be plain, they need not be lacking in aesthetic appeal, and they certainly must meet the challenge of change which is upon us.

Chapter 13 / *To Remodel or Not To Remodel*

Obsolescence can sneak up on a schoolhouse in two ways. The building may become *structurally* obsolete; it may become *educationally* obsolete; or, as in the case of many unfortunate buildings, both. In any event, the problem of just what to do with the old breed of building is a natural and sound concern of those involved in education.

An intriguing problem arises when the question of obsolescence is being considered. With education in a period of increasing change or transition, how long does it take for a building to become obsolete? A tour of almost any school district will reveal buildings 50 or 60 years old that are still considered structurally safe, so we know that many of our buildings are around for a long time. As a matter of fact, unless some unusual educator or architect with uncanny powers finds a way to build for free, it is an economic fact of life that buildings must be used for long periods of time. Ten years or so ago a leading school architect was heard to say that his dream was to build schools which would safely and automatically fall apart 25 years after they were built. Then they would be less likely to outlast the best years of

their lives dedicated to serving education. He may have been more nearly right than he and many others thought. In fact, in most cases, the schools which were built when he made that statement 10 years ago are already becoming obsolete — educationally obsolete. When one considers the fantastic number of schools built since 1947, the thought that many of them may be facing educational obsolescence is an appalling one. The "old" breed of school may not be very old after all. Many relatively new school buildings are already beginning to limit the educational programs they are attempting to serve.

Fixed Elements

The word *flexibility* has been moving around educational circles for quite a long while. Educators have for many years recognized the need for a degree of flexibility in their buildings, certainly not the degree now visualized, but some. Unfortunately—perhaps due to lack of vision, but more likely due to many unsolved technical and financial factors—our old friend flexibility has often been talked about but all too seldom asked to join the game.

During the last 15 or 20 years, school after school has been built with heavy load-bearing walls and partitions which, if removed, would

help our architect friend realize his dream of automatic disintegration. Fixed mechanical elements, fixed electrical elements, fixed this, and fixed that have joined forces to create facilities which limit rather than facilitate good educational programs. Forward-looking educators are becoming deeply concerned about this problem. They are wondering how to install needed electronic learning laboratories in rooms whose size and shape is wrong and whose electric outlets are not available. They are wondering how the badly needed resources center replete with its books, tape recorders, projectors, programed learning equipment, study carrels, and group research and seminar rooms can be stuffed into a space that now houses only books. They are scratching their rapidly graying heads searching for a way to get adequate ceiling height for large-group audiovisual lectures and wondering how in the world they can divide a room equipped with only one unit ventilator into two seminar rooms without rebuilding the mechanical system at the cost of a king's ransom.

THE "OLD BREED" — NEW VERSION

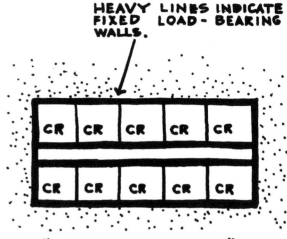

HEAVY LINES INDICATE FIXED LOAD-BEARING WALLS.

A "CELLS-AND-BELLS" CLASSROOM UNIT - A TYPICAL SITUATION.

All of this worry about buildings that are still operating on their first coat of paint! The fact that many nearly new facilities have been built without valid plans for interior change is reason for real concern. Fixed elements in existing buildings, whether new or old, are problems that may well cost many tax dollars to remedy. This problem is not selective; it applies to elementary and secondary facilities alike.

Remodel What?

Really, then, the problem of remodeling applies to buildings of all vintages, whether built in 1903, 1933, or 1963. In many ways they are all the same breed of cat; but, like plastic surgery, school remodeling works best on young faces. Age often determines whether structural remodeling can be undertaken at all and nearly always prescribes the kind of remodeling feasible. It would seem obvious that the newer buildings facing educational obsolescence and without serious structural, mechanical, and electrical aches and pains lend themselves better to the often minor changes that will help them become educationally young again.

This kind of remodeling must be undertaken periodically, and its cost will likely be relatively low.

Old buildings, however, unlike old generals, don't just fade away. They stay until their paint peels, their walls bulge, and their fine old steam pipes rattle. Often the only element in their existence that remains unchanged is their ever-increasing supply of occupants. Should these buildings nearing the end of their useful lives be remodeled?

Perhaps it would be useful to digress at this point in the text to consider definition. *Rehabilitation* or *remodeling* as used in this chapter is not the rehabilitation that is simply the process of restoring the facility to its original physical condition. The kind of remodeling considered here may well include such rehabilitation, but it goes much deeper. As discussed here, remodeling must make the facility capable of meeting the new educational requirements created by today's and tomorrow's dynamic societies. This is a very big order, indeed!

The Plan of Attack

Remodeling must be attacked with the same care and concern exercised in approaching the design of a new building. If the programing and design of a new fa-

cility represents a challenge, the job of converting old schools into useful facilities—facilities which will remain useful in this day of educational change—is a challenge and a half. Like the planning of the new facility, the remodeling job requires many keen minds. The best talents of both educator and architect should be secured at the very beginning. Their combined efforts should immediately establish the nature of the task facing the old facility. Only then can they determine whether it is up to the job.

Since the facility—whether new or old—is basically a teaching tool, a carefully considered educational specification must come first. It must establish the numbers and kinds of spaces which must be provided in the remodeled building and the curriculum content, teaching techniques, and instructional equipment to be used. The educational program itself will help to determine whether remodeling will adequately meet requirements or whether additional construction will be necessary; or, indeed, whether either of these procedures will pro-

"BEFORE" "AFTER"

REHABILITATION

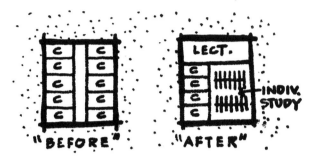

REMODELING BY FLOOR PLAN CHANGE

"BEFORE" "AFTER"

vide numerically adequate and educationally proper spaces. Thus, much as in the planning of a new facility, the educational specification is the point of beginning, but here the similarity begins to fade. When educational needs have been established, a thorough review of the facility to be used must be made to determine whether the old girl is up to a new task.

The evaluation procedure for an existing facility can conveniently be divided into two parts. First, a general physical examination should determine the state of the building's health; second, if it is healthy enough, a thorough examination should determine whether the needed educational program can be accommodated. An adequate health check-up should certainly obtain answers to these general questions:

1. Site
—Is the site large enough? Are better alternate sites available?
—Are visible site elements such as sidewalks, fences, and parking areas in adequate condition?
—Do existing utility services provide adequate capacity to meet program demands?
—Does the site drain properly?
—Are there subsurface soil problems which may cause struc-

tural difficulties in the buildings on the site?

2. Structure
—Are there any signs of deterioration or failure of footings, foundations, or piers?
—What is the structural framing system (steel, wood, or reinforced concrete)? Do such clues as moisture penetration of walls or roofs, sagging floors, sticking windows and doors, or cracking of walls or ceilings suggest the possibility of structural deterioration?
—What is the general condition of visible elements of the building such as windows, floors, wall and ceiling surfaces, the roof, flashings, spouts, lockers, and hardware?

3. Mechanical and Electrical Facilities
—Are such elements as heating, ventilation, and cooling systems; plumbing fixtures and piping; and electrical systems such as lighting, outlets, conduit, public address, and program in adequate condition? Are they accessible so they can be modified in a remodeling program without extremely high cost?

4. Code Requirements
Any evaluation of an existing building *must* include a highly detailed analysis of its ability to meet the requirements of applicable building codes. This analysis will answer such questions as—
—Are exit facilities such as corridors and stairways adequate to allow rapid and safe egress?

—Does the building provide fire resistive ratings required by the code?
—Do floors and roofs have the ability to carry loads established by code requirements?
—Are adequate lighting levels provided? Adequate numbers of plumbing fixtures? Acceptable numbers of air changes?

5. Cost
Needless to say, the cost factor is of prime importance and may well be the deciding factor in the final analysis.

An examination such as the one outlined above will help answer the crucial question: "Should the old gray mare be led away and shot, or will surgery and currying do the job?" A great deal will depend on just how old she is in the first place.

Life Begins At?

Chances are that the real old-timers—buildings built before 1910 or thereabouts—should be left alone. In many areas they are likely to be of wood-frame floor construction. The walls are probably load-bearing and not friendly toward relocation, and the mechanical and electrical systems most likely are just not suited to updating, but

THE ATTACK

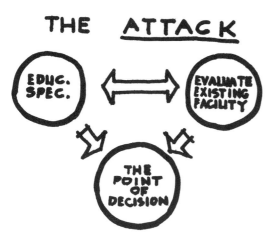

REMODELING
BY FLOOR PLAN CHANGE AND ADDITIONS

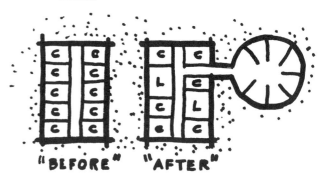

"BEFORE"   "AFTER"

rather are ready for total replacement. In new school construction, mechanical and electrical work may consume 30 to 35 percent of the total construction costs. In an extensive remodeling program, replacement costs of these elements can greatly exceed the cost of providing systems with equivalent capabilities in new facilities; and all of the structural problems of the old facility still remain to haunt the educator and the maintenance personnel. The cure can easily be worse than the disease, leaving a second-rate facility far from capable of meeting the educational needs which must be served.

Newer buildings—those built since World War I—however, may be less difficult. Their structural systems are far more likely to tolerate change; they are also more likely to meet safety standards established in current building codes; and though their mechanical and electrical systems will need work, it will be less extensive than for the real old-timers. These buildings, then, may deserve a long hard look.

Educational Requirements

At this point the new educational specifications should be examined and related to the existing facility. Again, there will be a question-and-answer session which may move along these lines:

—Does the educational program call for large-group lecture activities? If so, can large column-free spaces be achieved? Will they need sloped floors to provide proper sight-lines? Is there adequate ceiling height for projection of audiovisual material?

—Are small spaces needed for seminar purposes? Will heating, ventilating, and lighting systems serve adequately when existing classrooms are divided into smaller spaces?

—Will extension of usage of the facility into summer months for remedial, enrichment, vocational, continuing education, or other essential programs present needs for mechanical cooling which cannot be economically met?

—Will conversion to electric typewriters, installation of electronic learning laboratories, and increased use of audiovisual equipment overload existing electrical systems? Let's face it, many of the new tools for learning require utilities that simply do not exist in even some of our newer buildings.

—Do new areas of the curriculum require such spaces as science laboratories, plane-

tariums, and resources areas that will be difficult to fit into the framework of the existing building?

These questions are typical of the many areas in which educational need and facility must be considered *together.*

Additions

Perhaps the existing facility cannot be remodeled economically —given unlimited money, of course, almost anything can be accomplished—to provide certain types of spaces needed to serve educational needs. Then, if the site is adequate and if enrollment or program demands justify additional building space, an addition may become an excellent medium through which the old facility will meet new needs. Here is an excellent way to achieve the spaces so hard to find within the limitations of the old building— for example, large spaces with sloping floors, flexible learning areas, and greater ceiling heights. But additions are often impracticable because of the far too common problem of site limitation. In efforts to avoid unwarranted expenditures of funds, many school

ADDITIONS REQUIRE ADEQUATE SITE

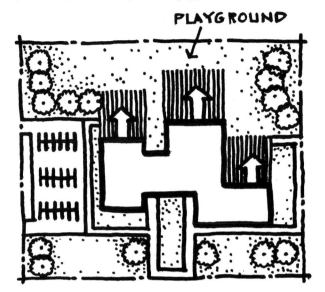

PLAYGROUND

ADDITIONS OFTEN ARE IN VISUAL CONFLICT WITH THE ORIGINAL BUILDING

districts have time and time again built buildings on sites which at first seemed adequate enough but later were consumed by building additions because of growing enrollments.

Compatibility

The total environment for learning—functional and visual—is as important here as in new buildings. Too often, remodeling and additions create a visual battle between the new and the old and the child is trapped in a no-man's-land of a visual environment. Often the new spaces are far superior visually to the old spaces that remain, and it is only natural for the child to associate the relative importance of subject material with the general quality of the environment within which it is offered. Thus, there is the danger of providing first class and second class spaces

which will create serious disturbances to both pupils and teachers. The remodeling project, then, requires a great deal of sensitivity in its planners if it is to provide a total visual environment of adequate quality. Beauty, as is discussed in another chapter of this book, is an essential ingredient of all schools, old or new.

The Big Question

Where remodeling is being considered, one must decide in the final analysis whether the cure is worse than the disease. As far as rehabilitation is concerned, it really

should be pretty much a continuing program. It is a simple fact that the pupils' and the taxpayers' best interests are served by keeping educational facilities in good and safe condition. The learning process is enhanced when housed in visually pleasant facilities. When remodeling is being considered, many things must be balanced. Each project must be carefully scrutinized under its own individual set of circumstances.

So, really, remodeling isn't a dirty word, after all. Given proper care and starting with an old facility of some merit, the old breed of school building may indeed come back to life and become an educational facility of a high degree of functional and visual quality.

Chapter 14 / Plant Management

During the first century of American public education, school buildings were built, operated, and replaced with little concern for *how* they were built, operated, or replaced. With a few notable exceptions, educators and lay leaders did not concern themselves with the long-term problems of school plant. During the last half of the 1800's, school boards often subdivided themselves organizationally into many subcommittees, much as many of the boards of control of the nation's colleges still do; one of these subcommittees would be responsible for buildings and grounds and for directing the business manager in the day-to-day care and repair of the plant. Within a decade or two after the turn of the century, school boards generally were reduced in size, which restricted their time for plant activities. By the "birthquake" years of the 1950's and the 1960's, school boards' plant-related activities were almost exclusively limited to planning and constructing new buildings, consolidation, and bond issues. The planning and construction of new facilities became of prime concern, overshadowing all operating and maintenance aspects of plant management.

In 1966 the public school educational plant in the United States had a dollar value in excess of $100 billion. This amount is being further increased at a rate in excess of $4 billion a year. The public school plant now cares for the educational needs of over 47 million youth, in addition to another estimated 50 to 75 million adults who use the buildings for continuing education, social activities, and recreational pursuits. The public educational plant of the United States is a big, valuable, institutional resource requiring and meriting the serious and prudent attention of both school board members and educational administrators.

A Basic Responsibility

The plant management function is not confined merely to the activities of the physical plant director's department; it requires that school boards develop operating policy and community support; administrators give supporting leadership and guidance; and faculty-student groups react to services rendered. Between 13 and 25 percent of all educational expenditures are normally devoted to providing for plant and plant-related services. Thus boards and administrators must seek constantly more positive management techniques with which to secure the maximum and most economical output from this fundamental educational resource—a charge which they assumed when they took office. The modern concept of plant management is one of the most exciting developments in current educational business management.

A careful examination of almost any urban or rural school will reveal many ways in which modern plant management can improve educational opportunity. Faculty members can identify needed educational services which, if provided by the plant division, will enhance their teaching. Management experts who have been commissioned to examine school plant operations have recognized the need for efficient modern plant management. Its value to the educational program has been clearly demonstrated time and time again.

American public education is typified historically by its local organization. Local citizens formulate policy and employ a chief admin-

istrator to enhance it in virtually all of the public schools in the nation. This fact bears heavily upon the management of the nation's school plant, just as it does on the instructional program. It is the local school board and its administrative force which must develop, adopt, and implement a policy of plant management which adequately cares for the physical plant entrusted to their keeping. This is true in one-room schools, just as it is true in plants having hundreds of classrooms. The policy of plant management maintained in the local school system is, of course, only one part of the total educational philosophy of the district, but in support of its value it can be pointed out that the physical plant is one of the most important and certainly the most costly tool used in the total educational process. The policy implemented by each local school system and school building staff controls substantially the degree to which the plant benefits the program, how costly the plant will prove to be to the community, and how long it will be before the buildings will be worn out and have to be replaced.

Unfortunately, the school districts which have, for one reason or another, not yet implemented a satisfactory policy of plant management far outnumber those which have. This chapter is directed to assisting those school districts which need to re-evaluate their plant programs. A partial reassessment will be undertaken of the role played by educational facilities in the educative process, and an attempt will be made to identify processes which school districts of all sizes might initiate to take better advantage of the educational opportunities available through competent plant management and to improve the economical management of plant facilities. Every conscientious school board and every thoughtful educational leader seeks to provide for the children in the district the best possible educational climate at the lowest possible cost. Good buildings may not be the primary component of any school system, but without them—and especially without good buildings which are well and economically operated—opportunities for teachers to teach and for children to learn are greatly reduced.

The Purposes of School Plants

Everyone knows that school buildings are built to provide housing for pupils. That is about where public understanding stops. But board members, administrators, and staff personnel must determine what service personnel are required to meet efficiently and economically the special buildings and grounds needs of each school's total program. While the basic purposes an educational plant serves may seem to professionals to be self-evident, it is important that they be clearly recognized by all, because these purposes, not the mere presence of properties, determine the school's plant management policy if it is to be constructive and enduring. The educational plant—both grounds and buildings—serves primarily the basic purposes of education by providing a maximally conducive-to-teaching and conducive-to-learning environment: one which is continuously maintained for the comfort, safety, and health of students, teachers, and patrons.

The school plant which has been designed and constructed adequately and is operated with constant effort to achieve the best educational setting within the op-

erational policy of the school is one which is designed, equipped, and operated to satisfy all of the human physical senses. Such facilities provide visual environments which enable the eyes to work accurately without unnecessary fatigue or injury; acoustical conditions which enable the ears to have discriminating access to all of the sounds which need to be interpreted; room space in which to work and relax comfortably without unduly interfering with the activities of others; thermal environments which are healthful and stimulating to a variety of forms of physical activity; an aesthetically pleasing environment which contributes to the enjoyment, peace, and serenity of the atmosphere in which children and teachers work; and an artistically developed environment which, by its very being, has positive impact upon the artistic and sociological pursuits of individuals in the school and community.

Achieving the Purposes of Plant

The attainment of constructively built and managed facilities, like every other worthwhile objective in education, requires the adoption and implementation of basic policy. The achievement of an ef-

fective educational plant management program is the responsibility of top management. Teachers, principals, and supervisors can assist in its development, but they cannot reasonably be expected to give plant management the required leadership.

A successful plant management program develops out of the educational policy of the schools. General management is provided by the board of education through the superintendent. In larger systems this responsibility may be delegated to an assistant superintendent in charge of business or plant management. In the typical larger school district a director of physical plant, referred to here as the plant manager, is directly responsible for the professional direction and the day-to-day administration of the plant management program. In small school systems the superintendent must function as the plant director concurrently with his other educational duties.

A well managed and educationally supportive plant management program is not easy to secure nor easy to continue in operation. It requires the development of an understanding of the function of education, the specific characteristics of the local situation, and the composition of the faculty and the student body. It requires extensive knowledge about the educational

program, the needs of youth, and the currently used methods of teaching. In addition, the operation of a successful plant management program requires the energies of an individual who is schooled and experienced not only in education, but also in management of property, purchasing, personnel administration, finance, and other areas related to business. A successful plant management program needs to be directed by a person with sufficient time, intelligence, and interest, not just to keep the plant out of the way of pupils, but to use the total plant resource to enhance teaching and learning opportunities maximally and emphatically. Regardless of building or school system size, plant management is needed by all school systems. The benefits which can accrue are the same to all districts; they only change in scope.

The Functions of the Plant Management Program

It is important to understand all of the functions of a plant management program because such a program can do so much to enhance the educational program. At any school an effective plant man-

133

agement program can improve teaching and learning opportunities by—

- —Making it possible to more completely utilize facilities and equipment.
- —Increasing the assignability of existing floor space, thus reducing the need to spend time and money on new construction.
- —Improving building services and reducing their cost.
- —Improving community relationships.
- —Providing maximum security.
- —Reducing safety hazards to persons and property.

A good plant management program, among other things, coordinates the broad range of plant-related activities which have all too often been scattered throughout many school positions and departments. However, the concept is more than an attempt to coordinate functions; it is also an attempt to centralize plant-related responsibilities within an organized program to keep as much of the program as possible in one department. An analogy might be a well run school system's personnel program. Many schools, departments, and persons are involved in aspects of the pro-gram, but responsibility for the total program is centralized in a personnel office with a director of personnel.

The major elements of a plant program can be divided into two groups. In the first group are the five functions which constitute the nature and scope of plant management. The second group contains six functions which are of equal importance but are managerial in nature and support the functions in the first group. The following functions are included in the first group:

1. *Determining the facilities needed to house the education program.* Economical operation—the effort to conserve maximum funds for long-range use of the program—demands that prudence be exercised in determining which facilities need to be newly constructed and which are to be rehabilitated. A scientific assessment of program, existing facilities, and space utilization practices is needed prior to the making of decisions as to whether to construct new facilities or to rehabilitate old facilities. This planned approach to the analysis of total program housing requirements is vital.

2. *Planning, financing, and constructing the facilities.* It is readily conceded that planning, financing, and constructing facilities is a responsibility of the board of education and its chief school administrator.

Yet, too often this responsibility is shifted to architects for almost all plant planning work, to board members for financing efforts, and to building contractors for most contract administration. Control over design decisions and construction judgments is too readily lost by the owner when responsibility for planning and constructing facilities is placed out of the hands of the educational administrators who should be held accountable and in the hands of a variety of paid planning consultants.

Plant management is as closely related to the financial program of a school system as it is to the educational program. It is in this area that some of the most unexpected expenditures and savings are encountered. Faculty salaries—the biggest single expense item of a school system—are established at contract time and budgeted accordingly, but many plant problems cannot be so precisely budgeted. Furthermore, because the best of administrative talent is not always applied to the plant management program, budgets in the physical plant area are often based almost exclusively upon expenditures of past years rather than in direct relationship to the long-range problems of plant maintenance and upkeep and their relationships to education. If a plant organization is evaluating periodically the physical plant conditions and the need for educationally related services, its line items in budget requests will vary upwards and downwards from year to year. A straight line projection of expenditures should not always parallel past expenses with allowance for additional facilities and rising costs. The charted line of new budget proposals will have ridges and peaks indicative of plant-related programs which hopefully will save money, of programs which reveal attempts being made to catch up on accumulated building defects, and of attempts to experiment with methods holding promise for other long-term savings.

In considering plant finances, it is well to note that new facilities are generally initiated because of enrollment growth or program change, and then, as a second thought, rehabilitation needs are added as an auxiliary item. In a modern plant management program, long-term projections for annual rehabilitation are developed and presented to the administration so that facilities can be modernized when it is most advisable and not just when new buildings are being planned.

3. *Operating and maintaining facilities.* The operation of plants has long been recognized as the most costly and time-consuming of all plant management responsibilities. In public elementary and secondary schools, operations expenditures account for approximately 9 percent of all current educational expenditures. Keeping a school plant operating on a daily basis involves crews of custodians; heating plant operators; mechanics; and, in larger plants, security men, elevator operators, and others.

The values which the operations services hold for the educational program are many. Often these are not as immediately recognized as are plant planning or space assignments. Although cleaning itself may seem to have little relationship to education, it does affect instruction both qualitatively and quantitatively. The care of grounds is another area often regarded as remote from teaching and learning, but any school system which has had grounds designed and maintained to promote science education, recreational education, or art education would, of course, dispute this assertion.

Such simple routines as the provision of messenger and porter services by maids and custodians affect the teaching-learning program. When movie screens, projectors, science demonstration units, and other pieces of equipment are not properly positioned by the opening hour of a class, the ensuing disturbance and waste of time obviously have an adverse effect on learning.

The upkeep of the plant—the maintenance function—is slightly less than half as costly as the operating program. Without a systematic, well-scheduled maintenance program, however, the life of the physical plant is substantially shortened and the education program suffers accordingly. Marks of a good maintenance program include such organized functions as periodic building inspections, an annual redecoration program, periodically performed maintenance, and the planned, periodic replacement of equipment and building components as part of a long-range program.

Maintenance and mechanical services also hold great value for the teaching-learning opportunity in every school system. Physical plant conditions must be maintained which ensure the safety of building occupants, which guarantee that emergency evacuation equip-

135

ment is constantly in operating condition, and which ensure that facilities and equipment will be operable at all times.

4. *Analyzing space usage and assignment practices.* The problem of properly using available space in school buildings is often not complex, but it still can be a vital issue, seldom understood or even seriously considered. The assignment and analysis of space requires the cooperative effort of school administrators, plant managers, and faculty. Only through such an effort can administrators secure improvements and increased space utilization at desirable quality levels, conservation of the resources of the institution, and the location of teachers and students in the most suitable working environment for every learning activity.

A plant management department needs daily space utilization and assignment information not only for the designing and construction of facilities but also to improve economically upon the manner in which operations and maintenance are scheduled and performed.

5. *Adapting the plant and plant services to changes in science and technology.* The fifth ingredient in a successful plant management program is constant adaptation of plant and plant service to scientific and technological developments.

Thus, as improved health standards are recognized, an alert plant management takes steps to include them in the institution's daily routine; as standards of comfort and convenience in daily living change, active plant management adapts plant design and the purchase of furnishings accordingly; as new teaching methods and equipment are developed, the modern plant program works to incorporate them into the school's physical environment.

Keeping plants up-to-date with current developments is dependent upon the use of a definitive, coordinated approach involving frequent reappraisals of what the schools are doing in the plant management field—how work is being done; how it might be done better; how changes should proceed; and what benefits, economies, or problems will result from projected changes.

Supporting the five functions of plant management, and of equal importance, are six supporting managerial functions. Each of these functions permeates the length and breadth of the entire plant management program.

1. Personnel recruitment, relations, and training
2. Purchasing of tools, equipment, materials, and furnishings
3. Insurance of plant and plant personnel
4. Safety of people and plant

5. Contracting — including specifying, negotiating, executing, and administering
6. Financial control.

Some school boards and their administrators will find it difficult because of the size of the system to have these supporting functions within a plant management unit. In many small school systems the superintendent of schools and a few custodians will be that unit. In larger school systems, however, the board and its administrator will do well to consider the benefits, both educational and financial, of centralized plant management operating as an integral part of the organizational structure of the school system.

The Plant Manager

The modern, comprehensive plant management program requires the employment of a highly competent and educationally oriented plant manager. The nature of the program calls for a person with an understanding of educational methods and objectives and the philosophy adhered to in his particular school district. Because such a large percentage of the plant

management staff's efforts is integrally and directly related to the educational program, the value of the manager's understanding of the educational processes can hardly be overstated.

The second major characteristic which the leader of a modern, comprehensive plant management program must possess is ability in the area of general personnel and business management. He must be a competent general administrator possessing balanced judgment and the ability to pursue detail while, at the same time, keeping the entire scope of the operation in perspective. It is of prime importance that he be able to orient himself as a member of the administrative team. The many responsibilities of the job, involving personnel and contract administration, budget and facility planning, insurance, and purchasing, ordinarily require that the plant manager be a college graduate. The possession of one or more degrees related to education or educational administration will help to solidify successful business and educational relationships with students, faculty, citizens, consultants, and business leaders of the community.

The specific characteristics of a school's plant management program should be a guiding factor in the selection and retention of a plant manager. The job responsibilities should govern the development of criteria for appointment and the inservice education opportunities made available for personal growth and development. These criteria will help to determine whether the plant manager's background should include studies and experiences in such specialized areas as horticulture, landscaping, food service management, and engineering as a background for the responsibilities he will assume as a member of the administrative team.

Since plant management requires the employment of a person who can analyze facilities, plan financial programs, recommend and plan building expansion and rehabilitation programs, and utilize the resources of people, money, and materials, it should be evident that one of the most needed characteristics is what might best be called managerial skill.

The Plant Management Staff

It takes an able, professionally educated staff to operate a modern school plant and enhance its educational opportunity to the maximum. It requires personnel capable of setting standards of performance

for the control of thermal conditions, visual conditions, spatial arrangements, acoustical conditions, and aesthetic requirements and of planning for adequate, properly located instructional equipment. If pupils or faculty members are not thermally, visually, and acoustically comfortable, their reactions to specific learning situations will be inhibited. Similarly, both students and faculty prefer to work and study in facilities which beckon to them, which by sheer attractiveness urge people to come in and be both physically and mentally comfortable. It is hard to be fully productive in quarters which produce mental and physical stresses and strains. When there are facilities which provide good seeing conditions; proper thermal controls; acoustical features productive of better hearing; adequate leg room; comfortable seating; and suitable, frequently updated and maintained instructional equipment, then so far as physical surroundings are concerned, educational production can be at its peak.

Modern plant management programs need supervisors capable of determining for top management what needs to be done to attain these conditions, how it should be done, and what it will cost. Careful consideration needs to be given to employee recruitment and selection, personnel characteristics, job placement, performance evaluation, work procedures, schedules and standards, job training, supervisory techniques, and employee morale. Salary schedules and other benefits such as job security, vacations, holidays, insurance, and sick leave should be competitive with comparable vocations in the community in order to attract persons of high caliber to the plant management staff.

Member of the Administrative Team

Despite the fact that school systems vary greatly in size and small school systems can afford to employ only a small administrative staff, each member of which must play several roles, it is still essential that the plant management concept expressed here be part of the administration policy of small schools as well as large schools. The employment of plant adminis-

trators who are capable of implementing the objectives of the schools in the everyday actions of their department and who manage the services of an educational institution is a strong indication of top management's desire to capitalize on an additional valuable, economical, and readily accessible program resource.

It should be kept in mind that the performance setting provided by each school system for the personnel of its plant management function is important not only to the objectives of the plant management program, but to the objectives of the educational system. In other words, top management's confidence in the value of the plant to the educational program and the value of plant personnel services to that program will be reflected in both the quality and quantity performance levels of the plant management department. The physical qualities which school systems are willing to incorporate in their new buildings will have direct effect upon the ability of a plant management program to function and succeed. Similarly, the amount of money which a school system is willing to spend annually on plant operation and maintenance and the amount of guidance which top administration gives to plant administrators will affect the plant manage-

ment output. Members of the board of education and members of the administration have just as great a responsibility to provide adequate money for plant management as they do for other areas of the total educational activities of school systems; it is a part of the total school program. Just as the administrative philosophy of a school system affects the development of academic pursuits, so also does it affect the success of the plant management function.

The plant manager does not replace the architect, the engineer, or the educator. Instead he becomes a member of the planning team—the interpreter between the pedagogical staff and the technicians, the superintendent's liaison between the school's staff and faculty and the architects and consultants.

Final Analysis

The ultimate goal of the plant management program, like other areas of the educational enterprise, is to improve educational oppor-

tunities for students. The character of the school building becomes more complex each year; there is increasing reliance upon automated devices and complicated mechani- cal systems which must be kept in good working order. Education is being extended to meet the educa- tional needs of all age groups; peo- ple are coming to school at all hours of the day and all times of the year. The efficient plant man- agement program is designed to increase the efficiency of this com- plex and highly specialized institu- tion and to provide a better learning environment for its students.

Chapter 15 / *Stock Plans and Standards*

Why not use stock plans? Nearly every superintendent of schools and his school building planning team, faced with a multiple building program, have been asked this question. It usually is suggested as an "innovation" by a new board member or a citizen group sincerely interested in saving the taxpayers' dollars or in getting better use of the money available. To the typical lay citizen with little or no experience in planning school buildings, the idea of developing one set of plans and using it over and over, thus saving all but one architect's fee, is appealing.

Actually there is nothing innovative about stock plans. They have been in existence for generations but have met with little success. In the face of this record of non-success, however, attempts are still being made to thrust this concept upon local school planners, and the question is still being asked, "Why can't stock plans work?" The proponents of stock plans, while sometimes advancing other arguments, base the support of their use mainly on two goals—the saving of planning time for the school district and the saving of taxpayers' dollars, the main element of which is elimination of the architect's fee.

Stock plans, for purposes of this publication, are defined as sets of building plans and specifications intended for duplication without modification except for foundation structure and site development. Typically, stock plans in this country have been developed by states and are generally made available to school districts at low cost. The term *stock plans* as used in this chapter is not intended to include *repetitive plans*. Repetitive plans are those used for buildings on two or three very similar sites within a single school district for which the planning was concurrent and for which the educational and community needs were relatively identical. Members of the AASA Commission on School Buildings believe that the use of repetitive plans, while not likely to save architectural fees, may, if used with caution, save time in carefully controlled situations.

History and Present Status

It is not known just when stock plans were first used in this country, but it is believed that the U.S. Department of Indian Affairs may have distributed the first stock school building plans in the mid- or late 1800's. A comprehensive survey of school building stock plan programs was made in 1951 by The American Institute of Architects Committee on School Buildings.

This survey [1] reported that as of November of that year—

10 states have limited stock plans available:

West Virginia	1-room
California	
Minnesota	2-room
Kentucky	4-room
Maine	
Arkansas	$10,000
Mississippi	$15,000
Oklahoma	"small construction"
Virginia	4-6-room
	7-10-room
North Carolina	special units

23 states do not use and never have used stock plans for school buildings:

Arizona	Nevada
Colorado	New Hampshire
Delaware	
Idaho	New Jersey
Illinois	New Mexico
Indiana	North Dakota
Iowa	Ohio
Kansas	Oregon
Louisiana	Rhode Island
Maryland	Utah
Massachusetts	Washington
Montana	Wyoming

[1] AIA Committee on School Buildings. "Stock Plans for School Buildings: A National Survey." *AIA School Plant Studies*. Washington, D.C.: The American Institute of Architects, 1962. p. 57. See also Bursch, Charles W. "Stock Plans for Schools—Substance or Shadow." pp. 60-62; and a later report, AIA Committee on School and College Architecture. "Why Standard Plans Don't Work." School Plant Studies Series #BT1-56.

15 states do not use but formerly used stock plans and have now abandoned them.

Alabama	Pennsylvania
Connecticut	South Carolina
Florida	South Dakota
Georgia	Tennessee
Michigan	Texas
Missouri	Vermont
Nebraska	Wisconsin
New York	

The 1960 AASA School Building Commission reported that—

An inquiry was sent to state school-building officials in 47 states in December 1958 by the Washington State Board of Education. Forty-one states responded. Of those states responding, only four indicated that they now have statutory provisions that particularly pertain to the use of modifiable stock plans for elementary-school buildings with four classrooms or smaller. Seven states indicated that stock plans had been used in past years for the construction of small elementary buildings but that the practice had now been dropped entirely.

This survey indicated there were six large school districts in the United States that had used in the past or were using at the present time modifiable stock plans in their building programs. The Los Angeles City school system is one example; it is experimenting with modifiable stock plans for basic units in elementary school construction. In California school plans must be checked and approved by the State Division of Architecture for earthquake resistance, a process which may require from three to five months. A savings in time, not in costs, was the reason for Los Angeles' instituting modifiable stock plans.

Five states reported some experience in redrafting and reshaping modifiable plans for a new site and a new locality. Their experience indicated that the average cost of revising an existing plan so that it will be usable for a new building was approximately 3 percent of the cost of the building. In additions, approximately 2 percent must be added for supervision and inspection cost.[2]

New York State's Department of Education, at the insistence of its legislature, introduced in the 1960's a set of nine stock plans prepared under the direction of the State Department of Public Works by private architectural firms. After over two years of availability, only two of the nine plans had been used for construction. Despite its light utilization, however, the New York State stock plan program cannot yet be labeled a failure. It contains many interest-

---

[2] American Association of School Administrators. *Planning America's School Buildings.* Washington, D.C.: the Association, 1960. pp. 190-91.

ing features. Under this plan, a local school district that chooses to participate has considerable opportunity to select a plan to meet its own educational program needs and some choice in how much of the plant is to be built now and how much is to be constructed later.

It is interesting to note that those persons responsible for the development of the New York State program designated their plans as "standard" rather than stock plans. They did this because their plans do leave some choices to the local school board. The plans do not contain foundation design drawings but clearly state that architects and engineers will have to be employed to complete the design, to recommend finishes, to prepare site development drawings, and to handle building department reviews. Furthermore, attempts were made to provide plans which would develop sound and attractive buildings. An advisory group of educators, architects, businessmen, and the project architect of the state's public works department worked with professional architects and engineers commissioned by the State of New York to design the nine sets of standard plans.

Although the plans are apparently not being used extensively, the program's sponsors believe they serve a useful purpose in providing a tool for discussion in local com-

munities. If considerable time is not wasted in debating the issue of stock versus individually drawn plans and the merits of one plan over another and in making site visits to stock-plan designed buildings, this purpose might be fulfilled. There would, however, appear to be many more advantageous uses for the valuable time of boards and educators planning new educational facilities.

Stock Plan Pitfalls

Prior to lending support to any proposed stock school building plan program, school building planners should consider the following reasons why modern school building conditions do not lend themselves to stock plans.

—Standard plans are rarely economical in the long run.
—They are not readily adjustable to variations in site nor to changes in curriculums and teaching.
—They can be helpful only in school districts whose needs and conditions exactly match the available stock building plans.
—They are too generally designed for a minimum level of quality.
—Like all school building plans in these days of rapid change, they become obsolete on the drawing board.

—They cannot possibly be designed to meet adequately a sufficiently wide variety of spatial relations, topographies or site shapes, nor to accommodate all of the possible access roads, adjacent streets, and nearby traffic patterns of many sites.
—They cannot take into consideration the location and direction of the most economical approach for all incoming utility connections.
—They cannot be economically or feasibly designed to accommodate the educational programs of many communities.
—They negate the development of a local sense of pride in a community's school buildings.
—They make impossible the use of local judgment on the optimum use of school sites and local school funds.
—They fail to consider adequately the possibility of difficult subsoil conditions, noise problems, and other extreme conditions. They can be protective only by overdesign.
—They negate the individual initiative and judgment of local faculties and citizen groups.
—They eliminate competent and competitive manufacturers from bidding and thus may increase costs by the delimitation of competition.
—They make it difficult to incorporate new and improved products and construction techniques.
—They do not eliminate necessity

for employing architects and engineers to adapt the stock plan to a new site with different soil conditions, topography, and location in relationship to all incoming utilities and to structural changes for snow, water, wind, and soil. An architect or engineer is needed to supervise construction, check payments to the contractor, advise the owner on construction and design problems, check drawings against performance, and approve samples of materials. Likewise, someone needs to make sure the stock plan conforms to local fire, health, and sanitation laws.

There may have been a period in the history of the United States when the use of stock school building plans could offer genuinely valuable assistance to local schools. Conditions are vastly different today. Many features of today's schools are totally incompatible with the stock-plan concept. Buildings are much larger and more complex; more and improved materials and equipment are available annually; and scientific and technological advances have produced new knowledges to meet the requirements of varying types of buildings and instructional innovations in modern educational programs.

Among persons who support the stock-plan concept are persons who believe that stock plans should be utilized in poverty-stricken, low-enrollment school districts which need small, low-cost buildings. This view should be reappraised. It is these very communities which need the most carefully planned educational facilities. New and better ways need to be found to finance an educational program—including facilities, curriculum, teachers, supplies, equipment, and many other resources—which will reach deep into the problems of such communities and provide them with the educational means to "leap frog" back into the mainstream of American society.

Recent Attempts To Reduce Cost and Time

Anyone who has studied school building planning in America knows that hundreds of planning and construction improvements have been made throughout the industry. These improvements have helped to reduce the cost of construction and the number of hours spent on planning. Reductions have served to off-set, in some degree, the spiraling costs resulting from the effects of inflation, the more comprehensive nature of modern school buildings, and increased labor costs. Of the hundreds of design and production improvements which have evolved in the school building field in the last decade, undoubtedly the most exciting have been the attempts to invoke the tremendous powers of mass production of American industry into the construction of school buildings.

Fabricated building components. Over the past ten years considerable attention has been given to prefabricated school buildings. Early efforts were disappointing. Some significant improvements have been made in the modern versions of these units, but the reduction in cost is still considerably less than might be expected. Out of these experiments, however, came a development which holds substantial promise when engineering and industrial skill was turned to the production of basic modules to be used in school building construction. Many companies today, for example, sell very usable, factory-fabricated, wall panel sections. Others provide lighting fixtures which integrate heating, ventilating, and cooling with the lighting function. Still others provide packaged boiler systems. These factory-built units are being drawn upon for use in school buildings by both the architectural and engineering professions. Every year more multifabricated innovations are being introduced, tried, tested, and retained or rejected by the school building industry.

Modular construction. In modular construction the basic module is repeated again and again throughout an entire building in order to simplify construction and cut costs. Elemental examples of a modular building unit are the standard brick and the partition studs established on 16" or 24" centers to receive 4' by 8' plywood sheeting. Larger modules reduce the number of operations and hence cut labor costs. Smaller modules, on the other hand, provide more opportunity to secure desirable space allocations. The usefulness of the modular unit in effecting economies in school building construction is now well established.

Mechanization. It is self-evident that the building process is being increasingly mechanized; motorized and automatically controlled equipment are used in both on-site construction and the manufacturing of component building parts. The combination of increase in size and completeness of building components with the development of faster and more capable mechanized tools is successfully stepping up the pace and lowering the cost of both new construction and rehabilitation.

Standardization of building products and material. The building industry has moved a long way in this area. Standardization helps school planners to keep the cost of schools down and reduces construction time. Today, for example, most lighting manufacturers produce typical school fixtures in identical sizes; roofing manufacturers do the same with roofing materials, as do companies selling wood, blocks, brick, steel, glass, and numerous other building products and materials. Thus, if one supplier, dealer, or manufacturing chain is

out of a product, one can get the same or equal material from other sources.

Standardized approaches to planning. Significant moves toward standardization of state and municipal building codes and the publication of standards by recognized organizations such as the American Standards Association, the Illuminating Engineering Society, and The American Institute of Architects have helped to simplify the steps and procedures in designing and building school structures. The National Council on Schoolhouse Construction has been a leading exponent of developing standard

performance guidelines which can be used by all school building planners. Its *Guide to School Plant Planning* is best known. This has been adopted by several states as their official school building code and has been used informally as the state school building code of many other states.

Unquestionably, standards, when carefully established and appropriately used, have been helpful in improving the quality of school buildings. However, there is the danger that the standard stated as a minimum may tend to become the maximum or the common procedure. Understanding this cautionary note, school planners will use performance standards as a take-off point to develop increasingly more suitable plans and products to meet the challenge of today's exciting educational progress.

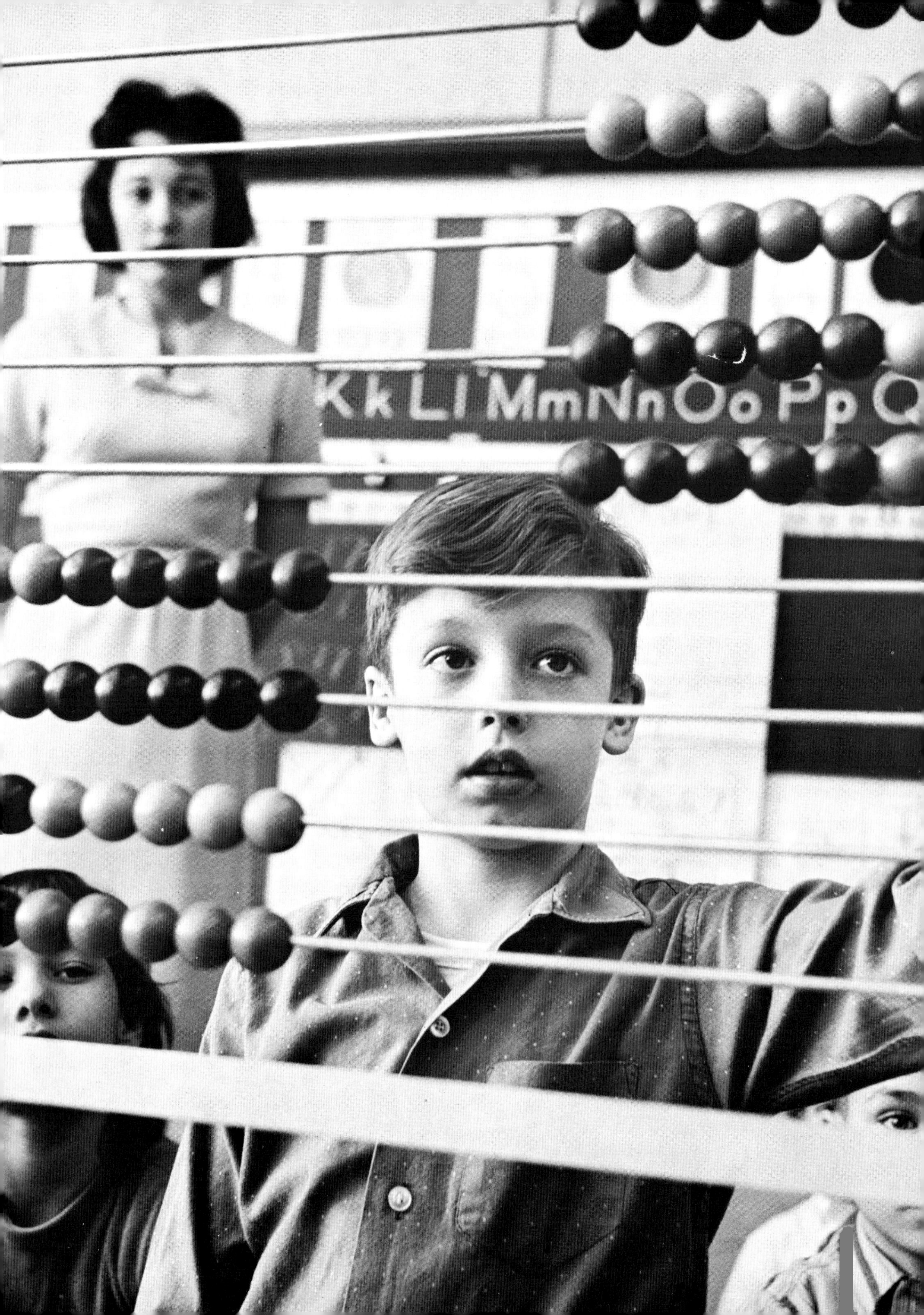
Kk Ll Mm Nn Oo Pp Q

Chapter 16 / *Dollars and Sense*

School building costs are of great concern to everyone engaged in the planning of a new school. Capital, or initial, costs receive most attention before the school is built, especially if it is necessary to vote bonds to finance it. However, after the school is completed and occupied and has served its community for many years, its initial cost is forgotten and the dollar facts are lost. Only the small tax obligation and the building itself have meaning. The achievement is the reality. Either the facilities serve well, or they don't serve well. Either the school is beautiful, or it is not beautiful. Operation and maintenance costs are then of more concern. But the primary concern is the educational quality of the building. During the generations of use of the school facilities, many will wish that the money had been more wisely spent, and often that more had been spent while they were at it.

Competition and Costs

The hard, cold facts of school building costs are of interest to all of us. We are especially interested —sometimes too interested—in seeing how costs can be kept low. The competition in building costs is intense. This competitive spirit hap-pily produces great efficiency and, hence, lower construction costs; it is also responsible for a continuous flood of new ideas, new building methods and techniques, and new ways to achieve facilities at reasonable cost. The person who considers school building costs too high is usually unaware of this intense competition and the published statistics which clearly show that there have been only relatively modest increases in school building costs during the years in which there has been considerable inflation.

In contrast to some fields, such as science, where research may be separate from application, building construction research is constantly going on in conjunction with actual building projects. This research is directed toward doing a job better and less expensively. When a new material or a new method proves to be better and cheaper, it is adopted, replacing less efficient materials and methods. For example, during the fifties the flat-roofed school building of lightweight construction and many standard factory-built parts proved to be more economical than the heavy, thick-walled schools of earlier decades. Consequently, these "modern" schools were built in great numbers throughout America. Thus, competitive forces tend to keep building costs at the lowest possible level within the current economic framework.

The Market

The economic conditions of the nation, the community, and the times have interesting implications for school builders that are not always readily understood by school administrators, board members, and citizens. After the school has been designed, using the most efficient materials and methods, building costs, as reflected by the bids received from contractors, are determined by the economic conditions of the country and the community in which the school is located and by the general level of building activity. If many factories, houses, apartments, and office buildings are under construction, the school project competes with them for materials, men, and contractors, and costs will be higher than if the school is bid during a time of relatively little building activity when everyone—manufacturers, suppliers, contractors, and the building unions —is anxious to build the school. The architect often gets blamed for prices that are too high or credited for low costs because of market fluctuations which are not within his control. He is often expected to predict costs when designing a school in January that will be bid in December, even though he cannot always know with accuracy whether prices will be up or down at that time. This presents a most difficult problem. Some school districts have avoided trouble by taking bids for the new building and then, if a bond issue is needed, asking the citizens to approve the necessary amount. For many districts this is not possible or practicable.

Quantity and Quality

Building costs are usually analyzed by establishing the total building area in square feet and the cost per square foot. When multiplied together these produce the building cost. In other words, cost is the product of quantity—square feet—multiplied by quality—cost per square foot. To obtain the total project cost, the cost of equipment, fees and other expenses, the cost of site development, and sometimes the cost of the land must be added.

When the total number of dollars available for a building is inadequate and a certain amount of space is required, quality must be adjusted. For example, if not over $720,000 is available for building construction and 40,000 square feet of space is required, quality must be limited to what can be bought for $18 per square foot in the current market. If, on the other hand, the community demands the level of quality represented by $20 per square foot and must work within the $720,000 limitation, the area must necessarily be limited to 36,000 square feet. The owner can control only two of the factors; the third is controlled by the building market conditions at the time of bidding. If one ignores these facts during the planning stages of a school building project, disappointment and recriminations will prevail on bid-opening day.

Estimating Costs

In estimating costs, the cost-per-square-foot method is convenient but can be no more than a rough rule-of-thumb approximation. It ignores the fact that kitchens, toilet rooms, and laboratories cost more than classrooms and unequipped shops. Sometimes the cost per square foot is computed separately for different areas of the building. Then the question arises, Should the cost of expensive mechanical equipment be reflected only in the cost of the space that houses it, or should the equipment cost be distributed over the areas served by the equipment? Further refinement leads us to a more accurate kind of cost estimating—the quantity survey.

In the quantity survey method of cost estimating, actual quantities of materials and their cost are calculated, appropriate dollar amounts are assigned for labor and subcontract items, and a final percentage is added for general conditions such as the prime contractors' supervision and profit. This process produces an itemized list which may be many pages long but which shows rather accurately the estimated cost for each item. Even this method is not infallible. Market conditions can only be anticipated. Bid amounts will be determined by many hundreds of prices the contractors collect immediately before the bid date, and the contractors cannot control the prices submitted by their subcontractors and suppliers.

The quantity survey is expensive, and the mass of data collected is unwieldy, so cost-per-square-foot figures continue to be most popular. One must remember, of course, that such figures vary widely from one part of the country to another, and cost cannot equitably be compared without applying appropriate adjustment factors, many of which are published in government publications and in magazines and books. It is interesting to note that some parts of the country that formerly enjoyed low costs—caused by low wages—are finding that their building costs are now rising toward levels prevalent in other parts of the country.

On "Cost Per Square Foot"

Considered alone, cost per square foot is often misleading. Claims of exceptionally low costs should be questioned. Who calculated the area? What did he include? Have some costs been hidden elsewhere? It is difficult and not always meaningful to compare cost-per-square-foot figures provided by different individuals who may have used different methods and formulas in their computations.

Even when the cost-per-square-foot figures are comparable, they may not be a true indication of the cost of construction. For example, the cost of two hypothetical elementary schools might be compared in the following manner: One school, which provides 120 square feet per pupil for 600 pupils, has a total gross area of 72,000 square feet.

Another school of 600 pupils provides 140 square feet per pupil, or a gross area of 84,000 square feet. The architect and owner of the second school may boast that their school cost only $16 per square foot since the total building cost was $1,344,000. However, the first school, which cost $18 per square foot, actually cost less for the total building. In other words, the first school cost $2,160 per pupil, while the second, even though it cost less per square foot, cost $2,240 per pupil. When compared in this manner, the first school actually cost $48,000 less, or $80 less per pupil.

A note of caution is in order. The foregoing is a comparison of cost only. The actual educational value to the community has not been compared. It is often true that the more spacious and more costly school is a better investment for the community. In considering only the building cost—unfortunately a commonplace, popular practice—the educational value may be ignored. The only significant figure is its cost in terms of the quality of the education of one child.

Total Building Cost

It is not only cost-per-square-foot figures that are misleading. Total building cost, taken alone without equipment, land, and site development, may not be a reliable

indication of relative value received. As an illustration, two elementary schools, each designed for 600 pupils, may be considered. Each school has the same building cost —the contract amounts for general, mechanical, and electrical work— in this instance, $1,296,000. The first school spends $100,000 for equipment, $20,000 for a site, and $60,000 for site development. The second school, with the same building cost, spends $136,000 for equipment, $80,000 for a site, and $90,000 for the development of that site. Thus, the total spent by the first school for building, equipment, site, and site development is $1,476,000, or $2,460 per pupil; and by the second school, $1,602,000, or $2,670 per pupil. Though both had identical building costs, the second school invested $126,000 more in the project than the first school, or an additional $210 for every pupil. Here is a dramatic example of how factors other than actual building cost can affect total project cost.

Total Project Cost

This analysis of cost can be carried one step further, to show that even total project cost is not always a true indication of the eventual cost of a building. For example, two school buildings are completed with an identical total project cost. The school in Community A, carefully planned, enjoys a number of inherently efficient features which will make possible lower operating and maintenance costs. These savings will be realized year after year, substantially lowering the cost of education for Community A, as compared to the costs incurred year after year by Community B. Community A's school was thoughtfully planned. Its kitchen and serving area was efficiently designed so that one less kitchen staff member will be needed. It is also skillfully designed to utilize and control natural forces for some of its lighting, heating, cooling, and ventilating, so that power consumption and operating costs are lower than for School B. Materials were more wisely selected for School A, and maintenance costs will be lower. True cost is long-range cost which considers both capital and operating cost. The advantages which yield lower long-range costs usually cannot be achieved without some additional capital outlay costs, but such additional capital outlay can produce enough long-range savings to make the ultimate cost to the community lower than it would otherwise have been.

True Cost

It should be kept in mind that because this chapter focuses on *cost* per se, there is danger of ignoring the benefits which may be derived in building the better, and hence more costly, building. The educational process has as its only product, people; cost is meaningful only when related to that product.

Rising Costs

The cost of education is rising; so is the cost of school facilities. It cannot be otherwise. Our population is increasing rapidly, the aspirations of each individual are growing, and the people's expectations from the schools are extending beyond any previous boundaries. Furthermore, the body of knowledge expands at an ever increasing rate and students must learn more and learn better than ever before. It is unreasonable to think that we can "hold the line" on the cost of education. It is equally unreasonable to think that we can spend the same amount for future school buildings that we spent in the past.

In the complex world of tomorrow, citizens will go to school more years and will enjoy a better education each of those years, and the schools will be of higher quality and better equipped. They will also cost more. In planning school buildings for tomorrow, top priority should be given not to merely keeping school costs down, but rather to choosing wisely how capital outlay funds are used. In planning new school facilities, thoughtful school planners will encourage citizens to look to the future and keep their educational expectations high.

Spending School Construction Money Wisely

Each community must analyze its own building needs. First, a long-range plan must be established for schools in coordination with the future plans of the total community. If the character of the area served by a particular school is temporary in nature or if there are indications that few people will be living there in the future or that needs are likely be markedly different in the future, then the proper decision may be to construct a low-cost, short-life building. This kind of short-term investment may call for portable or temporary structures or perhaps prefabricated demountable structures of high quality. The plan may call for amortizing the total building cost over a short period of time, and a low unit cost may be necessary.

On the other hand, the well-planned school serving a stable community having long-term future prospects will probably be a high-cost, long-life building. It will be designed to facilitate a higher quality education each year and ultimately will be the truly economical building. Many of the finest schools in America occupy buildings that are 40 years old; where the quality of the original building is high and the site is adequate, some of these plants can serve another 40 years with limited remodeling and periodic rehabilitation of existing space, along with necessary additions for enrollment and program growth.

Experience with good older buildings shows that even though the basic structural shell, exterior walls, structural floors, beams, and columns can serve well unchanged for generations, periodic changes in interior walls, equipment, lighting, and mechanical systems are necessary as educational needs change, as our standards of comfort change, and as our desires and tastes change. The basic structural shell, experience proves, is a very long-term investment; interior partitions, lighting, and mechanical systems are medium-term investments; and equipment and furniture are short-term investments, since they tend to wear out or become obsolete sooner.

For school construction money to be spent wisely, the quality school of the future should perhaps be designed specifically in recognition of three kinds of investment:

1. *The long-term investment.* Foundations, underground utilities, landscaping, the structural framework, exterior walls, and the backbone of the mechanical and electrical system will be designed to serve for many generations without major change and to accept expansion gracefully.

2. *The medium-term investment.* Interior partitions, doors, working-wall surfaces, built-in equipment, lighting fixtures, and air conditioning devices—all of which tend to wear out or become functionally obsolete in perhaps 20 years—will be designed to be replaced economically when new needs arise or when better equipment is available.

3. *The short-term investment.* Laboratory equipment, communications devices, instructional materials, and furniture, which are used intensively and wear out or become obsolete rapidly, will be replaced more often.

The modern office building considered to be the best investment by business is designed in this manner. The investor builds a permanent shell building; it has, as a long-range investment, permanent foundations, structural frame and floors, mechanical and electrical plant, and a utility core containing elevators, stairs, and toilets. Other than this utility core, virtually no interior partitions are part of the long-term investment; tenants will change, and each tenant's needs will change. When a tenant signs a lease, a medium-term investment is made in partitions and built-in equipment designed specifically for that tenant's own needs. The tenant makes short-term investments in furniture, typewriters, and materials which he expects to consume or wear out. In the planning of facilities, the needs of education might well be compared to the needs of business, with each department considered as a tenant. Since departments will change and grow, space provided for them must be flexible enough to adapt to changes and growth.

Tomorrow's school must have this kind of flexibility. It may require higher original capital costs, but the long-term investment will be sound and true economy in terms of product will be realized over the years.

Where the Building Dollar Goes

In the one-room school, almost all of the building dollar was spent on the foundation, floor, walls, and roof. A little money was needed for a heating stove. Lighting and ventilation were provided naturally, through the windows. The general contractor got all 100 cents of the dollar. For the larger schools that were built in the first decades of this century and that had central heating, ventilation fans, and electric lights, the general contract involved perhaps 80 cents of the building dollar. Recent progress in the mechanical and electrical trades has brought new equipment on the market that has exerted more and more influence on school design and consumed more and more of the school building dollar.

Today, for the automatically controlled, summer and winter air-conditioned school with high ventilation standards, with the world's finest plumbing and with high quality lighting design, mechanical and electrical contracts consume 30 cents or more of every building dollar, leaving only 70 cents or less for general contracts.

The upward trend will continue. We live in a world that expects ever more efficient lighting; better ventilation; improved plumbing; more elaborate, individually controlled air conditioning; and growing numbers of machines—computers, copiers, calculators, communications systems, and an endless procession of labor savers—all requiring buildings with increasingly greater mechanical and electrical capacity. Undoubtedly, the dollar will soon be divided 50-50, and in the future, mechanical-electrical expenditures predictably will climb above the amount spent for foundation, structural shell, roof, and interior space dividers.

If the general contract expenditure is to be considered stable, while the mechanical-electrical contract expenditure grows, then this comparison should be noted:

Percent of building dollar	1927	1967	1987
For general work	80%	70%	?
For mechanical-electrical	20%	30%	?

Investment in Beauty

Why is a school torn down? Some schools are considered unsafe or unclean and are therefore demolished. Some have permanently established room sizes and arrangements which no longer satisfy new educational requirements. Many buildings are demolished simply because they are ugly. The school building that is considered beautiful by the community lives longer. Beauty is an essential ingredient in the good-investment school.

Chapter 17 / *The Impact of Federal Legislation*

In his January 1965 message to Congress on federal support of education, President Johnson listed four major educational goals: to bring better education to the millions of disadvantaged youth who need it most; to put the best educational equipment and ideas within the reach of all students; to advance the technology of teaching and the training of teachers; and to provide incentives for those who wish to learn at every stage of their lives. For the schools, striving to meet these constant challenges, recently enacted federal legislation has made resources available for renewed attacks on a number of fronts. Almost every conceivable phase of the school program can now be touched in some way by one or more provisions of the various acts. "Innovative," "exemplary," "supplementary," "imaginative," "cooperative" have become bywords as school systems have applied for grants to plan or expand programs to meet the pressing needs which they have identified.

Recognizing that new educational programs usually require increased facilities or new kinds of facilities, some of the recent federal acts make provision for new construction to house the programs they are designed to activate. If school systems take full advantage of these opportunities and use creative and cooperative approaches in their planning, imaginative, forward-looking educational buildings and complexes which will strongly influence future school design could well be the result.

There are certain guiding principles established in federal legislation for aid to education that have implications for school design:

1. The first step in the design of any program is the identification of the vital needs of all children or adult learners in the area to be served and the extent to which current programs have failed to meet these needs.

2. Proof of these needs must be provided through research.

3. Imaginative, innovative, and exemplary programs are to be planned to meet these identified needs, and appropriate facilities designed to implement the programs.

4. Agencies applying for planning grants or for grants to implement their plans should familiarize themselves with the intent of Congress implied in the several acts and with the guidelines provided by the U.S. Office of Education. They should study all acts which could have relevance for the various aspects of their program and apply for funding through several sources, if appropriate. To assist school districts in interpreting the laws and applying the guidelines, state departments of education have set up offices which provide consultative services.

5. The planning of all programs must involve teachers, the community, and specifically the people being served.

6. Emphasis is placed on cooperative planning and activity of educational and community agencies throughout a region, rather than on local activity by a single small school district or agency alone.

7. The programs are to be designed to supplement existing programs, not to supplant them. Federal resources are not intended to finance already established activities.

8. Assistance to the poor and culturally deprived is stressed as a means of conserving all the nation's human resources.

9. Programs are to be designed to provide enrichment activities for all children.

10. Evaluative instruments must be designed and used to measure the degree to which the programs are meeting the needs for which they are intended.

11. Criteria for the evaluation and selection of instructional materials are to be established and applied.

12. Groups receiving federal grants are obligated to disseminate the results of their programs.

The importance of designing schools to meet the particular needs of the specific areas they serve is quite evident in these guidelines. Incentives provided in this legislation for the use of imagination and creativity in designing programs and facilities to meet special needs should encourage school districts to move ahead in planning school buildings with a forward look. Initial grants for planning and research will enable planners to survey existing facilities in school systems which have already experimented with new types of school building design. School districts are increasingly encouraged to develop experimental programs and facilities.

The research required for identification of needs, design of programs and facilities, and evaluation of results by the Economic Opportunity Act and Titles I, II, and III of the Elementary and Secondary Education Act demand more research facilities than most school systems now possess. The implication is obvious. A school district taking full advantage of the resources available through these acts may need to add a research assistant to the regular staff to serve one or several schools. The district's research program may require increased cooperation with other school districts and increased physical facilities.

Identification of children's needs nearly always provides insight into the types of individualized instruction various learners require. School buildings must provide facilities to permit the flexibility required by individual scheduling; facilities for individual study, such as study carrels and individual listening stations; small science and language laboratories for independent research and study; and a wider range of classroom sizes, from seminar room to lecture hall.

Perhaps most important of all the implications which the federal legislation has for school design and construction is the encouragement it provides of increased cooperative planning by school and community agencies and of the construction of educational facilities to serve a number of school systems within a region. The Elementary and Secondary Education Act of 1965 encourages the establishment of supplementary educational centers; other acts concerned with more specific needs, such as libraries and higher education facilities, provide assistance for types of construction which, with imaginative and cooperative planning, can well be incorporated

into educational centers to serve wide areas.

With the stimulus of federal funds, at least three types of centers can emerge:

1. *The Neighborhood Center.* The local kindergarten and elementary school can be designed to provide educational, cultural, and recreational activities for the immediate community, much as the rural one- or two-room school served former generations. The neighborhood-center school envisioned in the federal legislation performs an especially important function in areas of cultural and economic deprivation. The classrooms in the school are designed to accommodate both normal daytime classes and evening adult education groups. The center's multipurpose room is equipped to serve community groups in little theater activities, forums, study and discussion of community and national problems, concerts, and meetings of organizations. Gymnasiums and playground facilities are designed for use in the neighborhood recreational program six or seven days and evenings a week throughout the year. Since campus facilities will accommodate everything from lighted tennis courts to sandboxes, they must be laid out and zoned to provide protection and freedom for the small children who will play there. An art gallery is considered to be an important element of this

156

neighborhood center, and the library is designed and equipped with an extensive periodical, recording, and picture collection readily accessible to the community and available for loan.

2. *The Area Center.* The area center may include two or three junior high schools and a senior high school, located on an extensive campus. In addition, the campus would include a number of different types of playing fields, swimming pools, and picnic areas, and a branch library, all carefully designed for use by both the schools and the surrounding communities.

The junior high schools would contain small auditoriums, seminar rooms and classrooms, libraries, laboratories, shops, and cafeteria. Although each school would be a separate administrative unit, some facilities, such as the cafeteria or a highly specialized shop or laboratory, could serve several schools.

The senior high school would contain a large auditorium, a library, a small theater, classrooms varying in size from seminar rooms to lecture halls, laboratories, studios, galleries, shops, a cafeteria, and a computer center for schools on this campus and feeder schools.

In addition to the daytime activities in these buildings and the campus playing facilities, evening adult education, study, and tutorial centers for the youth of the area, and a wide variety of cultural and recreational activities would be conducted throughout the year.

3. *The Community-Wide Educational and Cultural Park.* The educational and cultural park would be designed to serve the schools and community by centralizing and expanding important services which supplement the elementary and secondary school facilities within a community or region. The park would be planned around a cluster of such institutions and facilities as a—

Community college

Branch of the state university

Museum

Central public library of the county or district

Regional educational and cultural resources center serving a county school system or several smaller school districts

Studio for educational television

Community theater

Science center and planetarium.

Associated with the educational park could be a school farm; so could camping and nature study areas of a state park located nearby.

Neighborhood centers within walking distance of every child or adult, easily accessible area centers offering a rich and varied program for young people and adults, and an educational park providing specialized services to teachers and cultural opportunities to the community would provide a total educational program for a large community or a region of small districts. This type of school complex is no longer just visionary, for with or without federal aid a number of communities are bringing long-term plans for such educational centers into reality. Educators are observing with great interest such centers as the Nova School in Florida, an area center similar in concept to that described here, and the Harkness Educational Center in Erie County, New York, an example of a regional resources center offering services to a number of cooperating school districts. The stimulus of federal planning grants, guidance from state education departments in the complex task of planning on a regional basis, and eventual adequate federal assistance in construction of facilities should bring more of these imaginative and forward-looking plans into reality.

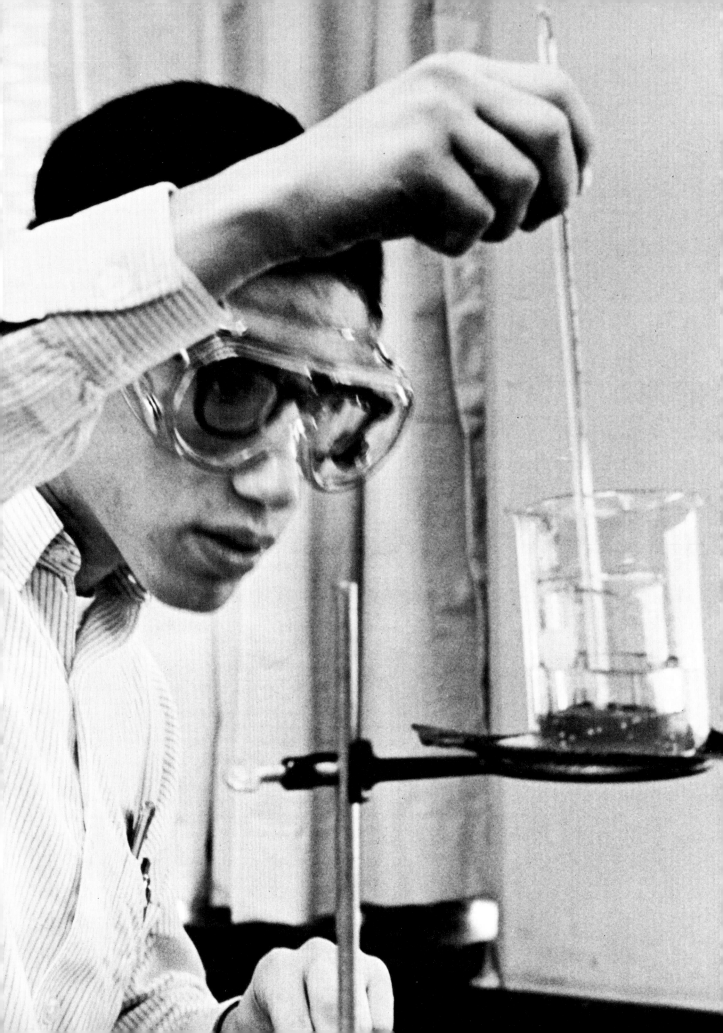

Chapter 18/*Ingredients of Excellence*

What makes a really successful educational facility? Ask a simple question and expect a simple answer? There isn't one! Schools are not simple any more. They have become a complex response to an even more complex set of circumstances. It was fairly general procedure not many years ago for an educator to hand his architect a list of required rooms on a couple of typewritten sheets, perhaps supplemented by a set of building standards developed by the maintenance department, and say, "Here is everything you need to know about our new elementary school." Secondary schools took a little longer. Those wonderfully simple days are gone forever. Our civilization and education have moved on down the road.

Those who are planning schools —educators, architects, school board members, and citizens—carry a heavy responsibility, for it is they who will either limit education through inadequate planning or free it by planning facilities which will serve the educational needs of students today and tomorrow.

What are the ingredients of planning excellence?

Creativity, imagination, and invention are essential in planning a facility that looks to the future, that makes effective use of the limited dollars available, and that provides an environment which excites the imagination and challenges the abilities of the teachers and children who use it.

Knowledge, background, and research must become a part of the planning and building process if the facility is to be an adequate home for the educational program, because the program itself must be based upon knowledge of the needs of the community and the traditions of the area and upon research into the nature of the future. The facility, in turn, must be based upon an equally broad foundation of knowledge so it may become a meaningful environment for education.

Understanding, grace, and judgment must be included among the ingredients of excellence. There must be an understanding of the needs of the child, stated with functional and visual grace so they become eloquent ambassadors of education. Judgment will eliminate the nonessentials and direct the planning toward the true imperatives of education.

Willingness and determination are indispensable; without strength of will, the entire process may fall by the wayside.

Facility planning, then, must join the growing parade in the quest for excellence. Those who participate in this important function of education must face up to their tasks—challenges which are vital and exciting.

Team Planning

If the planning processes of educational facilities are complex— and who is to deny that they are— who should be the planners? Since many areas of knowledge are required, it follows that many planners will be required. Given knowledgeable, capable planners, the support of the public, and effective communication among them all, the desired results should be attained. Planning is a real cooperative team effort. The team will be composed of a group of specialists whose combined fund of knowledge covers the whole spectrum of the planning concept. The members of the team must be flexible: it is difficult to draw definite lines of responsibility, and many duties will overlap. Even though the planning team must work as a single, unified entity, it will be subdivided into groups of

specialists who have particular abilities and who will contribute most in their own particular areas of ability and knowledge. Basically, the team is composed of the public, the educator, and the architect.

Ideally, the entire team should be assembled at its very beginning. Otherwise, the necessary interplay of abilities and knowledge will be inhibited, and the probability of success limited. Once the team is assembled, effective means of communication among its members must follow. If the educator has not established proper communication with the public, the bond issue may fail. If the educator and the architect do not fully understand each other's desires and limitations, the facility will surely suffer. Complete understanding is of paramount importance, and understanding can be reached only through proper communication.

The Public

During recent years much attention has been given to the role that lay citizens play in thinking through and solving public school problems. The contributions laymen have made to successful drives for raising funds for school buildings are well known. They have been equally effective in helping to develop educational philosophy, to plan the broad aspects of an instructional program, to select school sites, and to plan the school as a community center.

The ultimate responsibility for decision making remains vested in the citizens of the local community. In the final analysis, truly democratic government is based on the wisdom of its people. If its people know how to do a job better than that currently being done, this knowledge will find its way into the political arena, where it will result in wiser and more broadly conceived rules, regulations, and policies. The need to safeguard local control and at the same time to ensure adequate support from state and federal government sets in relief the problem of why we plan, what we plan, and how we plan a comprehensive program of education.

The responsibility for operating the school system consistent with the objectives of the community and within the limitations of legal obligations is vested in the governing board. The board represents the public and its interests and is the direct line of communication between the public and the superintendent. It keeps the public informed of the community's educational program, solicits financial support to implement the program, translates the objectives of the community into educational goals, and formulates policy in the public behalf.

The Educator

It is the administrators, the teachers, the nonprofessional personnel, and the pupils who are most intimately acquainted with the school building. They live in it and work in it for hours each day and through this close acquaintance are aware of its limitations as well as its outstanding features. Just as the housewife knows her kitchen, so do these people know the school plant. It is they more than the lay citizens of the community who understand the kinds of facilities needed and to whom school planners should turn for specific recommendations. School building facilities are tools in the hands of teachers. The quality of a teacher's work is affected by the tools with which he works. Since he lives with these tools and works with them day after day and year after year, he knows their advantages and disadvantages, knows what he needs and what he doesn't need, and can suggest practical improvements.

The educator team is a complex one. Its size will vary, depending upon the size of the school district and its staff or the size of the construction project involved. Under any circumstances, all of the various interest groups should be represented in one way or another—the administration, the teachers, the maintenance staff, and others. With such representation, it is inevitable that conflicts of interest will arise. If the chairman of the science department is worth his salt, he will insist that his department have just a little more space and that the space occupied by the social studies seminar room would be just right. In turn, the social studies man is just itching to lay his hands on the space occupied now, in preliminary plans, by the preparation-storage room for chemistry. At the same time, the teachers who have grown weary of sterile spaces in schools want stained wood paneling in the corridors and the head of maintenance prefers structural glazed tile. These are natural—even desired—conflicts. Each group has its own interests. They must be heard and balanced, and a well considered decision reached. It must be remembered, however, that the object is still learning—that is the reason the building is being built in the first place. Decisions must be made which will allow the

building to provide the best possible environment for learning.

Observers of school building construction programs in the past have noted a leadership pattern that may well be given attention at this point. In some districts where a number of building projects have been under way over a period of years, the superintendent assumes the leadership role in the early stages of planning, focuses attention on the instructional program as the fundamental consideration in designing the new school building, and continues to hold this dominant leadership role until the educational specifications are firmed up. Then, as final decisions about many features of the building have to be made, more and more consideration is given to mechanical equipment, to maintenance, and to custodial services. At this crucial stage in the planning process, the superintendent has backed away from his leadership responsibility and delegated this function to his top maintenance man, head engineer, or chief custodian.

Employees in the maintenance department often see the school building merely as a physical structure that must be kept clean, or-

derly, and in good repair. Maintenance is their job, their domain, their sphere of operation in the school plant. They are concerned about closets, cupboards, and corners that may be easy or not so easy to keep clean; about finishes and surfaces in corridors, stairs, and doorways where traffic is especially heavy; about fixtures; and about mechanical and service systems. They are aware of the provoking problems that arise when a toilet is stopped, a door lock jams, the heating system doesn't function, the power plant fails, or the roof begins to leak. These conditions are clearly visible, whereas many features of the plant pertaining to the teaching environment tend to be of an abstract nature.

It is perhaps for these reasons that attention shifts at this point from the educational program to maintenance and custodial service. This should not happen. Nothing is more demoralizing to good planning and more devastating to good architecture than to have one creative approach after another ruled out by a custodian or a maintenance man simply because of difficulty in maintenance and operation. By reason of their intimate acquaintance with the physical properties of the school plant, custodians, engineers, and maintenance people do have important contributions to make to 161

school plant planning. However, their contributions should come in the form of suggesting better ways to meet new problems in janitorial service and building maintenance rather than of vetoing new ideas and insisting on the perpetuation of existing features of buildings merely because they are familiar. School buildings are designed and constructed as tools for teaching, not specifically for the convenience of custodians and engineers. This, of course, does not mean to imply that their interests should not be fully and carefully considered. It simply means that they must be put in proper perspective.

All of this would indicate that the educator team must be organized with great care. It is neither good practice nor fair to the architect to place him in a position where he must face the head of the science department and tell him that he cannot invade the domain of social studies. The educator team must have a leader—a leader who has the authority of decision and the ability to reach it wisely. This does not mean that the architect should not meet with the members of special interest groups. If he is to be well informed and if he is to be put in a position to contribute most

heavily to the project, he must join in these meetings. It does mean that the leader of the educator team— the decision maker—also must be there.

The Architect

Like the educator, the architect has a rather highly complex organization replete with special interest groups which must be put in proper balance. He, too, must have a decision maker placed in much the same position as the leader of the educator team. He, too, must envision the building he is planning as an educational institution —an environment for learning.

The good architect will have a highly trained and highly diversified team. Because school design is not simple, the members of his team should either have or be able to obtain a high degree of specialized knowledge in the field of education as related to the facilities which will be required to serve it. The architect's team includes designers, draftsmen, specification writers, field inspectors, structural engineers, mechanical engineers, electrical engineers, acoustical engineers, landscape architects, color specialists, graphics designers, land use planners, building use planners, building code analysts, and zoning ordinance analysts. Some of the very large architectural firms have

people with this diversity of knowledge on their own office staffs. Smaller firms employ consulting firms to provide the necessary specialists. In either case, it is the architect who is the leader and the coordinator of the team and who carries the moral and legal responsibility for its performance.

The school district faced with the need for new educational facilities should secure the services of the most capable architect it can find. Excellent guidelines for selecting the architect and evaluating his work, as well as discussion of his responsibilities in planning and design, are presented in considerable detail in Chapter XI of *Planning America's School Buildings* [1] and *Facts About Your Architect and His Work.* [2]

Communication and Confidence

One of the best reasons for a careful and thorough architect selection procedure is to ensure confidence. When a school district has

---

[1] American Association of School Administrators. *Planning America's School Buildings.* Washington, D.C.: the Association, 1960. pp 155-85.

[2] The American Institute of Architects. *Facts About Your Architect and His Work.* Washington, D.C.: The Institute, 1958.

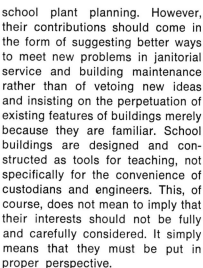

selected its architect, it has made a decision upon which much of the ultimate success of the project will depend. Once it is decided that the architect is the right one, his talents should be used in the best possible manner.

Here again, good communication is paramount. While he may have a degree of knowledge in these fields, the architect is not a superintendent of schools, a science teacher, a football coach, or an audiovisual specialist. Yet he must know a great deal about the function of these people if he is to design an effective educational facility. How is he to learn all of this —particularly in relationship to the manners and habits of a specific school district? The answer is not too difficult to find. It is through effective communication with the educator team—communication in such areas as the kinds of children who will attend the school, curriculum offerings and trends, teaching techniques and equipment, and policy. This kind of knowledge should not be just handed to the architect in the form of a written document. Rather, there should be much verbal exchange, field observations of actual educational procedures, and detailed conferences. If the educator has led the architect to a real understanding of his needs and dreams, they are far more likely to

be realized and a better architectural solution will result.

In turn, the architect has a great deal of communication of his own to do. The educator is not an architect. Architectural drawings and jargon are often unfamiliar to him. He may have difficulty reading and understanding technical drawings. The architect does not want the educator to be surprised when he sees the facility after it is built; he wants him to understand it as it is being planned. This requires a high level of communication through the media of perspective drawings, models, diagrams, and written data, which the person untrained in reading floor plans and wall elevations can understand. Proper communication on the part of the architect can convert the planning process from one of confusion and misunderstanding to one of excitement and pleasure for all of the participants.

The architect who maintains a continuing research program in educational facilities, attends seminars, visits school building exhibitions, visits outstanding school buildings across the nation, and

studies exhibits of school equipment will have much to contribute to the functional educational planning, too. He will understand much of the educator's language and may also recount experiences of other school districts for evaluation.

The ideal relationship between educator and architect, which will result in a fine educational facility, is one of confidence, ability, and communication. This relationship must start at the very beginning—at best before the site is selected, before the educational specifications are written, before concepts are reached and minds begin to close— and must continue long after the project is completed. A good architect will guard the finished project with a high degree of jealousy. He has several reasons for this continued interest in the project.

If he is a good architect, he has put a good deal more into the project than his ability and time. He has given some of his heart and spirit to the building. Having made this kind of effort, he is more than a little likely to feel somewhat maternal about it all. In fact, he should be downright proud of the building that he, the educator, and the community have worked so hard to create. Does it have to be said that this kind of pride is a desirable thing? Of course it is, and it should be en-

couraged. Furthermore, the architect's next job in either the original school district or another may well depend upon how well he performed on his last job. Others will judge him to a great extent on his completed work.

It should not be hard to understand the architect's deep concern and continuing interest in the buildings that he has worked so hard to create. He will want to know how well they are serving the pupils and the teachers; he will want to know how well they are being maintained. Sometimes he is faced with the prospect of the owner, who is often unaware of his interest and concern, requesting the maintenance department to add a few finishing touches. A dispensing machine is put here and a poorly lettered sign there, or a trophy case from the old high school is moved into the new entry lobby. Important landscaping, originally agreed to, is forgotten, and weeds begin to grow; furniture and equipment colors clash with the walls. So often the effective communication established during the programing and planning phase breaks down and a good building, well conceived, turns into a last-minute hodgepodge. The good architect may be offended by visually unsuitable elements such as these. Perhaps he is a bit oversensitive, but if changes in his building are made

in good taste, or if he is given the opportunity to assist in making them, his pride in his work will grow, and through this growth he will do his work increasingly well.

When the architect has done his job well and designed a building which lends itself to easy maintenance and then discovers that the owner is not keeping it in good condition, not only his pride but his livelihood is hurt. He does not dare take a prospective client to see the building because he may well be judged by a job which the owner has not done well and over which he has no control. The owner sometimes misunderstands an architect's fierce pride in his work. To the architect, it is his life's blood. He has an obligation to the educator, the public, and, above all, to the children to do his job well. If he has fulfilled his obligation, then the school district, in turn, is obligated to him as well as to others to maintain his work in good taste and with some degree of care. Most architects will virtually jump through hoops for the client who shares their interest and concern for a project.

The Challenge

As society moves with great rapidity toward a future far different from anything we have ever known, those involved in education face heavy responsibilities and thrilling challenges. Since facilities are shaped by education, and in some ways shape education, facility planners share in these challenges and responsibilities.

* * *

The capacity of cooperation for a common cause and for a common purpose has been a formidable power in the hands of the people of this country from the time of the early settlers' first toeholds on the Atlantic seaboard to the recent Freedom March in Alabama. It has been the source of social energy that has created and shaped institutions, nurtured learning, and opened doors to new and greater opportunities for successive generations of people. The leadership that is instrumental in bringing this power of cooperation to bear in a constructive manner on the basic problems that confront mankind is the leadership that will make the greatest and most enduring contribution to the well-being of the country.

Individually and collectively, the people of this country are looking to the schools for a contribution to developing the reservoir of creative power, kindling the vision, and perfect-

ing the skills needed to meet and deal with challenges arising on the forefront of cultural change. The headline on the front pages of the newspapers as this Commission was meeting for the first time—"Man Steps into Space"—is a challenge to people in every neighborhood and community in this country.

What do these and other overriding problems that have relevance to school policy, school programs, and school building planning mean to the superintendent, the architect, the school board member, and the citizen who has special interest in making schools better? There is no simple answer to this important question. Answers will be found by people as they join together in facing them, in seeking solutions, and in finding practical ways to

deal with them. In any event, it seems reasonable to assume that—

—The need for innovations will continue.

—Young people will go to school longer and learn more.

—Programs will be value oriented.

—The range of educational opportunities will be broadened.

—There will be more depth and thoroughness in many fields of instruction.

—The period of formal education will be extended beyond the twelfth grade.

—Adult education will be given more emphasis in community educational programs.

—The humanities—art, music, drama, literature, dancing—will be given new and greater emphasis because it is through these programs that young people in great measure will acquire deeper appreciation of the total culture and develop the sense of values needed to sustain their lives and guide their actions.

—Instructional methods will be revised again and again, making it possible for young people to learn more in less time.

—Curriculum revision will go on continuously, and provisions will be made for getting better instructional equipment and teaching materials into the hands of teachers and pupils when and where needed.

—And, finally, the success of superintendents, architects, school board members, and citizens in the community in planning their new school plants will depend in large measure on their discerning and understanding the ebbs and flows in the tides of cultural change that have relevance for the schools.

From Shirley Cooper's notebook.

Contributors

The Commission expresses its appreciation to the following individuals who have contributed to the development of this publication.

Margaret C. Austin, Staff Member, American Association of School Administrators, Washington, D.C.

JoAn Booth, Coordinator of School Communications, White Plains Public Schools, White Plains, New York

John Caffrey, Program Director, Education, Advanced Systems Division, System Development Corporation, Santa Monica, California

Thomas B. Doherty, Superintendent of Schools, Colorado Springs, Colorado

William J. Ellena, Associate Secretary, American Association of School Administrators, Washington, D.C.

Marian F. Graves, Director of Pupil Personnel Services, White Plains Public Schools, White Plains, New York

Katherine M. Klier, Curriculum Specialist, Baltimore County Schools, Towson, Maryland

Marilyn E. Ludwig, Staff Executive, Committee on School and College Architecture, The American Institute of Architects, Washington, D.C.

Jean R. Moser, Coordinator, Office of Special Studies and Programs, Baltimore County Schools, Towson, Maryland

Arthur R. Olson, Deputy Superintendent of Schools, Colorado Springs, Colorado

Jane Power, Staff Member, Publications Division, National Education Association, Washington, D.C.

Staff of Western States Small Schools Project, State Department of Education, Denver, Colorado

Illustrations

The Commission is further indebted to many individuals for their assistance in providing and permitting the use of the following drawings and photographs used to illustrate this publication.

American School and University; Carl Purcell, photo **viii**

National Education Association; Carl Purcell, photo **xii**

System Development Corporation, Santa Monica, California **2**

System Development Corporation, Santa Monica, California **3**

National Education Association; Joe Di Dio, photo **4**

National School Public Relations Association, NEA, from *The Schools and the Press;* Carl Purcell, photo **6**

System Development Corporation, Santa Monica, California **7**

System Development Corporation, Santa Monica, California **8, 9**

National Education Association; Carl Purcell, photo **10**

National Education Association; Carl Purcell, photos **12**

System Development Corporation, Santa Monica, California **13**

Evanston Township High School, Evanston, Illinois; The Perkins and Will Partnership, architects **15**

System Development Corporation, Santa Monica, California **15**

National Education Association; Carl Purcell, photo **18**

National Education Association; Carl Purcell, photo **20**

T. C. Abbott Elementary School, Ann Arbor, Michigan; The Perkins and Will Partnership and Kainlauri, MacMullan and Millman, associated architects; Bill Engdahl, Hedrich-Blessing, photo **21**

Birchwood Elementary School, Duluth, Minnesota; The Perkins and Will Partnership and Thomas J. Shefchik and Associates, associated architects; Harr, Hedrich-Blessing, photo **22**

Lincoln Elementary School, La-Porte, Indiana; The Perkins and Will Partnership, architects; Suter, Hedrich-Blessing, photo **24**

Roy J. Wasson Senior High School, Colorado Springs, Colorado; Bunts and Kelsey, architects; Guy Burgess, photo **25**

National Education Association; Carl Purcell, photo **26**

Birchwood Elementary School, Duluth, Minnesota; The Perkins and Will Partnership and Thomas J.

Shefchik and Associates, associated architects; Harr, Hedrich-Blessing, photo **28**

Abington High School, Abington, Pennsylvania; Caudill, Rowlett and Scott, architects; Lawrence S. Williams, photo **29**

Maine Township High School South, Park Ridge, Illinois; Caudill, Rowlett and Scott and McCaughey, Erickson, Kristmann and Stillwaugh, associated architects; Hedrich-Blessing, photo **29**

James K. Polk Elementary School, Alexandria, Virginia; Vosbeck-Vosbeck and Associates, architects; J. Alexander, photo **30**

T. C. Abbott Elementary School, Ann Arbor, Michigan; The Perkins and Will Partnership and Kainlauri, MacMullan and Millman, associated architects; Bill Engdahl, Hedrich-Blessing, photo **31**

Kennedy Junior High School, Natick, Massachusetts; Davies and Wolfe, Freeman and Flansburgh, associated architects **32**

Kennedy Junior High School, Natick, Massachusetts; Davies and Wolfe, Freeman and Flansburgh,

Subject Index

Name Index